HIGHER EDUCATION IN THE DIGITAL AGE

HIGHER EDUCATION IN THE DIGITAL AGE

Technology Issues and Strategies for American Colleges and Universities

James J. Duderstadt
Daniel E. Atkins
Douglas Van Houweling

AMERICAN COUNCIL ON EDUCATION
PRAEGER
Series on Higher Education

Library of Congress Cataloging-in-Publication Data

Duderstadt, James J., 1942–
   Higher education in the digital age : technology issues and strategies for
American colleges and universities / James J. Duderstadt, Daniel E. Atkins, and
Douglas Van Houweling.
     p. cm. — (American Council on Education / Praeger Series on Higher Education)
Includes bibliographical references and index.
ISBN 1–57356–520–2 (alk. paper)
  1. Education, Higher—Effect of technological innovations on—United States.
2. Information technology. 3. Education, Higher—United States—Data processing.
I. Atkins, Daniel E. (Daniel Ewell) II. Van Houweling, Douglas E. III. Title.
LB2395.7 .D83 2002
378.73—dc21   2002067830

Formerly ACE/Oryx Press Series on Higher Education

British Library Cataloguing in Publication Data is available.

Library of Congress Catalog Card Number: 2002067830
ISBN: 1–57356–520–2

First published in 2002

Praeger Publishers, 88 Post Road West, Westport, CT 06881
An imprint of Greenwood Publishing Group, Inc.
www.praeger.com

Printed in the United States of America

The paper used in this book complies with the
Permanent Paper Standard issued by the National
Information Standards Organization (Z39.48–1984).

10 9 8 7 6 5 4 3 2 1

Contents

Preface

Today our society and our social institutions are being reshaped by the rapid advances in information technology: computers, telecommunications, and networks. Modern digital technologies have vastly increased our capacity to know and to do things and to communicate and collaborate with others. They allow us to transmit information quickly and widely, linking distant places and disparate areas of endeavor in productive new ways. This technology allows us to form and sustain communities for work, play, and learning in ways unimaginable just a decade ago. Information technology changes the relationship between people and knowledge, and it is likely to reshape in profound ways knowledge-based institutions such as our colleges and universities.

Higher education has already experienced significant change driven by information technology. Our management and administrative processes are heavily dependent upon this technology, made all too apparent by the millions of dollars that our institutions spent reengineering their enterprise computer systems while preparing for the date reset of the year 2000. Research and scholarship also depend upon information technology, for example, the use of computers to simulate physical phenomena, networks to link investigators in virtual laboratories or "collaboratories," or digital libraries to provide scholars with access to knowledge resources. There is an increasing sense that new technology will also have a profound impact on teaching, freeing the classroom from the constraints of space and time and enriching the learning of our students through access to original source materials.

While this technology has the capacity to enhance and enrich teaching and scholarship, it also poses certain threats to our colleges and universities. Powerful computers and networks now have the potential to deliver educational services to anyone, anyplace, anytime, no longer confined to the campus or the academic schedule. Technology is creating an open learning environment in which the student has evolved into an active learner and consumer of educational services, stimulating the growth of powerful market forces that could dramatically reshape the higher education enterprise. Already, most students arrive on our campuses, computers and Palm Pilots in hand, expecting the same transparent efficiencies in their college education that they receive from dot-coms such as Amazon.com and Travelocity.com.

We are bombarded with news concerning the impact of information technology on the marketplace, from "e-commerce," to "edutainment," to "virtual universities" and "I-campuses." The higher education marketplace has seen the entrance of dozens of new competitors that depend heavily upon information technology. Examples include the University of Phoenix, the Caliber Learning Network, Sylvan Learning Systems, the Open University, the Western Governors University, and a growing array of "dot-coms" such as Unext.com and Blackboard.com. It is important to recognize that while many of these new competitors are quite different from traditional academic institutions, they are also quite sophisticated in their pedagogy, their instructional materials, and their production and marketing of educational services. They approach the market in a highly strategic manner, first moving into areas characterized by limited competition, unmet needs, and relatively low production costs but then moving rapidly up the value chain to more advanced educational offerings. These information technology (IT)-based education providers are already becoming competitors to traditional postsecondary institutions.

Today some suggest that in the face of rapidly evolving technology and emerging competition, the very survival of the university, at least as we know it, may be at risk. In an interview in *Forbes* several years ago, Peter Drucker suggested: "Thirty years from now the big university campuses will be relics. Universities won't survive. It is as large a change as when we first got the printed book."[1] William Wulf, president of the National Academy of Engineering, posed the question in a somewhat different way: "Can an institution such as the university which has existed for a millennium and become an icon of our social fabric disappear in just a few decades because of technology? If you doubt it, just check on the current state of the family farm."[2]

Ray Kurzweil, in his provocative speculation about the future, *The Age of Spiritual Machines*, predicts that over the next decade intelligent courseware will emerge as a common means of learning, with schools increasingly relying on software approaches, leaving human teachers to attend primarily to issues of motivation, psychological well-being, and socialization.[3] Eventually, in two or three decades, Kurzweil sees human learning accomplished primarily by using virtual teachers and enhanced by widely available neural implants.

While most believe that the university will survive the digital age, few deny that it could change dramatically in form and character. Knowledge is both a medium and a product of the university as a social institution. Hence, it is reasonable to suspect that a technology that is expanding our ability to create, transfer, and apply knowledge by factors of 100 to 1,000 every decade will have a profound impact on both the mission and the function of the university.

Clearly, the digital age poses many challenges and presents many opportunities for the contemporary university. For most of the history of higher education in America, we have expected students to travel to a physical place, a campus, to participate in a pedagogical process involving tightly integrated studies based mostly on lectures and seminars by recognized experts. As the constraints of time and space—and perhaps even reality itself—are relaxed by information technology, will the university as a physical place continue to hold its relevance?

More generally, are we entering just another period of evolution for the university? Or will the dramatic nature and compressed timescales characterizing the technology-driven changes of our time trigger a process more akin to revolution in higher education? Will a tidal wave of technological, economic, and social forces sweep over the academy, both transforming the university in unforeseen and perhaps unacceptable ways and creating new institutional forms to challenge both our experience and our concept of the university?

However, over the longer term rapidly evolving digital technology will enable us to build and sustain new types of learning communities, free from the constraints of space and time. We are on the threshold of a revolution that is making the world's accumulated information and knowledge accessible to individuals everywhere, a technology that will link us together into new communities never before possible or even imaginable. This has breathtaking implications for education, research, and learning and, of course, for our colleges and universities in the digital age. Higher education must define its relationship with these emerging possibilities in order to create a compelling vision for its future as it enters the new millennium. It is our collective challenge as scholars, educators, and academic leaders to develop a strategic framework capable of understanding and shaping the impact that this extraordinary technology will have on our institutions.

Despite the profound impact that this technology will have on higher education, information technology does not appear to be high on the agenda of priorities as seen by many leaders of our colleges and universities, or by the state and federal governments that support our institutions. Perhaps this is because of the highly complex, confusing, and almost overwhelming nature of the many issues that information technology raises for the university, for example, the financial investments required for IT infrastructure, the degree to which IT could transform traditional educational activities, and the new competitive threats that it stimulates within the higher education marketplace. It may also be the case that the current generation of university leaders, most of whom received their own educations and career experiences in the precomputer era, feel uncomfortable in dealing with these issues. It is also clear, however, that in the face of such rapidly evolving and profound technology-driven change, indecision and inaction are perhaps the most dangerous courses of all.

This book is intended to address these and related issues from a perspective appropriate for leaders of our colleges and universities who must make very real and imperative decisions and commitments for their institutions. This is an important point. While there have been countless conferences, articles, and books concerning the impact of information technology on higher education, these are all too frequently either so specialized as to be of interest primarily to the information technology professional or academic scholar or so generalized as to be of little practical use to those who must make decisions.

We seek instead to provide both possible visions for the future of higher education as well as pragmatic advice on how to cope with the complex, yet consequential, issues facing university leaders. In a sense, we are writing not from the perspective of information technology professionals or scholars but rather from our experiences as individuals who have led academic institutions and faced the considerable challenge and risk of making such decisions in the past.

While we have written this book at a sufficiently pragmatic level to be of practical use to university leaders, we also believe it important when discussing such a rapidly evolving subject to provide a glimpse of future possibilities. Put another way, we seek to be visionary without crossing the boundaries into science fiction yet also to be pragmatic without being trapped in the jargon of business IT professionals or the scholarly community. Most of all, we hope to provide a useful guide to the challenges and opportunities of the digital age as a context for the very real and demanding decisions that university leaders must face.

Although information technology presents many challenges and threats to the current nature of higher education, we have taken a more optimistic approach in this book. We suggest that colleges and universities should use the challenges presented by digital technology to stimulate actions that lead to opportunities to enhance their fundamental activities of education, scholarship, and public service. For example, although technology will threaten the current paradigm of the classroom lecture, it can also enrich the learning experience by enabling access to new resources such as original source materials or remote sites. It can facilitate more robust interactions between instructor and students through the formation of asynchronous learning communities. It can be viewed as a tool to help our best teachers become even better. It can stimulate a serious rethinking of pedagogy focused more on the student's learning experience than on content development and presentation.

This opportunistic philosophy captures well the fundamental intent of this book: to assist colleges and universities and their various stakeholders in responding to the challenges and opportunities presented by digital technology in a way that strengthens and enhances those traditional roles of higher education so important to our society.

The authors wish to acknowledge and thank their many colleagues for their advice and suggestions on this work. Gratitude is also due to Stanley Ikenberry, former president of the American Council on Education, who originally suggested the project, and to the Atlantic Philanthropies for its support of many of the activities important to its completion.

NOTES

1. Peter F. Drucker, interview, *Forbes*, 159 (1997), 122–28.

2. William A. Wulf, "Warning: Information Technology Will Transform the University," *Issues in Science and Technology* (Summer 1995), 46–52.

3. Ray Kurzweil, *The Age of Spiritual Machines: When Computers Exceed Human Intelligence* (New York: Viking, 1999).

PART I

Introduction

The impact of information technology will be even more radical than the harnessing of steam and electricity in the 19th century. Rather it will be more akin to the discovery of fire by early ancestors, since it will prepare the way for a revolutionary leap into a new age that will profoundly transform human culture.

—Jacques Attali, *Millennium*

There is little doubt that rapidly evolving information technology is transforming both our society and our social institutions. Corporations, governments, nation-states, and economies are all facing the challenge of change driven by digital technologies. Little wonder that tradition-bound colleges and universities tend to view the digital age more from the perspective of its threats than its opportunities.

There is a great deal of hype and exaggeration concerning both information technology and its impact on higher education. Scenarios range all the way from a world dominated by a commercial commodity marketplace for higher education services, to the replacement of traditional learning with neural implants à la *The Matrix*. In the near term, at least, most colleges and universities are likely to continue their traditional roles of education and scholarship in familiar ways. Here the "near term" should be measured in years rather than decades (or centuries, as is the case with some universities), since the relentlessly rapid pace of evolution of digital technology suggests a future of increasing uncertainty for the longer term.

Skeptics note that the university has been one of the most stable institutions in our civilization, surviving for a millennium through wars and plagues and technological change with its values and roles largely intact. Yet digital technology fundamentally transforms the way in which we create, manage, transfer, and apply knowledge. It modifies the way in which people communicate with one another. It liberates the formation of learning communities from the constraints of space and time. These are, of course, the core functions of the university.

In these introductory chapters we discuss the nature of information technology and summarize the current challenges and opportunities that it presents to higher education.

CHAPTER 1

Higher Education Faces
a Brave New World

A UNIVERSITY PRESIDENT'S NIGHTMARE

A Particularly Open Letter to the Faculty from the President
on the Occasion of the Closing of a University's Doors Forever[1]

May 2020

Dear Colleagues:

You are all aware of my deep regret, my personal sense of loss on this occasion. I've been with this institution for 22 years, and it's a small enough place that I know all of you personally. So enough of the official talk of declining enrollments and bad investments and infrastructure debt overload. I owe it to all of you to explain more particularly why we are closing our doors after a century and a half, and why this demise is taking place on my watch.

Friends, we have failed. We have been followers in a world that demands we be first. With hindsight our missteps seem clearer and the signposts to the road to success are better illuminated. But only with hindsight. So with these remarkable optics of hindsight, I give you a litany of what we should have done.

When Newt Gingrich was elected president a decade ago we should finally have seen the permanence of the stand Congress had taken several years earlier: that the new concept of public support for higher education had less to do with funding for student loans or universities than with opening up the "learning market" to new, leaner competitors who could deliver the specialized training programs corporations were looking for. And that

Gingrich's tongue-in-cheek promise of "a laptop in every lap," coupled with his appointment of Al Gore as Digital Information Czar, meant that the government itself was ready to do business with the CD-ROM makers and the edutainers because they could deliver skills training at low-cost and high-glitz. We should have recognized that the digital age was overtaking us.

When this university gave Bill Gates—a dropout—his eighth honorary doctorate, we should have recognized who in this digital age was overtaking us, and we should have listened to what he told our graduates: "Insist with both fists that your education puts you at the gate to your career." We should have remembered that in our age the prey always invites the predator to come to give a talk.

Gates's focus on being career-ready should have been our focus a decade ago when the University of Minnesota offered the first "guaranteed for life" degrees—lifelong learning contracts that warranted students would be kept current in their field. Instead we looked skeptically and decided this was something only professional schools could sell. But we underestimated both the drop in the life span of a college degree and the price students would pay to have that degree renewed again and again. Now Princeton, of all places, has had great success providing this "maintenance ed" to its graduates through its for-profit Princeton Professional Institute. We should have had a more accurate appraisal of the value of the degree we offer, for we have discovered too late in what low esteem it is held.

When the Gingrich administration pushed through Congress its voucher system for K–12 education in this country, we should have realized that economism was so rampant there was no reason to expect higher education to withstand the buffeting intact. Competition and choice became the buzz words in education—from Idaho's tax credits for home-schooling to the Nation of Islam's dominance of urban education. We couldn't have predicted that Tennessee would close its state universities and buy its higher education from the University of Phoenix, but we should have foreseen that such closings and failures lurked in the dark just ahead. We should have understood that the stakes were that high.

When ETS and Stanley Kaplan won in court the right to offer competency-based certification in medicine, we saw yet another sacred function of the university fall to the barbarians. What we should have foreseen was what a damn good job the barbarians were to make of it. Their online exams can be taken anywhere in the world by anyone who wishes, and they've teamed up with suppliers of various online and CD medical-education programs to guarantee student success. No longer do you have to go to medical school; instead, you have to diagnose pixilated patients and dissect digital cadavers. We should have better appraised the quality of our competition and met them head-on.

When those pixilated patients first became available in the '90s—and I remember my 12-year-old daughter conducting simulated surgery, mask and all, on those ADAM and EVE anatomy programs—we should have simply sat down and spent some time with them ourselves. We would have seen how completely engrossing they were and that they actually did teach, a mixture we as professors struggle mightily to achieve in the classroom. We would have also noticed that their interactive, hyperlinked, and multimedia nature allowed the student to learn at her own pace and in her preferred style—visual, textual, aural, whatever. Had we taken a closer look, we might have foreseen that most calculus classes in this country would today be taught in one semester instead of two—that the Newton's Whimsy program would let students approach the subject in the manner they found most efficient. We might have anticipated the interdisciplinary multimedia chairs that are now being endowed at so many universities. We might even have dreamed up Microsoft's announcement last year that it was endowing a Nobel Prize in multimedia education. Our greatest failure on this front was our failure to realize that freedom of choice was something the American collegiate population desperately desired. So now Motorola-Apple University—a university run out of an old warehouse in Hoboken—dominates multimedia education, and our beloved ivied walls are about to become barracks for our state's pettiest criminals.

Finally, when I compared the recent college experience of my son Aaron on this campus to the college experience of his girlfriend, Julianna, it was already too late. Aaron's experience was much like my experience 30 years earlier. But Julianna's. . . . She decided to live at home because the thousands of dollars she saved on room and board allowed her to accept admission to a more prestigious university. She took most of her courses in her family's den: broadcast courses, net-based courses, and interactive multimedia CD-ROM courses—what we once disparagingly called "edutainment." She passed exams given online by a company that used to be involved exclusively with SATs. Her Big Ten university, three-fourths of whose student body of 100,000 were distance-learners like her, gave her degree credit for this work. When she signed up for physics she was of course hooked into Rensselaer's gold mine—Physics 110 Online, now the introductory physics course for the majority of our nation's undergrads. (I suppose the fact that ours is one of the few universities in the country that hasn't lost half of its physics faculty to Rensselaer's course is now a moot point.) She majored in chemistry, spending eighteen months as an apprentice to a government researcher who worked halfway across the country and who freelanced as a student mentor. Aaron also majored in chemistry. He attended lectures, took notes, performed experiments in antiquated labs under the tutelage of TAs [teaching assistants]. Julianna had unlimited access to the Big Ten Digital Library. No doubt you're aware that my son's university paid millions of dollars to the Big Ten consortium to give him access to the world's largest virtual library.

When Julianna graduated in 3 years—now the national average for undergrads—she turned down three job offers so she could continue her research as a graduate student. Aaron had spent too much time in classrooms and was eager to do "real" work, as he called it. He had a hell of a well-rounded education behind him, but the only work he could find was a job as a lab assistant. I realized then that we had failed him and his fellow students, for all of the above reasons but also because we had failed to notice that a new form of literacy had arisen, a form in which text was only one in an array of media to be mastered by the educated person. I realized that we were no longer graduating literate students, and that realization has brought me to the greatest sorrow of my life: the realization that perhaps it is best we close our doors. To finish off the tale and make it mean more than it should, I'll add that Julianna is now a post-doc working with DuPont and the University of Maryland on photoactive molecules. Aaron has returned to school. He is working toward an MS/MFA in scientific visualization at Wisconsin. I may follow him.

This scenario, developed by writer Frank DeSanto several years ago as part of a strategic planning project sponsored by the Carnegie Foundation, is perhaps the ultimate nightmare for higher education leaders. Of course, some skeptics note that it took several decades for the overhead transparency projector to make it from the bowling alley into the classroom. Computers may also bounce off the classroom just like technology-based media such as television.[2] Yet today we have entered an era in which the new engine of economic prosperity is digital communication, enabled by the profound advances that we are now seeing in computers, networks, satellites, fiber optics, and related technologies. We now face a world in which billions of computers easily can plug into a global information infrastructure. These rapidly evolving technologies are dramatically changing the way that we collect, manipulate, and transmit information. They change the relationship between people and knowledge.

From a broader perspective, today we find a convergence of several themes: the importance of the university in an age in which knowledge itself has become a key factor in determining security, prosperity, and quality of life; the global nature of our society; the ease with which information technology—computers, telecommunications, and multimedia—enables the rapid exchange of information; and networking—the degree to which informal cooperation and collaboration among individuals and institutions are growing more rapidly than formal social structures, such as governments and states. We are also seeing a convergence of technology as first the telephone and then the television become computer appliances and hence windows into the Net. As a result, there is also a convergence in which computer, telecommunications, entertainment, and commerce are merging into a gigantic, $1 trillion infotainment marketplace. Although the university remains as an enduring social institution, providing our society with not only the educational and intellectual resources but also a link to the culture and values that sustain it, it has also become yet another element of an emerging and highly competitive global knowledge and learning industry.

THE AGE OF KNOWLEDGE

Today we have entered a new age, an *age of knowledge*, in which the key strategic resource necessary for prosperity has become knowledge itself, that is, educated people and their ideas.[3] The signs are all around us. Industrial production is steadily shifting from material- and labor-intensive products and processes, to knowledge-intensive products. A radically new system for creating wealth has evolved that depends upon the creation and application of new knowledge. We are in a transition period where intellectual capital, brainpower, is replacing financial and physical capital as the key to our strength, prosperity, and well-being.

Our rapid evolution into a knowledge-based society has been driven in part by the emergence of powerful new technologies such as computers, communications networks, and other digital devices.[4] Modern electronic technologies have vastly increased our capacity to know and to do things and to communicate and collaborate with others. They allow us to transmit information quickly and widely, linking distant places and diverse areas of endeavor in productive new ways.

Our world has experienced other periods of dramatic change driven by technology, for example, the impact of the steam engine, telephone, automobile, and railroad in the late nineteenth century, which created our urban industrialized society.[5] Never before have we experienced a technology that has evolved so rapidly, increasing in power by a hundredfold or more every decade, radically changing the constraints of space and time, and reshaping the way that we communicate, think, and learn.

Furthermore, unlike natural resources such as iron and oil that drove earlier economic transformations, knowledge is inexhaustible. The more it is used, the more it multiplies and expands. Knowledge is not available to all. It can be absorbed and applied only by the educated mind. Hence, as our society becomes ever more knowledge-intensive, it becomes ever more dependent upon those social institutions that create knowledge, that educate people, and that provide them with knowledge and learning resources throughout their lives.[6] Schools in general and universities in particular will play increasingly important roles as our society enters this new age. The increasingly sophisticated labor market of a knowledge-driven economy is driving new needs for advanced education and training. Even today roughly two-thirds of America's high school graduates will pursue some form of college education, and this will likely increase as a college degree becomes the entry credential to the high-performance workplace in the years ahead. There is an increasingly strong correlation between the level of one's education and personal prosperity and quality of life.

The age of knowledge holds an even deeper significance for higher education. In a sense, knowledge is the medium of the university. Through the activities of discovery, shaping, achieving, propagating, and applying knowledge, the university serves society in myriad ways: educating the young, preserving our cultural heritage, providing the basic research so essential to our security and well-being, training our professionals and certifying their competence, challenging our society, and stimulating social change. In a world in which knowledge and educated people have become the key to prosperity and security, there has been an increasing tendency for society to view the university as an engine for economic growth through the generation and application of new knowledge.

The university has survived other periods of technology-driven social change with its basic structure and activities intact, but the changes driven by evolving information technology are different, since they affect the very nature of the fundamental activities of the university: creating, preserving, integrating, transmitting, and applying knowledge. More fundamentally, because information technology changes the relationship between people and knowledge, it is likely to reshape in profound ways knowledge-based institutions such as the university.

THE IMPACT OF INFORMATION TECHNOLOGY
ON THE ACTIVITIES OF THE UNIVERSITY

Over the past several decades, computers have evolved into powerful information systems with high-speed connectivity to global communications networks. Public and private networks permit voice, image, and data to be made instantaneously available across the world to wide audiences at low costs. The creation of virtual environments, where human senses are exposed to artificially created sights, sounds, and feelings, liberates us from restrictions set by the physical forces of the world in which we live. Close, empathic, multiparty relationships mediated by visual and aural digital communications systems are becoming more common. They lead to the formation of closely bonded, widely dispersed communities of people interested in sharing new experiences and intellectual pursuits created within the human mind via sensory stimuli. Computer-based learning systems are also being implemented, opening the way to new modes of instruction and learning. New models of libraries are being provided to exploit the ability to access vast amounts of digital data in physically dispersed computer systems, which can be remotely accessed by users over information networks.

New forms of knowledge accumulation are evolving; written text, dynamic images, voices, and instructions on how to create new sensory environments can be packaged in dynamic modes of communication never before possible. The applications of such new knowledge forms challenge the creativity and intent of authors, teachers, and students. Technology such as computers, networks, wireless communications, and virtual reality may dramatically alter many of the current assumptions and thinking about the future nature of the university.

Several characteristics of information technology set it apart from earlier experiences with technology-driven change:

- It is active rather than passive;
- It radically changes the constraints of space and time (and perhaps reality);
- It exhibits an extraordinary rate of evolution, relentlessly increasing in power by factors of 100- to 1,000-fold decade after decade; and
- It unleashes the power of the marketplace.

Furthermore, this technology drives very significant restructuring of our society and social institutions through what John Seely Brown and Paul Duguid[7] term the 6-D effects of *demassification, decentralization, denationalization, despecialization, disintermediation,* and *disaggregation.* Perhaps we should also add a seventh "D," *democratization,* since digital technology provides unusual access to knowledge and knowledge services (such as education) hitherto restricted to the privileged few. Like the printing press, this technology not only enhances and broadly distributes access to knowledge but in the process shifts power away from institutions to those who are educated and trained in the use of the new knowledge media.

Although it has been slow in coming, we are beginning to see the impact of technology on university teaching. Today's "digital generation" of students, media-savvy, are demanding new forms of pedagogy. They approach learning as a "plug-and-play" experience; they are unaccustomed and unwilling to learn sequentially—to read the manual—and instead are inclined to plunge in and learn through participation and experimentation. Although this type of learning is far different from the sequential, pyramidal approach of the traditional college curriculum, it may be far more effective for this generation, particularly when provided through a media-rich environment. It challenges the faculty to design technology-rich experiences and environments based upon interactive, collaborative learning.

Sophisticated networks and software environments can be used to release the classroom from the constraints of space and time and make learning available to anyone, anyplace, anytime. The simplest approach uses multimedia technology via the Internet to enable distance learning. Yet many believe that effective computer-network-mediated learning will not be simply an Internet extension of correspondence or broadcast courses. Since learning happens most effectively in the presence of communities, the key impact of information technology may be the development of computer-mediated communities that are released from the constraints of space and time. There is already sufficient experience with such asynchronous learning networks to conclude that, at least for many subjects and when appropriately constructed, the computer-mediated distance learning process is just as effective as the classroom experience.[8]

The attractiveness of computer-mediated distance learning is obvious for adult learners whose work or family obligations prevent attendance at conventional campuses. Perhaps more surprising is the degree to which many on-campus students are now using computer-based distance learning to augment their traditional education. Broadband digital networks can be used to enhance the multimedia capacity of hundreds of classrooms across campus and link them with campus residence halls and libraries. Electronic mail, teleconferencing, and collaboration technology is transforming our institutions from hierarchical, static organizations to networks of more dynamic and egalitarian communities. The most significant advantage of computer-mediated distance learning is access. Perhaps we should substitute "distributed" for "distance" learning, since the powerful new tools provided by information technology have the capacity to enrich all of education, stimulating us to rethink education from the perspective of the learner. The rich resources and new forms of social interaction enabled by information technology create the possibility of the objective of "better than being there" for distributed learning environments.

Distance learning based on computer-network-mediated paradigms allows universities to push their campus boundaries outward to serve learners anywhere, anytime. Those institutions willing to and capable of building such learning networks could see their learning communities expand by an order of magnitude. In this sense, the traditional paradigm of "just-in-case" degree-based education can be more easily replaced by the "just in time" and "just-for-you" customized learning paradigms, more appropriate for a knowledge-driven society in which work and learning fuse.

In the near term, at least, traditional models of education will coexist with new learning paradigms, providing a broader spectrum of learning opportunities in the years ahead. The transitions from student to learner, from teacher to designer-coach-consultant, and from alumnus to lifelong member of a learning community seem likely. With these transitions and new options will come both an increasing ability and responsibility to select, design, and control the learning environment on the part of learners.

So, too, information technology is reshaping the nature of research. Today, problems that once required the computational capacity of rooms of supercomputers can be tackled with a laptop computer. The use of information technology to simulate natural phenomena has created a third modality of research, on a par with theory and experimentation. Some of the most powerful applications of this technology have been in the humanities, social sciences, and the arts. Scholars now can use digital libraries to access, search, and analyze the complete collection of scholarly journals or digital images of artistic objects. Social scientists are using powerful software tools to analyze massive data sets of verbal and visual materials collected through interviews and field studies. The visual and performing arts are exploring the new power of technologies that merge various media— art, music, dance, theater, architecture—and exploit all the senses—visual, aural, tactile, even olfactory—to create new art forms and artistic experiences.

The preservation of knowledge is one of the most rapidly changing functions of the university. The computer—or more precisely, the "digital convergence" of various media from print, to graphics, to sound, to sensory experiences through virtual reality—will likely move beyond the printing press in its impact on knowledge.[9] Throughout the centuries, the intellectual focal point of the university has been its library, its collection of written works preserving the knowledge of civilization. Today such knowledge exists in many forms—as text, graphics, sound, algorithms, and virtual reality simulations—and it exists almost literally in the ether, distributed in digital representations over worldwide networks, accessible by anyone, and certainly not the prerogative of the privileged few in academe.

The library is becoming less a collection house and more a center for knowledge navigation, a facilitator of information retrieval and dissemination.[10] In a sense, the library and the book are merging. One of the most profound changes will involve the evolution of software agents, collecting, organizing, relating, and summarizing knowledge on behalf of their human masters. The legal and economic management of digital information is rapidly becoming one of the most critical and complex issues facing higher education.

THE FORM, FUNCTION, AND FINANCING
OF THE UNIVERSITY

Colleges and universities are structured along intellectual lines, organized into schools and colleges, departments and programs that have evolved over the decades (some would suggest following more the structure of nineteenth-century science and literature rather than twenty-first-century knowledge). Furthermore, the governance, leadership, and management of the contemporary university are structured to reflect this intellectual organization as well as academic values of the university such as academic freedom and institutional autonomy rather than the command-communication-control administrative pyramid characterizing most organizations in business and government. The "contract" between members of the faculty and the university also reflects the unusual character of academic values and roles, the practice of tenure being perhaps the most visible example.

We have suggested that information technology is already having great impact on the university. It has modified its fundamental activities of education, scholarship, and service to society quite significantly. Digital technology has created new channels of communication throughout the university and with the broader society through mechanisms such as electronic mail, chat rooms, and Web site conferences that largely bypass traditional administrative arrangement and external relationships. Technology is also transforming the manner in which information concerning the university, its people, and its activities is gathered, stored, and utilized.

Just as the university is challenged in adapting to new forms of teaching and research enabled by rapidly evolving information technology, so, too, its organization, governance, management, and its relationships to students, faculty, and staff will require serious reevaluation and almost certain change. For example, the new tools of scholarship and scholarly communication are eroding conventional disciplinary boundaries and extending the intellectual span, interests, and activities of faculty far beyond traditional organizational units such as departments, schools, or campuses. This is particularly the case with younger faculty members whose interests and activities frequently cannot be characterized by traditional disciplinary terms.

Beyond driving a restructuring of the intellectual disciplines, information technology is likely to force a significant disaggregation of the university on both the horizontal (e.g., academic disciplines) and vertical (e.g., student services) scales. Faculty activity and even loyalty are increasingly associated with intellectual communities that extend across multiple institutions, frequently on a global scale. New providers are emerging that can far better handle many traditional university services, ranging from student housing, testing, and evaluation to facilities management and health care. Colleges and universities will increasingly face the question of whether they should continue their full complement of activities or outsource some functions to lower-cost and higher-quality providers, relying on new paradigms such as e-business and knowledge management.

It has become increasingly important that university planning and decision making not only take account of technological developments and challenges but also draw upon the expertise of people with technological expertise. Yet all too often, university leaders, governing boards, and even faculties ignore the rapid evolution of this technology, treating it more as science fiction than as representing serious institutional challenges and opportunities. To a degree this is not surprising, since in the early stages, new technologies sometimes look decidedly inferior to long-standing practices. For example, few would regard the current generation of computer-mediated distance learning programs as providing the socialization function associated with undergraduate education in a residential campus environment. Yet there have been countless instances of technologies, from personal computers to the Internet, that were characterized by technology learning curves far steeper than conventional practices. Such "disruptive technologies" have demonstrated the capacity to destroy entire industries, as the rapid growth e-commerce makes all too apparent.[11]

So, too, colleges and universities will need to reconsider a broad array of policies that have become antiquated in the digital age. Clearly, those policies governing intellectual property, whether created through research or instructional activities, require a major overhaul. Traditional patent, copyright, and technology transfer policies make little sense in a world in which the digital products of intellectual activity can be reproduced an infinite number of times with perfect accuracy and at almost zero cost.[12]

Furthermore, the relationship between the university and its faculty, staff, and students needs to be reconsidered. The university will face a major challenge in retaining instructional "mind-share" among its best-known faculty. Although we have long since adapted to the reality of those faculty getting release time and very substantial freedom with regard to research activities, there will be new challenges as instructional content becomes a valuable commodity in a for-profit postsecondary education marketplace. Do we need new policies that restrict the faculty's ability to contract with outside organizations for instructional learningware? Can these policies be enforced in the highly competitive marketplace for our best faculty? Is it possible that we will see an unbundling of students and faculty from the university, with students acting more as mobile consumers, able to procure educational services from a highly competitive marketplace, and faculty members acting more as freelance consultants, selling their services and their knowledge to the highest bidder?

Beyond this, we will face an ever-mounting challenge in helping our students and faculties keep abreast of the extraordinary pace of technology evolution. Many universities are simply unprepared for the new plug-and-play generation, already experienced in using computers and Net-savvy, who will expect—indeed, demand—sophisticated computing environments at college. In the old days we would wait for a generation of professors to pass on before an academic unit could evolve. In today's high-paced world, when the doubling time for technology evolution has collapsed to a year or less, we simply must look for effective ways to reskill our faculties or risk rapid obsolescence.

In positioning itself for this future of technology-driven change, universities should recognize several facts of contemporary life. First, robust, high-speed networks are becoming not only available but also absolutely essential for knowledge-driven enterprises such as universities. Powerful computers and network appliances are available at reasonable prices to students, but these require a supporting network infrastructure. There will continue to be diversity in the technology needs of the faculty, with intensive needs arising not only in science and engineering but also in parts of the university such as the arts and humanities where strong external support may not be available.

All universities face major challenges in keeping pace with the profound evolution of information and its implications for their activities. Not the least of these challenges is financial. It is of particular note that 40 percent of all new investment in capital facilities in our society today goes to acquire and support such technology. This need for investment in information technology applies to universities just as much as it does to the commercial or government sector, and it poses just as much of a challenge. As a rule of thumb, many organizations have found that staying abreast of this technology requires an annual investment of 10 percent or greater of their operating budget. For a very large campus, this can amount to hundreds of millions of dollars per year.

Historically, technology has been seen as a capital expenditure for universities or as an experimental tool to be made available to only a few. In the future, higher education should conceive of information technology both as an investment and as a strategic asset, critical to a university's academic mission that must be provided on a robust basis to the entire faculty, staff, and student body. Colleges and universities could learn an important lesson from the business community: investment in robust information technology represents the table stakes for survival in the age of knowledge. If an organization is not willing to invest in this technology, then it may as well accept being confined to a backwater in the knowledge economy, if it survives at all.

Few universities have a sustainable financial model for investing in information technology. Accustomed to a budgeting culture driven by faculty appointments and physical facilities, they are unable to cope with investments that become obsolete on timescales of years rather than decades. Rather, they tend to lurch from one crisis to the next in their attempts to provide the IT infrastructure demanded by students and faculty, without a strategic sense of direction as they face the choice between "bricks" and "clicks."

THE POSTSECONDARY EDUCATION ENTERPRISE

The "e-economy" is growing at an annual rate of 175 percent. It is estimated that by 2004, the e-economy will be $7 trillion, roughly 20 percent of the global economy. Beyond providing the graduates and knowledge needed by this digital economy, the contemporary university must be able to function in an increasingly digital world, in the way that it manages its resources, relates to clients, customers, and providers, and conducts its affairs. Put another way, "e-commerce," "e-business," and the "e-economy" must become an integral part of the university's future if it is to survive the digital age.

In the past, most colleges and universities served local or regional populations. While there was competition among institutions for students, faculty, and resources—at least in the United States—the extent to which institutions controlled the awarding of degrees, that is, credentialing, gave universities an effective monopoly over advanced education. However, today all of these market constraints are being challenged. The growth in the size and complexity of the postsecondary enterprise is creating an expanding array of students and educational providers. Information technology diminishes the barriers of space and time, and new competitive forces such as virtual universities and for-profit education providers enter the marketplace to challenge credentialing.[13]

In higher education, just as in other sectors of our economy, the Internet is redefining the basis for competitive advantage and survival. It is redefining boundaries and blurring roles. This technology, coupled with the emergence of new competitive forces driven by changing societal needs (e.g., adult education) and economic realities (the erosion in public tax support), is likely to drive a massive restructuring of the higher education enterprise. From the experience with other restructured sectors of our economy such as health care, transportation, communications, and energy, we could expect to see a significant reorganization of higher education, complete with the mergers, acquisitions, new competitors, and new products and services that have characterized other economic transformations. More generally, we may well be seeing the early stages of the appearance of a *global knowledge and learning industry*, in which the activities of traditional academic institutions converge with other knowledge-intensive organizations such as telecommunications, entertainment, and information service companies.

The size of the education component of this industry, consisting of K–12, higher education, and corporate learning, is enormous, estimated at over $740 billion in the United States and $2 trillion globally.[14] It is growing rapidly, driven by the increasing importance of human capital to our knowledge-driven economy. Business leaders are united in their belief that there is no bigger challenge in the global marketplace today than how to obtain, train, and retrain knowledge workers. The new economy is a knowledge economy based on brainpower, ideas, and entrepreneurism. Technology is its driving force, and human capital is its fuel.[15]

A key factor in this restructuring has been the emergence of new, aggressive, for-profit educator-providers that are able to access the private capital markets (over $4 billion in the year 2000). Most of these new entrants, such as the University of Phoenix and Jones International University, are focusing on the adult education market. Some, such as Unext.com, have aggressive growth strategies beginning first with addressing the needs for business education of corporate employees. Using on-line education, they are able to offer cost reductions of 60 percent or more over conventional corporate training programs since they avoid travel and employee time off. They are investing heavily (over $100 million in 2000) in developing sophisticated instructional content, pedagogy, and assessment measures, and they are likely to move up the learning curve to offer broader educational programs, both at the undergraduate level and in professional areas such as engineering and law. In a sense, therefore, the initial focus of new for-profit entrants on low-end adult education is misleading, since in five years or less their capacity to compete with traditional colleges and universities may become formidable.

THE CHALLENGE OF UNIVERSITY LEADERSHIP IN THE DIGITAL AGE

Today's university leaders face many important questions and decisions concerning the impact of information technology on their institutions. For example, they need to understand the degree to which this technology will transform the basic activities of teaching, research, and service. How should the university integrate information technology into its educational programs at the undergraduate, graduate, and professional school level? Will e-learning environments affect traditional teacher-centered instruction and promote more student-centered learning? How will the residential campus experience be affected? What will become of the classroom? Will information technology alter the priorities among various university activities, for example, the balance of educational activities related to socializing high school graduates compared to the rapid growth in the need for advanced education of adults in the high-performance workplace? Has information technology brought us to an inflection point in recasting the social contract for scientific research and in finding and utilizing new tools and methods for tackling major research problems?

More pragmatically, what kind of information technology infrastructure (hardware, software, staffing) will the research university need, and how will it finance the acquisition and maintenance of this infrastructure? How should the university approach its operations and management to best take advantage of this technology? How can institutions better link planning and decision making with likely technological developments and challenges? How do university leaders get the attention of faculty and governing boards concerning the imperative nature of these issues? How can one provide students, faculty, and staff with the necessary training, support, and equipment to keep pace with the rapid evolution of information technology? What policies does the university need to reconsider in light of evolving information technology (e.g., intellectual property, copyright, instructional content ownership, and faculty contracts)?

There are important questions concerning the broader higher education enterprise. How do colleges and universities address the rapidly evolving commercial marketplace for educational services and content, including, in particular, the for-profit and dot-com providers? What alliances are useful for colleges and universities in this rapidly changing environment? With other academic institutions? With business? On a regional, national, or global scale? Will more (or perhaps most) universities find themselves competing in a global marketplace, and how will that square with the responsibilities of publicly supported universities? What is the role of universities with respect to the "digital divide," the stratification of our society and our world with respect to access to technology?

The list of questions and issues seems not only highly complex but sometimes overwhelming to university leaders, not to mention the state and federal governments that support higher education in America. Surveys suggest, however, that despite the profound nature of these issues, information technology usually does not rank high among the list of priorities for university planning and decision making.[16] Perhaps this is due to the limited experience that most college and university leaders have with this emerging technology. It could also be a sign of indecisiveness and procrastination. As the pace of technological change continues to accelerate, indecision and inaction can be the most dangerous course of all.

As information technology continues to evolve at its relentless, indeed, ever-accelerating pace, affecting nearly every aspect of our society and our social institutions, organizations in every sector are grappling with the need to transform their basic philosophies and processes of how they collect, synthesize, manage, and control information. Corporations and governments are reorganizing in an effort to utilize technology to enhance productivity, improve quality, and control costs. Entire industries have been restructured to better align with the realities of the digital age.

To date, the university stands apart, almost unique in its determination to moor itself to past traditions and practices, to insist on performing its core teaching activities much as it has done in the past. Our limited use of technology thus far has been at the margins, to provide modest additional resources to classroom pedagogy or to attempt to extend the physical reach of our current classroom-centered, seat time-based teaching paradigm. It is ironic indeed that the very institutions that have played such a profound role in developing the digital technology now reshaping our world are the most resistant to reshaping their activities to enable its effective use.

THE DARWINIAN WORLD OF DIGITAL TECHNOLOGY

The digital age poses many challenges and opportunities for the contemporary university. As previously stated, for most of the history of higher education in America, we have expected students to travel to a physical place, a campus, to participate in a pedagogical process involving tightly integrated studies based mostly on lectures and seminars by recognized experts. Yet, as the constraints of time and space and monopoly—and perhaps even reality itself—are relieved by information technology, will the university as a physical place continue to hold its relevance?

In the near term it seems likely that the university as a physical place, a community of scholars and a center of culture, will remain. Information technology will be used to augment and enrich the traditional activities of the university, in much their traditional forms. To be sure, the current arrangements of higher education may shift. For example, students may choose to distribute their college education among residential campuses, commuter colleges, and on-line or virtual universities. They may also assume more responsibility for, and control over, their education.

For the longer term, however, it is clear that should the evolution of digital technology continue at its relentless, exponential pace, the very nature of the university, just like our society, will change very profoundly. Here we must take great care not simply to extrapolate the past but instead to examine the full range of possibilities for the future. There is clearly a need to explore new forms of learning and learning institutions that are capable of sensing and understanding the change and of engaging in the strategic processes necessary to adapt or control it.

No one knows what this profound alteration in the fabric of our world will mean, both for academic work and for our entire society. As William Mitchell, dean of architecture at the Massachusetts Institute of Technology (MIT), stresses, "the information ecosystem is a ferociously Darwinian place that produces endless mutations and quickly weeds out those no longer able to adapt and compete. The real challenge is not the technology, but rather imagining and creating digitally mediated environments for the kinds of lives that we will want to lead and the sorts of communities that we will want to have."[17] It is vital that we begin to experiment with the new paradigms that this technology enables. Otherwise, we may find ourselves deciding how the technology will be used without really understanding the consequences of our decisions.

Information technology poses certain risks to the university. It will create strong incentives to standardize higher education, perhaps reducing it to its lowest common denominator of quality. It could dilute our intellectual resources and distribute them through unregulated agreements between faculty and electronic publishers. It will almost certainly open up the university to competition, both from other educational institutions as well as from the commercial sector. Information technology will also present extraordinary opportunities as it rapidly becomes a liberating force in our society, not only freeing us from the mental drudgery of routine tasks but also linking us together in ways that we never dreamed possible. Furthermore, the new knowledge media enable us to build and sustain new types of learning communities, less constrained by space and time barriers. This technology will distribute more broadly access to the unique resources of the university for teaching and scholarship. Higher education must define its relationship with these emerging possibilities in order to create a compelling vision for its future.[18]

We believe that there is a need to address the impact of information technology on the university and the issues that it poses to university leaders in such a way as not only to enhance their understanding but to enable them to make decisions and take action. This book has been written, in part, in a pragmatic vein because of the urgency of the near-term technology issues facing higher education. However, it is also important to recognize the limitations of simply assuming that what exists at present—or in the past—will continue to influence the future and instead attempt to identify the key trends and possibilities that may characterize the longer-term future of higher education in the digital age.

NOTES

1. This scenario, written by Frank DeSanto, was developed for the Vision 2010 Project, directed by Daniel E. Atkins and sponsored by the Carnegie Foundation for the Advancement of Teaching <http://www.si.umich.edu/V2010/scen-ne.html>.

2. John Seely Brown and Paul Duguid, "Universities in the Digital Age," *Change* (July 1996), 11–19.

3. Erich Bloch, National Science Foundation, testimony to Congress, 1988.

4. A word here to address those concerns sometimes raised about the precision of the language used to describe digital technology. Webster's dictionary defines:

- *Data*: Factual information (such as measurements of statistics) used as a basis for reasoning, discussion, and calculation.
- *Information*: The communication or reception of knowledge or intelligence; knowledge obtained from investigation, study, or instruction.
- *Knowledge*: The fact or condition of knowing something with familiarity gained through experience or association; acquaintance with or understanding of a science, art, or technique; the fact or condition of being aware of something.
- *Wisdom*: Accumulated philosophic or scientific learning; the ability to discern inner qualities and relationships; a wise attitude or course of action.

5. Carolyn Marvin, *When Old Technologies Were New* (New York: Oxford University Press, 1988); Robert Pool, *Beyond Engineering: How Society Shapes Technology* (New York: Oxford University Press, 1997).

6. Derek Bok, *Universities and the Future of America* (Durham, NC: Duke University Press, 1990).

7. John Seely Brown and Paul Duguid, *The Social Life of Information* (Cambridge: Harvard Business School Press, 2000).

8. *On-Line Education: Learning Effectiveness and Faculty Satisfaction*, Proceedings of the 1999 Sloan Summer Workshop on Asynchronous Learning Networks, John Bourne, ed. (Nashville: Center for Asynchronous Learning Networks, 2000).

9. James Dewar, "The Information Age and the Printing Press: Looking Backward to See Ahead," Report R8014 Rand Corporation, Santa Monica, CA, February 2001.

10. "Books, Bricks, and Bytes," *Daedelus* 125, no. 4 (1996), v–vii.

11. Clayton M. Christensen, *The Innovator's Dilemma* (Cambridge: Harvard Business School Press, 1997); Christensen contrasts "sustaining" and "disruptive" technologies. Well-managed companies are excellent at developing the sustaining technologies that improve the performance of their products in ways that matter to their customers. Disruptive technologies, however, are distinctly different from sustaining technologies. Disruptive technologies change the value proposition in a market. When they first appear, they almost always offer lower performance in terms of the attributes that mainstream customers care about. Disruptive technologies have other attributes that a few fringe (generally new) customers value. They are typically cheaper, smaller, simpler, and frequently more convenient to use. Therefore, they open up new markets. With experience and sufficient investment, the developers of disruptive technologies will always improve their products' performance; they eventually are able to take over older markets. This is because they are able to deliver sufficient performance on the old attributes, while adding some new ones.

12. John Perry Barlow, "The Economy of Ideas: A Framework for Rethinking Patents and Copyrights in the Digital Age," *Wired* 2, no. 3 (March 1994).

13. Stan Davis and Jim Botkin, *The Monster under the Bed* (New York: Touchstone, 1995); Ted Marchese, "Not-So-Distant Competitors: How New Providers Are Remaking the Postsecondary Marketplace," *AAHE Bulletin* (May 1998); David Collis, "When Industries Change: Scenarios for Higher Education," in *Forum Futures 1999* (New Haven, CT: Forum for the Future of Higher Education, 1999), 47–72; David Collis, "New Business Models for Higher Education," in *The Internet and the University*, ed. Maureen Devlin, Richard Larson, and Joel Meyerson (Boulder: Educause, 2001), 97–116.

14. Michael T. Moe, *The Knowledge Web* (New York: Merrill-Lynch, 2000).

15. An interesting data point: compare the market-capitalization per employee of three companies: General Motors at $141,682; the Walt Disney Company at $743,530; and Yahoo! at $33 million! Indeed, the top 10 Internet companies have

a market cap per employee of over $38 million. The reason is simple: in the knowledge economy, the key asset driving corporate value is no longer physical or financial capital but rather intellectual and human capital. (Ibid.)

16. Convocation on Stresses on Research and Education at Colleges and Universities (Government-University-Industry Research Roundtable and National Science Board) (Washington, DC: National Academy of Sciences, 1997), <http://www2.nas.edu/guirrcon/>.

17. William J. Mitchell, *City of Bits: Space, Place, and the Infobahn* (Cambridge: MIT Press, 1995), <http://www-mitpress.mit.edu/City_of_Bits>.

18. James J. Duderstadt, *A University for the 21st Century* (Ann Arbor: University of Michigan Press, 2000).

CHAPTER

The Evolution of Information Technology

Although the past century was a period of rapid technological change in areas such as transportation and energy, the exponential growth of digital technology and its impact on knowledge, the very fabric of contemporary society, set it apart. Social institutions such as business, government, and, of course, universities, which traditionally change on timescales of years, if not decades, have great difficulty in coping with a technology that doubles in power every one to two years.

This characteristic of exponential growth is important to stress, since it is difficult to understand and appreciate just how rapidly information technology is evolving. Four decades ago, one of the earliest computers, ENIAC, stood 10 feet tall, stretched 80 feet wide, included more than 17,000 vacuum tubes, and weighed about 30 tons. The University of Michigan has 10 percent of ENIAC on display in a glass case looming over students in the lobby of the computer science department. But today you can buy a musical greeting card with a silicon chip more powerful than the ENIAC computer. Already a modern $1,000 notebook computer has more computing horsepower than a $20 million supercomputer of the early 1990s.

To members of today's university faculties, the extraordinary pace of evolution of this technology has more personal significance since their careers, indeed, their lives have both spanned and been shaped by the history of this technology. They have experienced firsthand the "technology turns" in:

- Computing paradigms from mainframes, to minicomputers, to micro-computers, to microchips

- Supercomputers from the IBM Stretch, to CDC Star, to Crays, to ASCI White and the Japan Earth Simulator
- Network technology from Ethernet, to Arpanet, to NSFnet, to Internet, to Internet2
- Human-machine interfaces from keypunched cards, to teletype terminals, to graphical displays, to GUIs, to virtual reality CAVEs
- Access from batch processing, to time-sharing, to personal computing, to client-server, to distributed processing, to wireless mobility
- Personal computers from the TRS 80 and Apple II, to the IBM PC and Macintosh, to Pentium PCs and PowerPC Macs
- Operating systems from Unix, to MS-DOS, to Mac OS, to Windows, to Linux
- Personal computing from time-sharing terminals, to desktop workstations, to notebook computers, to personal digital appliances, to ubiquitous computing

All university activities, from research to teaching, from administration to communication, have been influenced by this technology from the earliest days of our careers. The activities of scholars, teachers, and administrators were reshaped by each new "killer application" (killer app):

- E-mail
- word processors
- spreadsheets
- symbolic mathematical tools such as Mathematica or Maple
- idea processors
- presentation software
- Web browsers
- data warehouses and data mining
- Net-based telephony and video streaming

Looking back over the past several decades, it is hard to imagine how university teachers, scholars, and administrators could have functioned without these tools, yet the extraordinary evolution of digital technology continues to accelerate.

THE STATE OF THE ART

The early development of the digital computer was driven very much by national security applications such as the design of nuclear weapons and the breaking of military codes. In fact, ENIAC itself was designed to perform the very complex calculations describing the radiation-hydrodynamics of the first hydrogen bomb. For decades, these applications drove the development of computer technology, with a standing order at nuclear weapons laboratories such as Los Alamos or Livermore for delivery of model serial number one of each new computer design. Although computationally intensive applications such as the simulation of nuclear systems, cryptography, astrophysics, meteorology, and genomics continue to drive the state of the art in supercomputer development, the evolution and applications of digital technology have extended into every sector of our society.

From Mainframes to Microchips

The earliest applications of the technology involved large mainframe computers ("big iron") designed for scientific computation or business data processing. During the early years these computers, typically filling a large room or even a building, were operated in batch mode, in which users would bring programs or software on punch cards to be loaded in the computer, with output printed on paper. However, during the 1960s time-sharing operating systems were developed that allowed a large number of users to simultaneously access the mainframe computer through teletype or video displays, utilizing small slices of its operating cycle.

With the development of semiconductor and then integrated circuit technology, it was possible to dramatically reduce computers from the size of a room to that of a refrigerator, leading to so-called minicomputers such as the Digital Equipment Corporation's PDP and VAX designs. These were typically operated by individual departments or user groups rather than the broader enterprise. Major breakthroughs were also occurring in software, such as the development of the Unix operating system and the Ethernet for local area networks.

By the 1970s, miniaturization had evolved to the point where it was possible to build "microcomputers" the size of a typewriter. Although the early applications of these small computers were limited, entrepreneurs such as Gordon Moore and Bill Gates saw the potential of personal computing, and today's industry giants such as Intel and Microsoft are the result. The technology continued to shrink, and it became possible to fabricate an entire computer on a single integrated circuit microchip. This has led to an explosion of applications of digital technology, from the microprocessors and sensors used in the modern automobile (which now consists of more computers and electronics than steel and glass, at least in cost), to tiny wireless devices such as cellular phones and Palm Pilots, to chips so tiny that they can be implanted in the human body.

For the first several decades of the information age, the evolution of hardware technology followed the trajectory predicted by "Moore's law"— a 1965 observation/prediction by Intel founder Gordon Moore that the chip density and consequent computing power for a given price double every 18 months.[1] Although this was intended to describe the evolution of silicon-based microprocessors, it turns out that almost every aspect of digital technology has doubled in power roughly every 12 to 18 months, with some technologies such as optical computing, telecommunications, and wireless technology evolving even more rapidly.

Put another way, digital technology is characterized by the extraordinary pace of *exponential* evolution in which characteristics such as computing speed, memory, and network transmission speeds for a given price increase by a factor of 100 to 1,000 every decade. Furthermore, the technology becomes ever smaller and ever more connected.

The evolution of digital technology has been characterized by such exponential growth for over 50 years. But can we expect it to continue? Will Moore's law continue to hold? After all, if information technology continues to evolve at its present rate, by the year 2020, the $1,000 notebook computer will have a computing speed of 1 million gigahertz, a memory of thousands of terabits, and linkages to networks at data transmission speeds of gigabits per second. It will have a data processing and memory capacity roughly comparable to that of the human brain.[2] It will be so tiny as to be almost invisible, and it will communicate with billions of other computers through wireless technology.

To be sure, computer technologists are notoriously poor at predictions (as exemplified by the famous 1950s claim by IBM's Thomas Watson that the world would never need more than a few computers). Even today digital technology has reached some formidable goals. For example, the information density on hard drives is doubling every year. Today we can put a gigabyte of data on a disk the size of a quarter. Bandwidth is continuing to increase rapidly, with 100 Mb/s local networks routine and 10 Gb/s network backbones common. Software algorithm development is also moving ahead at a pace even faster than Moore's law, and with open source software paradigms, applications software is advancing rapidly.

We can confidently predict the general features of digital technology evolution over the next several years, at least, as characterized in Table 2.1.

To illustrate, it is useful to consider several specific areas of digital technology.

Table 2.1
Projected Evolution of Digital Technology

	Today	Soon
Internet Backbone	Gb/s	Tb/s
Local Networks	Mb/s	Gb/s
Access	100 Kb/s	100 Mb/s
Wireless	14 Kb/s	2 MB/s
Desktop computer	GHz	THz
Super computer	10 Thz	PHz
Databases	Tb	Pb

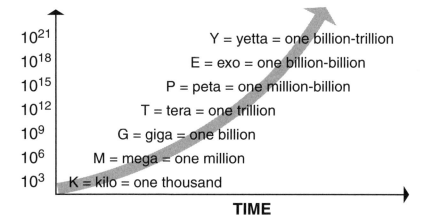

$$10^{21}$$
$$10^{18}$$
$$10^{15}$$
$$10^{12}$$
$$10^{9}$$
$$10^{6}$$
$$10^{3}$$

Y = yetta = one billion-trillion
E = exo = one billion-billion
P = peta = one million-billion
T = tera = one trillion
G = giga = one billion
M = mega = one million
K = kilo = one thousand

TIME

Hardware

The evolution of computer hardware can be illustrated by considering scientific computing and the evolution of supercomputers, the very high end of computing designed to address the most computationally demanding applications. This technology is usually driven by defense applications such as nuclear weapons development. In an effort to comply with the Comprehensive Test Ban Treaty, the United States has launched a major program to maintain the integrity of its current nuclear weapons stockpile by using supercomputers to simulate weapons performance, and this has triggered a major new evolutionary surge in supercomputer development in the Department of Energy known as the Advanced Simulation and Computing Initiative (ASCI). Typical of today's powerful supercomputers is an IBM machine known as ASCI White, installed at the Lawrence Livermore

National Laboratory, where it is used to simulate nuclear explosions. ASCI White consists of an interconnected cluster of 512 machines and covers an area equivalent to two basketball courts. Within each machine are 16 microprocessors that share access to a single memory. Together, ASCI White's 8,192 processors can perform calculations at the rate of 12 trillion operations per second.[3] This is roughly equivalent to the combined computing power of 30,000 desktop personal computers (PCs).

A further evolutionary advance is already in development, simulated by the new field of proteomics, the calculation of how proteins fold into the distinctive shapes key to biological function. The protein folding calculation is formidable even by the standards of nuclear weapons design, and hence an entirely new architecture of supercomputers is being developed by IBM—known as Blue Gene, naturally enough. This machine will be 100 times faster than ASCI White—with a speed of 1 million billion operations per second—a "petaflop" computer[4] (which not only is the equivalent of 2 million of today's personal computers but is also comparable to the processing power of the human brain—and to Kurzweil's predictions for the personal computer of the year 2020).

Blue Gene's processors and memory will sit side by side on the same chips. One might even consider Blue Gene to be an enormous "smart memory"—a collection of 36,864 memory chips, each containing 16 Mb of memory and 32 processor "cores," with each processor capable of running eight separate calculations at once. Blue Gene will be self-healing in the sense that it will diagnose and fix any hardware failures. This machine is expected to be up and running by 2006, with "exoflop" and "yettaflop" machines (perhaps distributed over networks) almost certain to follow.

Beyond processing power, both storage and bandwidth are evolving rapidly to handle the enormous flow of data created by research instrumentation such as Earth-observing satellites, high-energy physics particle accelerators, and digital video data archives. For example, when the Large Hadron Collider comes on-line in 2005, the collisions of its subatomic particles will generate a data stream of six petabytes every year, much of which must be transported to research centers around the world. To put this in perspective, it might be noted that a petabyte is equivalent to the capacity of 1 million PC hard-drives or a stack of CD-ROMs nearly 2 km high.

Yet storage technology is keeping pace with these demands. With microdrives in the gigabyte range and today's laptops with 100 Gb hard-drives and DVD removable media drives, it is now possible to walk around with data equivalent to that of a city library. The areal density of data that one can store on a magnetic or laser disk continues to double every 12 months.

In fact, today's personal computers are increasingly provided with CD or DVD read/write drives, since it is cheaper simply to burn a CD to transfer large amounts of data to another machine than to transfer it via networks or floppy disks. This foreshadows the day, soon coming, in which data storage becomes so cheap that there is no point of erasing it anymore. Imagine a world of "forget-nothing" technology, in which you can walk around with a camera on your shoulder recording everything you see or hear for essentially permanent storage. (Of course, then the challenge becomes how one sorts through this massive amount of data, but that is a problem for software engineers and librarians.)

As computers increase in power and shrink in size, some of the most interesting applications occur in consumer products. For example, the contemporary automobile is more computer than car, with dozens of sensors and computers controlling all aspects of its operation and maintenance. Gaming consoles such as the Sony Playstation and Microsoft X-Box are actually very powerful special-purpose computers. (In fact, the Sony Playstation 2 was first classified as a supercomputer and subject to export restrictions.) Since history has shown that today's laptops typically have the processing power of a state-of-the-art supercomputer of a decade earlier, we can well imagine commodity-priced personal digital devices with the power of IBM's Blue Gene by the year 2020.

Display technology is also evolving rapidly, with the next generation of 10 megapixel displays achieving resolutions that make them literally better than paper (and more akin to 35mm film resolution). With developments such as electronic ink and flexible integrated circuit substrates, future displays may have the convenience of paper as well. Wall-sized displays and surround sound systems are appearing that promise to make teleconferencing far more effective. Perhaps most significant, new "heads-up" human–machine interfaces are being developed that use lasers to paint images directly on the retina. One can imagine that full 360-degree immersive interfaces worn as glasses (or perhaps even implants) will soon be possible that will remove entirely the limitations of conventional video displays.

Software

Software is also evolving rapidly. Although we typically view software as lagging behind hardware development, in truth, applications such as the spreadsheet in the late 1970s (VisiCalc), the word processor in the 1980s, and the Internet browser in the 1990s provide ample illustration that such "killer applications" can drive hardware evolution (e.g., the Apple II, IBM PC, and DSL-broadband technologies). Today's applications and operating systems consist of millions of lines of computer code developed by teams of hundreds of software engineers.

There has been considerable progress in developing effective approaches to software development, including the automation of certain aspects of programming. Furthermore, new approaches to software development hold great promise. So-called genetic algorithms can be developed using a process akin to natural selection to allow the algorithms to improve themselves with experience. Open source software development, in which the software code is shared with others in the public domain so that a large user community can participate in its development, is also increasingly popular, as evidenced by the success of the Linux operating system.

Networks

The most dramatic impact on our world today from information technology is not in the continuing increase in computing power. It is due to the increase in bandwidth, the rate at which we can transmit digital information. From the 110 bps (bits per second) modems of the 1970s, we now routinely use wired and wireless 10 Mbps local area networks in our offices and houses. Gigabit-per-second networks now provide the backbone communications to link local networks, and with the rapid deployment of fiber-optic cables and optical switching, terabit-per-second networks are just around the corner. Laboratory demonstrations have achieved the bandwidth of more than eight terabytes per second over a single optical fiber, with a theoretical limit of 100 TB/s capable of serving 4 million personal computers, each viewing a unique High Definition Television (HDTV) program. At the turn of the century, fiber-optic cable was being installed throughout the world at the astounding equivalent rate of over 3,000 mph! In a sense, the price of data transport is in free fall, and with rapid advances in photonic and wireless technology, telecommunications will continue to evolve very rapidly for the foreseeable future.

One of the most important advances in information technology and telecommunications has been the Internet. During the early years of network technology, only a few thousand academics and government scientists used the collection of federal and private networks such as DARPAnet and Bitnet, both because of incompatible communications protocols and the difficulty in identifying and specifying various computers on the network. The networks were used primarily to provide access to mainframe computers and supercomputers.

Several events changed all of this, however. First, a standard communications protocol, TCI/IP, was adopted and allowed the various national networks to be merged into a single Internet. Second, technologies such as Gopher and Domain Name Service (DNS) were developed that made user access more transparent since no longer did one have to know the actual address of a computer in order to communicate with it. As a result, use of the Internet by academics and industry grew rapidly in the late 1980s and early 1990s. Two additional technologies, the World Wide Web, developed by high-energy physicists at CERN in Europe, and the Mosaic Web browser (later to become Netscape), developed by the University of Illinois, employed graphical methods and hyperlinks to make the use of the Internet even simpler, and the commercial world moved in rapidly to exploit it, as evidenced by the "dot-com" explosion of the late 1990s.

The key to the Internet was the use of low-cost, open standards for its development, in contrast to earlier networks using proprietary technology. No one firm or government agency or individual owns or controls Internet protocols or the rules for connecting to it or using it. Anyone can connect to the Net as long as he or she complies with these protocols. As more and more people linked into the Internet, it became more and more valuable. (The network analog to Moore's law is Metcalfe's law, named after Robert Metcalfe, the developer of Ethernet technology, which states that the value of a network is proportional to the square of the number of users.) The Internet not only has the potential to provide each user access to text, voice, and video at relatively low cost but also can enable broadcast to others on the network. In essence, the Internet allows each user to be both a consumer and a producer.

Accelerating this trend is the development of wireless technology to create small, mobile devices to access the Internet such as personal digital appliances (e.g., Palm Pilots) and Net-enabled cellular phones (so-called G-3 or third-generation technology). In fact, there is a sense that personal computers, now the most common way to access the Internet, will increasingly be replaced by so-called thin client systems that utilize relatively inexpensive commodity products such as cellular phones to access the Internet for sophisticated applications performed by network servers.

The emergence of broadband technology is certain to be a powerful catalyst in the Internet. The current drippy faucet of data that we receive over telephone lines will be replaced by a river of data from coax and fiber links. Cable companies, telephone companies, satellite/wireless distributors, and Internet service providers are locked in a battle over standards, protocols, open access, and data bandwidth. Most important will be the delivery of "always on" services, so that customers can access the Net in the same way that they use a television or other electrical appliances.

Since the introduction of the browser, the growth of the Internet has been staggering, doubling in number of users (servers) every six months. Already the Internet links together hundreds of millions of people, and estimates are that within a few years, this number will surge to billions, a substantial fraction of the world's population, driven in part by the fact that most economic activity will be based on digital communication. Bell Laboratories suggests that within two decades a "global communications skin" will have evolved, linking together billions of computers that handle the routine tasks of our society, from driving our cars to monitoring our health.

Access to computers and the Internet and the ability to use this technology are becoming increasingly important to full participation in America's economic, political, and social life. The challenge will be not only to handle the congested pathways that result from billions of users and devices and countless as yet unimagined applications but to provide robust connectivity to all members of our society rather than only to the prosperous and technological elite.

A Communications Medium

The nature of human interaction with the digital world—and with other humans through computer-mediated interactions—is evolving rapidly. We have moved beyond the simple text interactions of electronic mail and electronic conferencing, to graphical-user interfaces (e.g., the Mac or Windows world), to voice, to video. With the rapid development of sensors and robotic actuators, touch and action at a distance will soon be available. The world of the user is also increasing in sophistication, from the single dimension of text, to the two-dimensional world of graphics, to the three-dimensional world of simulation and role-playing. With virtual reality, it is likely that we will soon communicate with one another through simulated environments, through "telepresence," perhaps guiding our own software representations, our digital agents, to interact in a virtual world with those of our colleagues.

When we think of digitally mediated human interactions, we generally think of the awkwardness of E-mail or perhaps videophones, but as William Wulf puts it, "Don't think about today's teleconference technology, but one whose fidelity is photographic and 3-D. Don't think about the awkward way in which we access information on the network, but about a system in which the entire world's library is as accessible as a laptop computer. Don't think about the clumsy interface with computers, but one that is both high fidelity and intelligent."[5]

This is a very important point. A communications technology that increases in power by 100fold decade after decade will soon allow human interaction with essentially any degree of fidelity that we wish—3-D, multimedia, telepresence, perhaps even directly linking our neural networks into cyberspace, à la *Neuromancer*,[6] a merging of carbon and silicon.

THE IMPACT OF INFORMATION TECHNOLOGY ON SOCIETY

The penetration of digital technology into our society has proceeded at an extraordinary pace. In less than a decade the Internet has evolved from a research network, to a commercial infrastructure now reaching a significant fraction of our population and essentially all of our schools and businesses. Access to computers and the Internet and the ability to use this technology are becoming increasingly important to full participation in our nation's economic, political, and social life. Furthermore, the transition from phone links to broadband and eventually fiber optics will transform the frustrating pinging of modem-connectivity to a torrent of gigabit-per-second data flow over fiber optics into our homes, schools, and places of work.

Consider for a moment the following exercise. Think through your day's activities, from the moment when you wake until you return to bed at the end of the day. Try to identify the various ways that you encounter computers. While most of us first think of the trusty old computer workstation on our desktop, it does not take much further reflection to realize that we are surrounded by computers. Our radio-alarm clock contains a computer. Our watch is really a computer with a timing circuit. Our house is chocked full of computers—they control the temperature, make our coffee and toast, tune our television. The modern car is more computer and electronics these days—at least by cost—than it is metal and plastic. Our pager and cellular phone are computers. Our workplace is filled with computers. Even our credit card is becoming a tiny computer, capable of tracking our expenditures.

More specifically, IBM estimates that by 2004 there will be over 1.3 billion Net-enabled cellular phones or personal digital appliances (e.g., Palm Pilots) in the world.[7] In fact, almost every place in the world will have robust wireless access to the Internet—except for the United States, where our continued reliance on traditional telephone networks and our archaic practices and regulations have limited the growth of wireless technology. Estimates are that by the end of the decade, the number of people linked into the Internet will surge to billions, a substantial fraction of the world's population, driven in part by the fact that most economic activity will be based on digital communication.

Over the next decade, we will evolve from "giga" technology (in terms of computer operations per second, storage, or data transmission rates) to "peta" technology (1 million billion or 10^{15}).[8] We will denominate the number of computer servers in the billions, digital sensors in the tens of billions, and software agents in the trillions. The number of people linked together by digital technology will grow from millions to billions. We will evolve from "e-commerce" and "e-government" and "e-learning," to "e-everything"!

These, then, are the characteristics of information technology driving rapid and radical change in our world: the expansion from millions to billions of people using technologies such as the Internet; the shift of our world from 9 to 5 to 24/7 operations, always on, never off; the applications enabled by a "peta" technology; and the near-term possibility of telepresence. So, too, we face many challenges, not the least of which arise from our limited understanding and imagination. We still do not understand well the impact of human–machine interactions associated with the Internet, not to mention telepresence and virtual environments. Technology-driven productivity threatens to create a supply that now overwhelms demand. Our society increasingly suffers from knowledge indigestion, as the information overload associated with the digital revolution threatens to swamp us.

As William Mitchell, dean of the School of Architecture at MIT, suggests, "The emerging civic structures and spatial arrangements of the digital age will profoundly affect our access to economic opportunities and public services, the character and content of public discourse, the forms of cultural activity, the enaction of power, and the experiences that give shape and texture to our daily routines. The worldwide computer network—the electronic agora—subverts, displaces, and radically redefines our notions of gathering place, community, and urban life."[9]

The Digital Economy

The impact of digital technology on economic activity is profound. The transformation of business has typically been determined by the costs of transactions and transportation, and digital technologies are driving these down rapidly. In fact, some suggest that we are in the midst of a transition from the old economy, based on physical and financial capital and characterized by the pace dictated by transportation, to a new economy, global in extent, based on intellectual capital, and changing at a pace determined by the almost instantaneous speed of telecommunication.

If technology is the driver of the new economy, then human capital is its engine. The driving forces of the new economy are computers, telecommunications, health care, and instrumentation, and all depend heavily upon highly skilled knowledge workers, constituting roughly half of their workforce. Our e-economy is based on innovation and entrepreneurialism, on intellectual capital, on brainpower. As a recent Merrill Lynch report suggests, in a very real sense, e-commerce has become to the knowledge economy what railroads were to the Industrial Revolution.[10] The Net is building "knowledge tracks" that link the marketplace and business with knowledge centers such as schools and universities.

Beyond its dependence upon intellectual capital, the e-economy creates enormous incentives to reengineer activities. For example, IBM estimates that it saved over $300 million in 2000 by shifting its $14 billion of purchasing activities to the Internet. There are staggering increases in efficiency possible, if one can reengineer work to take advantage of technology. Note here the implications for the university, which has largely avoided reengineering the academic enterprise.

Other important trends characterize the e-economy. The tempo is accelerating faster than many organizations and social institutions can handle, yet it is not possible to stop the world. People are increasingly comfortable with technology and automated services, and they will demand these of the marketplace. Governments and universities will find their "customers" (citizens, students, staff) unhappy with old-fashioned forms, slow responses, and dated presentations. Students have no interest or tolerance for things being done the old ways. There is an increasing expectation of choice and relevance.

Of comparable significance to higher education is the way in which technology lowers the barriers for new competitors in the e-economy. There is an increasing move, enabled by information technology, toward selective outsourcing, more dynamic team building, and more interactive communications. Globalization is a growing fact of the marketplace; professionals work or move across borders as needed, utilizing the network to keep in touch with their employers and colleagues. There is increasing use of independent sources of information and new intermediaries (rating agencies, marketplaces, and brokers).

Major economic shifts require new technology platforms. The joining of computers and communications has only begun, and it has already redefined the value chain in many industries, just as it will do in higher education. We are entering the era of the temporary, recombinant, virtual organization—of business arrangements that demand good computing and telecommunications environments rather than large, permanent home offices. It will no longer be straightforward to distinguish between work time and "free" time or between production and consumption or between knowledge creation and transmission, that is, in the case of the university, between research and teaching.

Changing Lifestyles

Information technology has already stimulated profound changes in our lifestyles.[11] We sense the loosening constraints of space and time. Many of us have already discarded the burden of the daily commute in favor of "telecommuting" via our computer, modem, and fax. Others are finding that they have become tethered to their workplace with the electronic umbilical cord of pager and cellular phone. Electronic mail, voice mail, and fax are rapidly replacing "snail mail." Whether it is a university department, a commercial enterprise, or an individual, all are increasingly identified not by phone number or address but rather by the address (URL) of their Web site.

An interesting feature of these new communications technologies is the manner in which they shift and merge synchronous and asynchronous communication. Face-to-face human conversation is, of course, spatially coherent and strictly synchronous. In asynchronous communication, words are not heard as they are spoken but repeated at some later point, as are replies. While synchronous communication is frequently allowed and facilitated by electronic communication (e.g., two-way video), asynchronous communication sometimes has advantages. For example, E-mail allows one to reflect on a message before responding. Asynchronous communication over the Internet not only allows broadcasting to large numbers of people but furthermore allows the recipient to retrieve the message at a more convenient time and place. It also reduces barriers to global interaction across time zones. The increasing tilt toward electronic asynchrony will have increasingly dramatic effects upon lifestyle and workplace. For example, an on-line forum unfolds over an indefinite period, among dispersed participants who log in and out at arbitrary moments, through uncoordinated posting and receipt of E-mail messages. We have yet to see the full motion video and audio possibilities that await the bandwidth that we will soon have through cable modems and DSL; also to come are the new Net appliances, such as the portable Net in a phone, and a host of wireless technologies. Electronic interaction will become increasingly multimodal, as when videoconferencing combines sound and vision. Robotic actuators combined with audio and video sensors will provide telepresence.

Other aspects of our daily activities have changed dramatically. In the digital age, economic activity is driven by the production, transformation, distribution, and consumption of digital information. The physical marketplace is rapidly being augmented by "virtual" marketplaces based on networks, and computers are emerging as sites of economic activity. However, there is an important difference; digital information is unlike other economic goods—natural resources, human labor, property—in the very interesting respect that it cannot be used up. Use actually multiplies rather than diminishes digital products. Digital products can be reproduced an infinite number of times with perfect accuracy at essentially zero cost.[12] The concepts of property, copyright, patents, and laws—all based on physical manifestations—may no longer apply. The media with which we are all familiar, from books to television, are one-way propositions; they push their content at us. The Net is two-way, push and pull.

The Net is also the first medium that involves multiple forms of communication and cognition. This past century's concept of "literacy" grew out of our intense belief in text, a focus enhanced by the power of one particular technology—the typewriter or the printing press. These became great tools for writers but terrible ones for other creative activities such as sketching, painting, notating music, or even mathematics. The typewriter prized one particular kind of intelligence, but with the Net we suddenly have a medium that honors multiple forms of intelligence—abstract, textual visual, musical, social, and kinesthetic.

A third and unusual aspect of the Net is that it leverages the small efforts of the many with the large efforts of the few. At Michigan, our undergraduates use the Net to help high school students with their English composition courses. Maricopa Community College in Phoenix has found a way to link senior citizens with elementary pupils. At Hewlett Packard engineers use the Net to help K–12 students with science and math problems. The small efforts of the many—the seniors—complement the large efforts of the few—the teachers.

The Cybersphere

The most important feature of information technology is its ability to release people and their activities from the constraints of space and time.

The Internet, the World Wide Web, and their successors are evolving rapidly into a global digital network, a "cybersphere," interrelating people and their activities through robust, albeit ubiquitous, computers, networks, and intelligent hardware and software. To quote Mitchell once again, this will be a community "unrooted to any definite spot on the surface of the earth, shaped by connectivity and bandwidth constraints rather than by accessibility and land values, largely asynchronous in its operation, and inhabited by disembodied and fragmented subjects who exist as collections of aliases and agents."[13]

The cybersphere will be a global community, with physical infrastructure and users scattered widely across different political and cultural units, increasingly free from the norms and laws of nation-states. Because its electronic structure is so modular, geographically dispersed, and redundant, the cybersphere is essentially indestructible. The pervasiveness of networked computers depends primarily on access being affordable and on people's interest in having that access. If one has a computer, Internet connectivity costs are substantially less than the computer's cost, since each node is independent and has to handle its own financing and its own technical requirements.

This worldwide, electronically mediated environment in which networks are everywhere and in which most of the artifacts that function within it have intelligence and communications capabilities will pose great challenges to traditional societal institutions, but it will also create extraordinary opportunities. Nations that seek to remain economically competitive and prosperous will race to invest in the new electronic infrastructure, just as in the past they invested in public infrastructures such as railroads, highways, and airports. Nations dependent upon totalitarian governments and controlled economies may rapidly find themselves toppled by the free flow of information characterized by the global e-economy. The Internet, like the printing press, vastly improves the access, quality, and speed of information, enabling the individual to develop knowledge as never before. As with any force of mass distribution, the Internet will propel power toward the individual, devolving it away from the institution.

INFORMATION TECHNOLOGY AND THE UNIVERSITY

The digital computer was first developed in the laboratories of university scientists and engineers. Hence, it is not surprising that the earliest computers were designed for the solution of particular research problems such as complex mathematical equations arising in physics and engineering. As a consequence, few university faculty and students had direct experience with digital technology during its early years. Both the design and the development of the hardware and the programming of computers—much of it in low-level machine language—were frequently done directly by faculty and their graduate students.

This began to change in the early 1960s with the appearance on campus of large, mainframe computers such as the IBM 704 series, capable of more general applications. Although more faculty and students had access to such machines, their cost, size, and complexity demanded unique facilities (temples) attended by specialized staff (priests). To use these machines, one first had to obtain an account, then use a keypunch to prepare a deck of cards containing the program and data, submit these as a "batch job" to the computer center temple, and then wait for hours (sometimes days) for the job to be run by the priests on the computer and the output to be available as printed stacks of paper. Although some programming continued to be done in machine language or assembly language, the appearance of higher-level languages such as FORTRAN and COBOL simplified programming considerably. However, few off-the-shelf programs were available, and the use of computers required considerable knowledge of programming. At roughly the same time, computers also began to appear at larger universities to support business operations such as accounting and payroll processing. Business and administrative computing was generally kept quite separate from academic computing.

The most significant breakthrough of the 1960s was the introduction of time-sharing operating systems that allowed large numbers of users to simultaneously access mainframe computers remotely, through teletypes or CRT-display terminals. Hundreds or, on some campuses, even thousands of faculty and students could acquire accounts for use of computing resources. Not only did this stimulate a more pervasive use of the computer in research, but computer assignments also began to appear in the curriculum, particularly in disciplines such as engineering. Nevertheless, computing was still an extremely expensive activity and usually under central control.

The monopoly of "big iron" mainframe computers was broken in the 1970s with the introduction of small (desk-size rather than room-size) minicomputers based on integrated circuit technology. Although computers such as the Digital Equipment Corporation's VAX minicomputer were first used for highly specific scientific research such as data collection and analysis, the introduction of operating systems such as Unix allowed them to support a number of users through local area networks, enabled by networking technology such as Xerox's Ethernet. The relatively modest cost (hundreds of thousands of dollars rather than millions of dollars), infrastructure requirements, and software support allowed individual departments or research projects to acquire their own computing systems, but most use was still in the physical sciences and engineering, where external research sponsors such as the National Science Foundation (NSF), the Department of Defense (DOD), and the Department of Energy (DOE) provided the funds to acquire these computing systems.

As solid-state electronics continued to become ever more powerful and yet compact, it soon became possible to build an entire computer no larger than a typewriter. At first these microcomputers were used primarily as expensive workstations for scientific and engineering applications such as software development and computer-aided design, but soon the price of the technology dropped sufficiently low that computers designed for personal use began to appear. The early personal computers of Radio Shack (the TRS-80) and Apple (the Apple II) caught the imagination not only of hobbyists but also of software developers (Bill Gates and Paul Allen). When IBM entered the market with its first PC in the early 1980s, the personal computer was already moving rapidly both into the business community and into higher education driven by new applications such as word processing (WordStar) and spreadsheets (VisiCalc). Although many university professors first regarded the personal computer as an amusing toy, with its simple programming languages (BASIC), color displays, and primitive processing capability (at least compared to mainframe or minicomputers), the low cost and portability of these systems, along with their potential to link into more robust on-campus networks and support student instruction in computer systems, led to rapid expansion of their use in academic programs. They also provided a convenient entry point for many students and faculty into information technology.

Two examples from our experience at the University of Michigan illustrate these features. Although one might think of engineering faculty and students as among the most intensive users of computer technology, during the early 1970s most students experienced digital computing only in a few specially designed courses because of the cost of using time-sharing systems and mainframe computers. Furthermore, even in a discipline such as engineering, most faculty experience was of the "precomputer" era, and only a small fraction of the College of Engineering faculty were actually computer users (more frequently assigning these tasks to graduate students). To remedy this situation, in our roles as deans we first convinced the university to let us add a small fee onto student's tuition bill ($100 per term) to provide them with access to workstation and microcomputer technology. These new resources enabled us to make available to students on an unrestricted basis a number of state-of-the-art computing clusters, consisting not only of sophisticated workstations such as Apollo and Sun but also of next-generation personal computers such as the Apple Lisa and IBM PC.

To address the needs of faculty, we offered to buy each faculty member a personal computer. In fact, we encouraged them to take these computers home, if they wished. As we expected, essentially all of our faculty took advantage of this offer, and in the privacy of their home, many became introduced to computing for the first time, rapidly ramping up the use of information technology in both our instructional and research programs. Furthermore, as we also anticipated, the presence of computers at home in effect extended the working environment for our professors, and their productivity increased very substantially, far exceeding the modest investment that we made in their personal computers.

There was one additional benefit of this program that we did not anticipate. Since we placed no restrictions on the use of these home computers, the families of many of our faculty also became computer-literate. In fact, the teenage sons of one of our faculty members became so interested in programming their father's Apple II that they began to explore how to write software to manipulate the screen display pixels to modify digital images. Their software program soon became popular enough that they worked out an agreement with a large software company to produce and distribute the software as a commercial product. You may even have heard of it: Photoshop! The current medium of digital photography and video today is largely a consequence of such software.

Although personal computers and workstations rapidly became a standard tool for faculty, students, and staff, yet another evolutionary step occurred during the 1980s, when universities began to link these together in networks. Soon electronic mail became a common form of communication across the campus and beyond using early national networks such as DARPAnet, Bitnet, and CSnet. Software such as computer conferencing and document sharing software created new forums for discussion and collaboration. Although powerful computer workstations could meet the scientific computation needs of most faculty, there were still those with computational requirements that pushed the state of the art, and national supercomputer centers were established and linked to the campuses with networks such as NSFnet.

The rapid increase in network activity on the campuses posed a very significant challenge to university administrations to design, finance, and install the "wire plant" for digital technology. This was made even more imperative with the breakup of AT&T and the need for larger campuses to assume greater responsibility for their telecommunications environment. Furthermore, the fact that the technologies characterizing academic computing, administrative computing, library operations, and telecommunications were converging suggested the need to rethink the organization and management of the broader information and communications technology infrastructure. Since the costs associated with this infrastructure were enormous, ranging in the tens to hundreds of millions of dollars for larger institutions, these were strategic issues rising to the level of the president and governing boards of institutions. Although many of these issues were also being faced by corporations in the commercial sector, the great diversity of activities and needs characterizing the university, coupled with their highly decentralized management culture (a "creative anarchy"), presented particular challenges in higher education that most colleges and universities continue to face to this day.

The 1990s were a time of further technology change in higher education, as mainframes provided a shrinking proportion of computer power, replaced first by client-server networks and then by Web-client systems based increasingly on commodity personal computers or personal digital appliances (e.g., Palm Pilots) accessing intelligent networks. The Internet, coupled with technologies such as the browser and wireless mobility, has made information technology a pervasive need in every activity, at every level, and to all members of the university community. The diversity of needs of the university appears to be driving a fragmentation process, away from the centralized IT-telecom organizations of the early 1990s and toward local IT environments coupled by common network protocols and interoperability.

The continued evolution of the technology makes it clear that universities will continue to face an array of questions concerning not only the diversity of campus needs and the design, development, and financing of the necessary digital infrastructure but more significantly how it will affect the most fundamental activities of the university (teaching, research, and outreach) as well as its organization and function. These, of course, are the principal topics of this book.

TECHNOLOGICAL POSSIBILITIES FOR THE NEAR TERM (10 YEARS OR LESS)

Are there any limits to the evolution of information technology? It is likely that silicon devices will run into fundamental constraints within a decade or two. So, too, single optical fibers face fundamental data transmission limits of about 50 terabits per second. Some suggest that Moore's law won't survive beyond 2010 because power consumption is doubling or tripling with each generation of chips, yet scientists at Bell Laboratories believe that they have the technology to extend silicon technology for at least another decade or so. Others note that physical theory shows that we are far from any fundamental limits to computing. Announcements of advances in such areas as quantum computing and molecular electronics appear regularly.

Furthermore, as Kurzweil[14] notes, the exponential growth of computing goes back at least a century. Although a particular technology such as the vacuum tube will reach limits, it is quickly succeeded by a new technology. In fact, Kurzweil points out that we are currently in the fifth paradigm to sustain exponential growth in computing, including electromechanical calculators, relay-based computers, vacuum tubes, discrete transistors, and now integrated circuits. He believes that the next (sixth) paradigm shift is already apparent: building chips in three dimensions rather than the flat chips used in today's technology.[15]

Just as the rapid miniaturization of electronics to the micrometer scale has been the key to the evolution of information technology over the past several decades, there has been dramatic progress in extending this technology to the nanometer scale by building logic circuits from individual carbon nanotube molecules and assembly logic circuits from semiconductor nanowires. Until now one of the major challenges facing molecular electronics was the assembly of individual molecules or molecular-scale structures into functional logic circuits, but this was achieved in 2001.[16] The very small size of molecules makes it possible, in principle, to fit a trillion molecular devices in a square centimeter.

It is likely that new technologies such as molecular computing (the use of individual molecules as computing elements), quantum computing (using quantum states to represent data), biocomputing, and new materials such as nanotubes will take over from current silicon technology as we begin to encounter limits. Of course, if we cease to have new technology paradigms, and the curve describing the evolution of information technology begins to level off, we will have a very different twenty-first century from that predicted for continued exponential growth in digital technology.

Part of the challenge is that the various elements of information technology such as processing speed, bandwidth, storage, and human–machine interfaces tend to evolve at quite different exponential rates. "Riding the exponential" becomes the key feature of the technology, since this never lets up. Whichever aspect (e.g., processing speed, bandwidth, storage) is rising the fastest will determine the nature of the technology.[17] As a consequence, the most fundamental nature of information technology will also likely change. For example, if bandwidth continues to increase more rapidly than processor speed, it may soon be possible to regard the network (perhaps the entire Internet) as one very large computer. This could lead to true location transparency, in which people no longer care (or even know) whether they are working on their own computer or the network. As another example, if storage continues to evolve at its current pace, there may be little need for erasing data (e.g., for Read/Write memory elements).

Wireless Technology and Ubiquitous Computing

Mark Weiser and John Seely Brown suggest that when future historians document our times, they may conclude that "[t]he history of computers is quite simple. In the beginning there was the computer. Then it disappeared."[18] Of course, it didn't go away completely. It just became part of the physical background, forming part of ordinary objects such as tables, chairs, walls, and desks. Or it became a part of the social background, providing yet another part of the context of work. This second phase of the history of the computer is already under way. The modern car is, after all, really a four-wheeled computational platform.

Information technology—computers, networks, and such—is rapidly becoming ubiquitous, disappearing into the woodwork just as electricity did a century ago.[19] Today we do not look for the wires to hook up a light bulb to a power source. Rather we just throw a switch (or perhaps just enter a room that senses our presence), and the light goes on. Now that chips with supercomputer power and high bandwidth networks are becoming cheap commodities, information technology also is becoming so pervasive in our everyday life that it is becoming invisible, taken for granted even as we become more dependent upon it. Furthermore, as more functions are loaded onto the microchip, such as wireless and GPS (global positioning satellites) technology, these devices will find more unexpected applications. For example, such a chip mounted as a sensor on a device would not only know where it was at any moment but could actually tell you about it. The current slogan of "an IP on every cockroach" suggests that we may soon be able to characterize any and all objects by an Internet Protocol address!

Today wireless technology faces near-term challenges such as the different protocols used in the United States and the rest of the world and the archaic policies governing the digital spectrum. Sooner or later, market pressures will sweep aside these constraints to allow 3G (third generation) and beyond technologies providing broadband connectivity to mobile digital devices. The ubiquitous computing environment will become more and more focused on the individual. People will not have to be out of touch as they travel from home to work. Rather, wireless technology will keep them always connected. (Think of earphones and radios as a precursor.) Furthermore, one can imagine more sophisticated interfaces such as the use of eyeglasses as a heads-up optical display or the use of laser beams focused directly into the retina. The least aggressive future makes use of near-term technologies such as microphones (speech), eyeglasses (vision), and earphones (hearing), but perhaps someday we will bypass all of this to develop an interface directly to the auditory and optical nerves, which have a bandwidth of roughly 1 Mb/s.

There will be an increasing array of digital appliances at the interface between humans and the environment, many directly interacting with our senses. Of course, these are likely to have significant impact on our society. After all, if our eyeglasses and earphones can see anywhere there is a microscopic camera and microphone—or if the science fiction concept of neural implants become reality—then why do we need to be at any particular place? Perhaps the competitive advantages of regional areas or institutions will be increasingly determined by the robustness of connectivity to the Net. Of course, in a world with pervasive, always-on, wireless connectivity, we must design the technology so that it truly fades into the background, capturing our attention only when necessary (so-called calm technology[20]). Otherwise the distracting din of digital appliances will bring society to a halt.

Perhaps the ultimate example of ubiquitous computing will be the myriad computers and networks that attach themselves to us to extend our personal capabilities. Imagine a "bodynet" of computers and other devices distributed throughout our clothing—perhaps even embedded in our body—seamlessly linked in a wireless bodynet that allows them to function as an integrated system and connected to the worldwide digital network.[21] At some point our very nervous system may plug into the Net. This fusion of the carbon and silicon worlds may or may not evolve into a *Neuromancer*[22] blend of physical space and cyberspace such that electronic existence masks the physical world. However, it is clear that these two personal "realities" will be superimposed and intertwined in very complex ways.

The Evolution of the Net

The most important feature of information technology is its ability to release people and their activities from the constraints of space and time.

The Internet, the World Wide Web, and their successors are evolving rapidly into a global digital network, a global communications skin, interrelating people and their activities through robust, albeit ubiquitous, computers, networks, and intelligent hardware and software.

Of course, we face near-term technological challenges. The current Internet was built for a world of a few million users, utilizing relatively low-speed communications links with limited function (such as the World Wide Web and Web browsers). To accommodate the traffic generated by billions of users (not to mention trillions of digital devices) using applications requiring Gb/s bandwidths will require very significant technological evolution. However, just as the DARPAnet led to the NSFnet and more advanced networks, finally resulting in the commercial Internet, today efforts are under way, such as the Internet2 organization, Project Abilene, NSF's VBNS program, and advanced U.S. government networks, that can lead eventually to a commercialized advanced Internet.

The most significant near-term technology shift will be from electronics to optical networks. Although much of today's Internet is already based on photonics through the use of fiber-optic transmission, the introduction of optical switching and eventually optical computing should increase bandwidths by a factor of 1,000 or more. It is somewhat daunting to imagine what a data stream of 60 Gb/s into the house or the office would imply in terms of both end-use technology and applications, but it will clearly be possible within a couple of decades.

Yet another shift will be in the nature of the World Wide Web. Most of the content on today's Web is designed for humans to read, not for computer software to manipulate in meaningful ways. The creator of the Web, Tim Berners-Lee, suggests the need for a semantic Web[23] that will bring structure to the meaningful content of Web pages, creating an environment where software agents roaming from page to page can readily carry out sophisticated tasks for users. The development of the semantic Web will involve areas such as knowledge representation and artificial intelligence, but the foundation for such evolution has been laid with the development of extensible Markup Language (XML) as the successor to HTML and the use of Resource Framework (RDF) protocols. The real power of the semantic Web will be realized when people create programs that collect Web content from diverse sources, process the information, and exchange the results with other programs. Just as with the Web itself, the effectiveness will increase exponentially as more machine-readable Web content and automated services become available.

Universities are continuing to play an important role in the evolution of the Internet through the Internet2 project (www.internet2.edu), managed by the University Consortium on Advanced Internet Development (UCAID), a consortium of more than 200 research universities, 70 corporations, 30 government laboratories, and linkages to over 30 nations. The original goal of Internet2 was to create the next-generation Internet focusing on the needs of the research community, much in the spirit of the early DARPAnet as the precursor to the first Internet. For many applications, particularly in the emerging areas of e-science, the commercial Internet is simply not evolving rapidly enough in available bandwidth. Hence, Internet2 was designed to be a closed system test bed for developing and deploying advanced network applications and technologies, accelerating the creation of tomorrow's Internet. Its purpose is to create a leading-edge network capability for the national research community, enable revolutionary Internet applications, and ensure the rapid transfer of new network services and applications to the broader Internet community.

To date, its activities have focused on operating the Abilene backbone network (currently running at 10 Gb/s), developing the necessary network middleware, and capitalizing on the enhanced features of the network for advanced applications. Currently, Internet2 members are collaborating on advanced applications such as videoconferencing, multicasting, voice-over-IP, digital libraries, remote instrument control, and middleware development. For example, it has explored the use of advanced network technology in medicine, including not only real-time consultation using advanced graphics but also telesurgery. As astronomy has shifted from the photographic plates to charge-coupled detectors, thereby resulting in collection of data in digital form, it has become possible to distribute the observations of both terrestrial and satellite observatories to scientists anywhere in the world via advanced networks. Data-intensive applications such as high-energy physics or the SHOAH project (with petabytes of data in the form of interviews with Holocaust survivors) can be distributed over the network.

In this regard, it should be remembered that earlier disruptive technologies such as the World Wide Web and Napster were first incubated in universities. Through efforts such as Internet2, higher education has the only scalable platform capable of truly collaborative efforts to create and capture evolving technology, since unlike business and government, Internet2 is not hindered by fire walls or unnecessary regulation. Internet2 is currently supporting the efforts of several million faculty members, students, and staff in incubating new disruptive technologies.

While technology is necessary for such advanced applications, it is rarely sufficient. We will need new organizations and policies that are capable of dealing with the distributed, ubiquitous nature of advanced network technologies. Over the longer term it will be essential to propagate these technologies and organizations into the commercial sector to access capital resources and serve the broader needs of society, but we already have in the evolution of the current Internet an excellent model of such technology development and propagation.

Perhaps more significant will be conceptual issues such as the use of the Internet. For example, will it evolve primarily as a broadcasting medium, like television, where people have limited availability of programming, and interaction occurs in only modest ways using primitive technologies such as E-mail and chat rooms? Or will it lead to a *Snow Crash* world of avatars interacting in virtual spaces?[24] Or it may—and probably will—evolve in directions that we cannot even imagine.

The limitations that define the old Internet will eventually be surpassed. If the end-to-end, symmetric architecture of the Internet is sustained, it will become a new medium, based on peer-to-peer technologies that allow many-to-many communication, anything flows to anyone—from anywhere to anywhere—anytime. Individuals will be able to innovate in wireless space on their own without worrying about intermediaries. The end-to-end principle characterizing the Internet is likely to penetrate the wireless world. This will empower individuals and reduce the amount of hierarchical structure that people need to work with one another (with obvious implications for corporations, governments, and, of course, universities). In a sense, it will create a new kind of information fabric in which learning, working, and playing converge. Intelligence and technology will be truly distributed. Access to knowledge and knowledge resources will be democratized.

Software Agents and Avatars

The tendency of digital information to multiply and propagate rapidly through digital networks can also be a challenge. Already the vastness of the Internet and the access that it provides to storehouses of information threaten to overwhelm us. As anyone who has "surfed the Net" can testify, it is easy to be amused but often difficult to find exactly what you need. Further, living and working in a knowledge-rich—indeed, knowledge-deluged—world will overload our limited human capacity to handle information.

The Net is already a complex and interesting organism that has evolved far beyond human comprehension. It is more than just a medium incorporating text, graphics, and sound. It incorporates ideas and mediates the interactions among millions of people. It can already do things that no human can explain.

As a result, it will become increasingly necessary to depend on intelligent software agents or avatars to serve as our interface with the digital world. Many already use primitive constructs such as filters for electronic mail or Web-crawlers to search through databases on the Net. With the use of artificial intelligence and genetic algorithms, one can imagine intelligent agents dispatched by a user to search the digital networks for specific information. These agents will also represent their human user, serving as avatars, in mediating the interaction with the agents of other human users. The logical Web will require an avatar habitat. Agents in the network will be always on, always aware, and always attuned to one's needs. The logical part of the cybersphere will be a personal agent or avatar or an agent for a work group.

There are a couple of interesting possibilities here. Since software agents are easy to reproduce, one can imagine a cyberspace quickly flooded with billions of agents—similar to the software viruses that can propagate and cripple computer systems. There is already evidence of "wars" between software agents, where agents from one group of users seek out and destroy those from others. Perhaps the most significant evolutionary stage will occur if the distributed processing power of networks allows the appearance of "emergent behavior," wherein agents begin to exhibit self-organization, learning capability, and intelligent behavior. The predictions of science fiction of Clarke's HAL 9600 in *2001: A Space Odyssey* or Gibson's *Neuromancer* and the possibility that we may be unable to distinguish which of our colleagues in cyberspace are flesh-and-bones and which are silicon may be only a few decades away.

THE LONGER TERM FUTURE OF DIGITAL TECHNOLOGY

If there is one lesson that the history of digital technology has taught us, it is the difficulty in making predictions. Invariably, we tend to overestimate—and overhype—the near-term progress of the technology, while underestimating its longer-term evolution and impact. In part this is due to a tendency to take today's technology as given and attempt to extrapolate it into the future. We tend to overestimate what is feasible in the very short term because of implicit assumptions that gloss over difficulties. Over the longer term, our predictions are disrupted by unanticipated technological discontinuities. Too frequently, we assume that something will not change just because today's technology will not allow it.

While the longer-term future of digital technology may be uncertain, several characteristics of this technology are clear. First, its evolution will continue to be governed by exponential growth, whether tracking along the silicon trajectory predicted by Moore's law or switching over to another exponential growth trajectory associated with a new technology such as optical computing or quantum computing. Physical theory shows that we are still far from any fundamental limits to computing technology. Although there are potential limits, from a practical point of view, we are currently so far away as to still see infinite horizons. Within our lifetimes we can depend on using a wireless device to reach anyone in the world and having any request for information answered with the touch of a button. To be more extreme, we would note that Kurzweil estimates that a one-inch-cube computer of nanotube circuitry in theory could be 1 million times more powerful than the human brain.[25]

Second, we know that this technology not only tends to get faster but simultaneously also tends to get smaller. Hence, it is likely to become far more ubiquitous, with digital devices and software applications (and agents) multiplying in number even as they grow in power. In contrast, the applications of digital technology, such as the Net, tend to become more global, more interconnected, and more pervasive.

As John Seely Brown puts it, not only will the Net be as fundamental to society as electrification, but it will be subject to many of the same diffusion and absorption dynamics as that earlier medium. In the same way that electricity became a transforming technology, the Net will be a transformative medium just as important. Here again we have a story of gradual development followed by an exploding impact. We are just at the bottom of the S-curve takeoff. The years ahead are likely to present huge opportunities for entrepreneurs, corporate or academic, who will see things differently and will drive this chaotic, transformative phenomenon. Our challenge and opportunity, then, are to foster an entrepreneurial spirit toward creating new learning environments—a spirit that will use the unique capabilities of the Net to leverage the natural ways that humans learn.

There has never been a similarly rapid, sustained change in technology, especially one with such broad implications. We need to work harder to imagine the impact of evolving digital technology on all aspects of our civilization. We particularly need to do so for the university.

NOTES

1. Peter J. Deming and Robert M. Metcalf, *Beyond Calculation: The New Fifty Years of Computing* (New York: Springer-Verlag, 1997).

2. Ray Kurzweil, *The Age of Spiritual Machines: When Computers Exceed Human Intelligence* (New York: Viking, 1999).

3. In scientific computation, the particular operations used in solving equations are called "floating-point operations," in the sense that they involve decimal quantities. Hence, the measure of computing speed is called flops, for floating point operation per second. ASCI White has a speed of 12 teraflops, while Blue Gene will have a computing speed approaching 1,000 teraflops.

4. Although the speed of computers is usually measured in computation cycle frequency or hertz (e.g., the current generation of PCs run at about 1 Ghz or 1 billion cycles per second) or operations per second (a giga operation/second), the speed of supercomputers is usually measured in the number of arithmetical operations or floating point operations that they can perform per second, abbreviated "flop." Hence a "petaflop" computer is capable of performing over 1 million-billion floating-point operations per second.

5. William A. Wulf, "Warning: Information Technology Will Transform the University," *Issues in Science and Technology* 11, no. 4 (Summer 1995), 46–52.

6. William Gibson, *Neuromancer* (New York: Ace, 1984).

7. Stuart Feldman, "Technology Futures" Workshop on IT and the Future of the Research University, National Academy of Sciences, Washington, DC, 2001; <http://www.researchchannel.com/programs/na/itfru.html>.

8. Put another way, a petabyte of data is roughly equivalent to the capacity of a stack of CD-ROMs nearly 2 km high.

9. William J. Mitchell, *City of Bits: Space, Place, and the Infobahn* (Cambridge: MIT Press, 1995).

10. Michael Moe, *The Knowledge Web* (New York: Merrill Lynch, 2000).

11. Mark Stefik, *Internet Dreams* (Cambridge: MIT Press, 1996), 412.

12. John Perry Barlow, "The Economy of Ideas: A Framework for Rethinking Patents and Copyrights in the Digital Age," *Wired* (1993).

13. Mitchell, *City of Bits*, 167–68.

14. Kurzweil, *The Age of Spiritual Machines*.

15. Thomas H. Lee, "A Vertical Leap for Microchips," *Scientific American* 286, no. 1 (2002), 52–61.

16. Greg Y. Tseng and James C. Ellenbogen, "Toward Nanocomputers," *Science* 294 (November 2001), 1293–94.

17. Larry Smarr, private communication, 2001.

18. Mark Weiser and John Seely Brown, "The Coming of Calm Technology," in *Beyond Calculation: The Next Fifty Years of Computing*, ed. Peter J. Deming and Robert M. Metcalf (New York: Springer-Verlag, 1977), 75–86.

19. John Seely Brown and Paul Duguid, *The Social Life of Information* (Cambridge: Harvard Business School Press, 2000).

20. Mark Weiser and John Seely Brown, "Designing Calm Technology," *PowerGrid Journal* 101 (July 1996), <http//powergrid.electriciti.com/1.01>.

21. Mitchell, *City of Bits*.

22. Gibson, *Neuromancer*.

23. Tim Berners-Lee, James Nendler, and Ora Lassila, "The Semantic Web," *Scientific American* (May 2001), <http://www.sciam.com/2001/0501issue/0501berners-lee.html>.

24. Neal Stephenson, *Snow Crash* (New York: Bantam Books, 1992).

25. Kurzweil, *The Age of Spiritual Machines*.

PART II

Issues, Trends, and Themes

The biggest danger is that higher education may be the next railroad industry, which built bigger and better railroads decade after decade because that is the business it thought it was in. The reality was that it was in the transportation industry, and it was nearly put out of business by airplanes. Colleges and universities are not in the campus business, but the education business.
—Arthur Levine, President of Teacher's College, Columbia University

Typically, most discussions concerning information technology and higher education deal primarily with IT's impact upon instruction, for example, on-line distance education or virtual universities. However, the roles of the contemporary university are broad and diverse, ranging from educating the young, to preserving our cultural heritage, to providing the basic research essential to national security, economic prosperity, and social well-being, to training our professionals and certifying their competence, and to challenging our society and stimulating social change. Knowledge is the medium of the university in the sense that each of its many roles involves the discovery, shaping, transfer, or application of knowledge. In this sense, it is clear that the rapid evolution of information and communications technologies will reshape all of the roles of the university. To understand the future of the university in the digital age, it is important to consider the impact on each of its activities.

In an effort to adopt this broader perspective, we have organized our discussion of issues, trends, and themes concerning the impact of digital technology into three layers. First we discuss the impact of information on the fundamental activities of the university: teaching, scholarship, and public service. Next we consider its impact on the organization, management, and financing of the university. Finally we offer some observations concerning the impact on the broader postsecondary education enterprise.

Furthermore, to provide guidance for addressing the array of strategic issues facing colleges and universities, we conclude this section with a brief discussion of several alternative visions for the future of higher education.

CHAPTER

The Impact of Information Technology on the Activities of the University

The university is defined, in part, by the many roles that it plays in contemporary society. Universities provide an education for our citizens. They produce the scholars, professionals, and leaders needed by our society. Universities also preserve and transfer our cultural heritage from one generation to the next. They perform the research necessary to generate new knowledge critical to the progress of our nation. They provide service to society across a number of fronts such as health care and economic development that draw on the unique expertise of our institutions.

Although it is customary to identify the primary activities of the university as the triad of teaching, research, and public service—or in more contemporary terms as learning, discovery, and engagement[1]—from a more abstract perspective, each of the activities of the university involves knowledge. More precisely, teaching, research, and public service can be regarded as simply the current manifestations of the more fundamental roles of *creating, preserving, integrating, transmitting,* and *applying* knowledge. From this more abstract viewpoint, it is clear that while the fundamental knowledge-based roles of the university do not change over time, their particular character does change over time—and change quite dramatically, in fact, as higher education evolves. The evolution of higher education in America, from the early colonial colleges, to the land-grant universities, to statewide university systems, to research universities, to cyberspace universities, illustrates this continuity of change.

It is not surprising that powerful new digital technologies, which in effect are knowledge media, have the potential for major impact on each of the many and varied activities of the university. After all, this technology was developed in part in our campus research laboratories by our faculty, and many of the earliest applications of information technology have been developed and deployed on our campuses. Yet, in truth, the instructional activities of the university have tended to resist technology-driven change. Earlier technologies that were supposed to drive radical change—television, computer-assisted instruction, wireless communications—have bounced off the classroom without a dent.

Yet, as we have suggested, digital technology will eventually have a transforming impact on the activities of the university, because of both its unusual and relentless pace of evolution and the manner in which it relaxes traditional constraints such as space and time. There are already signs that the traditional classroom lecture-based format of university learning is evolving in response to the opportunities offered by digital technology. Recent surveys indicate that almost half of all college classes today use Internet resources as part of their syllabus, and over one-quarter have Web sites. Most students and faculty interact regularly using E-mail or conferencing software. Even more profound transformations will be driven by today's generation of students who seek highly interactive, collaborative, and customized learning experiences.

One can easily identify changes occurring in the other activities of the university. Digital technology has provided the scholar with powerful new tools to solve complex problems, simulate natural phenomena, and interact with colleagues. The library is becoming less a repository and more a center for knowledge navigation. Our capacity to reproduce and distribute digital information with perfect accuracy and with essentially zero cost has shaken the very foundations of copyright and patent law and threatens to redefine the nature of the ownership of intellectual property.[2] Digital communications networks are allowing universities to extend their array of public services far beyond the campus and even the state to encompass the nation or even the world.

In this chapter we consider how information technology is reshaping the various activities of the university.

EDUCATION

Despite the great diversity in colleges and universities, in learning environments, and in curricular content, most of us have a very specific notion of a college education. Stated in the most simplistic terms, this consists primarily of four years of study, divided into 30 semester hours a year, five courses per semester. These courses are selected either to meet the requirements of a particular area of concentration or major (e.g., psychology or physics or philosophy) or from more general survey courses designed to broaden one's education. Most of these courses are taught in a lecture format, augmented by occasional seminars, discussion sections, and laboratories.

The teaching function occurs primarily through a professor's lecturing to a class of students, who in turn respond by reading assigned texts, writing papers, solving problems or performing experiments, and taking examinations. A few students might also take advantage of faculty office hours for a more intimate relationship, but this is rather rare for most students. The technology used is primitive, for the most part, consisting primarily of books, chalk boards, oral lectures, and static images, occasionally assisted by audiovisual equipment and limited electronic communication.

Furthermore, beyond a very limited use of technology, few faculty members utilize or are even aware of the rapidly expanding scientific basis for learning from neuroscience and cognitive psychology. One of our colleagues observed that if doctors used science the way that college teachers do, they would still be trying to treat disease with leeches. Imagine the reactions of a nineteenth-century physician, suddenly transported forward in time to a modern surgery suite, complete with all of the technological advances of modern medicine. Yesteryear's physician would recognize very little—perhaps not even the patient—and certainly would not be able to function in any meaningful way. Contrast this with a nineteenth-century college professor transported into a contemporary university classroom. Here everything would be familiar—the same lecture podium, blackboards, and students ready to take notes. Even the subjects—literature, history, languages—would be familiar and taught in essentially the same way.

From Computer-Aided Instruction to Cyberspace Learning Communities

Although it has been slow in coming, we are beginning to see early signs of the impact of technology on education. Here we should clarify our terminology, since technology-assisted or computer-mediated instruction is frequently interpreted as on-line education, as exemplified by the asynchronous learning networks or virtual universities now springing up in higher education. The computer has been used to augment traditional classroom instruction for decades. Early applications such as the computer-aided instruction Plato system developed by the University of Illinois aimed to use the computer to enhance learning by automating routine drills such as language repetition or self-paced instruction. However, these were generally both resource-intensive and of marginal utility in augmenting conventional classroom instruction.

For many years universities have utilized passive telecommunications technology such as television to extend teaching to people unable or unwilling to attend campus-based classes. In its simplest form, such broadcast technology-assisted learning is really a "talking heads" paradigm, in which faculty lectures are simply delivered at a distance, through either live transmission or videotape. There have been efforts to broadcast such instruction on public television ("sunrise semesters"), augmented by written correspondence. A more effective approach utilized on-site teaching assistants to work directly with the students. Some distance learning allowed the use of student feedback via telephone or two-way video interaction with the instructor (in the case of live transmission).

It is not surprising that the early efforts to utilize digital technology in higher education simply replaced the broadcast of lectures over television with passive lecture courses either distributed on CD-ROMs or streamed from Internet Web sites. Although there was usually some opportunity for student interaction and feedback through E-mail or chat rooms, the pedagogy was still very much based on the transfer of knowledge in a lecture format. The aim was to use digital technology to perform ordinary tasks more efficiently, such as providing course syllabi and readings or linking students with instructors.

The real power of digital technology can be achieved only when we take advantage of the shift from the one-to-many character of broadcast media, to the many-to-many ability of digital networks. To this end, the most productive early applications of digital technology in higher education involved using computer conferencing, electronic mail, listservs (threaded discussions), and other computer-based collaboration technology to link together both students and faculty in highly interactive learning communities, unconstrained by geographical location or time.

The most significant advantage of such computer-mediated learning is access, the degree to which it frees learning opportunities from the constraints of space and time. It is understandable why the convenience of anytime-anyplace learning technologies is important to adult learners whose work or family obligations limit access to the residential college experience, an increasing number of on-campus students are also using on-line learning to augment their classroom experiences, since they, too, seek both the convenience and the learning resources provided through the Internet.

Distributed learning has a deeper significance than simply relaxing the barriers of space and time. Because of its interactive nature, it transforms learning from simply absorbing new knowledge to the act of creating knowledge. It provides new mechanisms for rich social interactions that simply could not exist if restricted to face-to-face contact. It provides both students and faculty with access to learning resources far beyond the boundary of the campus itself. Imagine, for instance, conducting a course on the public health implications of AIDS with the on-line participation of students from African countries or a course in archaeology augmented by virtual reality tours of various excavation sites around the world.

Students already make extensive use of digital technology for informal learning, typically without the involvement or even the awareness of the faculty. They build study groups, in some cases spanning several academic institutions, working together to seek information, answer questions, and develop learning skills. In a very real sense, such study groups based on computer networks are providing students with greater control over their educational experiences. They also represent a trend in which students construct their own consortia of learning resources—and academic institutions—just as the faculty build their own research consortia. Of course, these network-based student groups represent an important step toward active student learning. (In fact, when students are asked how they could best spend time on their college academic programs, they invariably rank student study groups at the very top, far above individual study or class attendance.)

Virtual reality—the use of visual, audio, and tactile sensations to create a simulated total sensory experience—has become common both in training and simulation and in gaming. However, higher education is more likely first to make use of distributed virtual environments,[3] in which computers create sophisticated, three-dimensional graphical worlds distributed over networks and populated by the representations of people interacting together in real time. Such software representations of people in virtual worlds are known as *avatars*. Here the goal is not so much to simulate the physical world but to create a digital world more supportive of human interaction. The software required for such distributed virtual environments is social in nature. It is not so much designed to simulate reality as to enable conversation and other forms of human collaboration.

These shared virtual worlds could radically alter the way that we work, learn, and play. For example, one might imagine teaching a course in

French language and culture through a distributed virtual environment representing a street in Paris. The virtual street could be lined with buildings, shops, restaurants, museums, and apartments. Language students and teachers would be represented by avatars in this world, along with native speakers or even software agents. Students entering this virtual world could practice a foreign language and experience its culture by speaking with other people in a nonthreatening environment.

One can imagine a host of other virtual environments that could support the human interactions necessary in learning communities. Even today we already have virtual environments that simulate university campuses, complete with registration offices, classrooms, coffeehouses, and recreation facilities.

Although we generally think of distributed learning as most useful to adult learners whose work or family obligations prevent their attendance at conventional campuses, online learning has also become important within the traditional residential campus environment. Both on campus and off, an increasing number of students and faculty members have access to broadband networks that allow them not only to access university resources such as libraries and student services, but also to form online learning communities through electronic mail, listservs, and other collaboration technologies.[4] Their educational, research, and other university activities span both the physical campus and cyberspace.

Even more important, on-line learning communities stimulate students to become more actively involved in the learning process, with the potential to significantly transform the way that learning occurs in the university, enabling the faculty to design and implement learning processes and environments that are far more effective than the traditional classroom lecture-based paradigm. Computer-based simulations and role-playing exercises give students hands-on experiences in any subject. Networks provide ready access both to vast knowledge resources as well as to original source materials. The flexibility of network-based communication allows faculty members to tailor teaching styles to each student's needs, shifting the faculty member's role from a source of information to a supervisor or coach of the learning process. Perhaps most significantly, it has moved the consideration of learning once again to center stage in higher education, even in those research universities long dominated by concerns of scholarship rather than teaching.

To date, there has been relatively little attention given to the way that information technology might reshape the cognitive process of learning. Furthermore, few seem to recognize that information technology may break the long-accepted linkage between economic measures such as expenditure per student or students per faculty and educational quality. There seems to be limited awareness of just how different a generation of students raised in a world of interactive electronic media are from their parents—and their teachers.

The Digital Generation

The traditional classroom paradigm is being challenged today, not so much by professors, who have by and large optimized their teaching effort and their time commitments to a lecture format, but by our students. Members of today's digital generation of students have spent their early lives immersed in robust, visual, electronic media—Sesame Street, MTV, home computers, video games, cyberspace networks, MUDs and MOOS, and MP3 players. Unlike those of us who were raised in an era of passive, broadcast media such as radio and television, today's students expect—indeed, demand—interaction. They prefer to learn by doing, mastering new tasks through what we might regard as play. Their nonlinear style of learning seems inconsistent with the rigid, sequential approach of the traditional college curriculum, building a pyramid of prerequisites that must be mastered in order. Yet, there is some evidence that the highly experiential and interactive approach to learning by the digital generation may be particularly effective in a media-rich environment.

John Seely Brown and his colleagues at Xerox PARC have studied the learning habits of the plug-and-play generation and identified several interesting characteristics of their learning process.[5] First, today's students like to do several things at once—they "multitask," performing several tasks simultaneously at a computer such as Web site browsing and E-mail while listening to music or talking on a cellular phone. Although their attention span appears short, as they jump from one activity to another, they appear to learn just as effectively as earlier generations. Furthermore, it is clear that they have mastered a broader range of literacy skills, augmenting traditional verbal communication skills with visual images and hypertext links. They are particularly adept at navigating complex arrays of information, acquiring the knowledge resources that they seek and building sophisticated networks of learning resources. Some observers suggest that this may lead to problems later in life as the digital generation sacrifices qualities such as patience and tranquillity, but, of course, patience and tranquillity have never been characteristics of the young. Asked about their elders' concerns, the typical response of the digital generation is "Get over it!"[6]

Indeed, there is even research that suggests the presence of a physiological difference between the brains of the "digital generation" and those of us from twentieth-century generations.[7] More specifically, it has been known that early exposure of infants and young children to various stimulation can actually affect their neurological development—the evolution of their neural networks. Children raised in a media-rich, interactive environment tend to think and learn differently because they are physiologically different from us. Their brains are wired in different ways. Our styles of learning are not theirs.

For example, to those of us from "precomputer" generations, encountering a hardware or software problem in our personal computer activities usually leads first to a frantic search through a nearby operating manual. After wasting many minutes—if not hours—we finally throw up our hands in resignation and look for the nearest teenager for help. The plug-and-play teenager sits down at our computer and, after a few minutes of "playing," solves our problem. Of course, if we were to ask, "Show me how you did that so I can fix the problem the next time it arises," we usually get a look of surprise, along with the suggestion that if the problem happens again, we simply call for help, and the student will come back and play a bit more until it is fixed.

Brown observes that this type of discovery-based learning approaches the bricolage concept suggested by Levi-Strauss, in which the learner develops the ability to find tools or resources to address a practical need.[8] It combines knowledge navigation, discovery, and judgment in a highly sophisticated way, supported by both technology (computer networks) and social skills (learning communities).

Today's students are different from earlier generations. They are citizens of the digital age. Unlike earlier generations, numbed into passive submission by the vast wasteland of broadcast media, the members of the digital generation are accustomed to reading, analyzing, authenticating, contextualizing, separating useful information from junk, composing their thoughts, criticizing, and building and navigating through complex knowledge webs. They are curious, self-reliant, contrarian, focused, able to adapt, and technology-savvy. They learn by experimentation and participation, not by listening or reading passively. They take no one's word for anything. Rather, they embrace interactivity, the right to shape and participate in their learning. They are comfortable with the uncertainty that characterizes their change-driven world.[9]

To be sure, for a time, such students may tolerate the linear, sequential lecture paradigm of the traditional college curriculum. They still read what faculty assign, write the required term papers, and pass our exams, but this is decidedly not the way that they would choose to learn. They prefer to learn in a highly nonlinear fashion, by skipping from beginning to end and then back again, and by building peer groups of learners, by developing sophisticated learning networks in cyberspace. In a very real sense, they build their own learning environments that enable interactive, collaborative learning, whether we recognize and accommodate this or not.

However, their tolerance for the traditional classroom and four-year curriculum model may not last long. Students will increasingly demand new learning paradigms more suited to their learning styles and more appropriate to prepare them for a lifetime of learning and change. There are already signs that the entire classroom experience—that is, the transmission of knowledge content associated with courses—may soon be packaged through electronic media as a commodity and distributed to mass markets, much like today's textbooks. What will happen the first time a student walks into the dean's office and states: "I have just passed all of your exams after taking the Microsoft Virtual Physics course, developed by three Nobel laureates, rather than suffering through your dismal classes taught by foreign graduate teaching assistants. I now want you to give me academic credits toward my degree"?

One can imagine the impact of millions of students from the digital generation as they seek the interactive, collaborative, and convenient learning experiences that they have already experienced from other digital media. We should not underestimate the impact of the plug-and-play generation on the university. After all, their use of digital technologies such as Napster and other peer-to-peer applications quickly overloaded our IT infrastructures and threatened the recording industry. Their use of the Net and other digital resources is already far more sophisticated than among most faculty and staff. They will drive rapid and profound change in higher education since they will demand that we adapt the university to their learning needs and characteristics through market forces.

The Nature of Learning in the Digital Age

The new interactive resources provided by emerging information technology represent the wave of the future for our society. As our knowledge base expands, isolated individuals will increasingly lose their ability to know everything that they need to grapple with complex challenges. We must equip our students with the ability to exploit these new technologies. They must learn the difficult art of communicating across disciplinary and cultural differences in the pursuit of common goals, discovering which collaborative tools serve us best for our different purposes. The new literacy enabled by digital technologies is rapidly becoming an essential skill in a knowledge-driven society and a responsibility of higher education.

The reality of our new students, diverse and often technically savvy, requires new educational approaches. Encouragingly, our growing base of technology has begun to create the possibility of new, more flexible roles for both students and faculty, within and beyond the classroom. Richard Lanham calls the social, technological, and theoretical challenges that these changes create an "extraordinary convergence," catalyzing fundamental shifts in higher education, allowing more interactive learning, and giving students the ability to interrogate or even create knowledge instead of simply absorbing it.[10]

The new knowledge media may fundamentally change what it means to be a professor and a student at our universities. Faculty members may become more like coaches or consultants than didactic teachers, designing learning experiences and providing skills instead of imparting specific content. Even our introductory courses may take on a form now reserved for only the most advanced seminar classes, thereby allowing more personal interaction. Not only do these new technologies create educational opportunities, but they also represent the literacy of our future. The medium of intellectual communication is in the process of evolving from the journal article to more comprehensive multimedia and even interactive documents. These shifts portend vast changes in the ways that information is manipulated and interaction is structured in our society. Universities cannot call themselves successful unless they provide students with the fundamental skills that they require in the twenty-first century.

In these new learning paradigms, the word *student* becomes largely obsolete, because it describes the passive role of absorbing content selected and conveyed by teachers. Instead, we should probably begin to refer to the clients of the twenty-first-century university as active *learners*, since they will increasingly demand responsibility for their own learning experiences and outcomes. Further, as we noted in the previous section, our students will seek less to "know about" (after all, in many ways they are more sophisticated at knowledge navigation in the digital age than their teachers) and more to "know how." There is strong evidence that the traditional class lecture approach to college education is one of the least effective forms of learning. Studies show that the more that one is involved in the learning experience, the more that one learns. One such study[11] found that only 5 percent of the information content conveyed by a lecture is retained, rising to 20 percent when augmented by audiovisual presentations and only 30 percent even when demonstrations are used. In contrast, when students learn by doing, they retain 75 percent. When they teach others, they retain 90 percent!

The hyperlearning model proposed by Perelman[12] may be more typical of the learning paradigms of the future than today's classroom-based curriculum in which students move along together in lockstep. In Perelman's model, learning consists of a number of learning modules or stations. Students employ the modules of their choice until a certain level of competence is achieved rather than competing with other students for a grade.

In a similar sense, the concept of a *teacher* as one who develops and presents knowledge to largely passive students may become obsolete. Today, faculty members who have become experts in certain subfields are expected to identify the key knowledge content for a course based on their area of interest and to organize and then present the material, generally in a lecture format, in this course. Frequently, others, including graduate teaching assistants and professional staff, are assigned the role of working directly with students, helping them to learn, and providing them with guidance and counseling. In a future increasingly dominated by sophisticated educational commodities and hyperlearning experiences, the role of the faculty member will shift. In these new paradigms the role of the faculty member becomes that of nurturing and guiding active learning, not identifying and presenting content. That is, they will be expected to inspire, motivate, manage, and coach students.

More specifically, faculty members of the twenty-first-century university will find it necessary to set aside their roles as teachers and instead become designers of learning experiences, processes, and environments. In the process, tomorrow's faculty members may have to discard the present style of solitary learning experiences, in which students tend to learn primarily on their own through reading, writing, and problem solving. Instead, they may be asked to develop collective learning experiences in which students work together and learn together, with the faculty member becoming more of a consultant or a coach than a teacher.

Many believe that effective computer-network-mediated learning will not be simply an Internet extension of correspondence or broadcast courses. John Seeley Brown and Paul Duguid of Xerox PARC believe that this model of the virtual university overlooks the nature of how university-based learning actually occurs.[13] They suggest that it is a mistake to think of learning as information transfer, the act of delivering knowledge to passive student receivers. Brown and Duguid see the learning process as rooted in both experience and social interaction. They believe learning requires the presence of communities.

This is likely to become the value of the university—to create learning communities and to introduce students into these communities. Undergraduates are introduced to communities associated with academic disciplines and professions. Graduate students and professional students are involved in more specialized communities of experience and expertise. From this perspective, one of the important roles of the university is to certify through the awarding of degrees that students have had sufficient learning experience with a variety of communities.

Once we have realized that the core competence of the university is not simply transferring knowledge but developing it within intricate and robust networks and communities, we realize that the simple distance-learning paradigm of the virtual university is inadequate. The key is to develop computer-mediated communications and communities that are released from the constraints of space and time.

In true learning communities the distinction between teachers and students blurs. Both groups become active learners, working together to benefit each other. While this duality is commonplace at the level of graduate education, where graduate students frequently learn more about a specialized subject than their faculty advisers, it is far less common in undergraduate education. Yet, we have long known that some of the most significant learning occurs when one also serves as a teacher. Advanced undergraduates should be encouraged to assume such teaching roles, not only to other undergraduates but even on occasion to faculty members themselves.

Such learning communities seem better aligned with how learning really should occur in a university. The classroom paradigm is usually dominated by one-way information flow from the faculty member to the student. Learning is not simply information transfer. It involves a complex array of social interactions in which the student interacts not only with the faculty member but also with other students, the environment, and possibly objects as well, for example, books! The role of the university and the faculty should be to facilitate the formation of learning communities, both through formal academic programs and through social, extracurricular, and cultural activities that contribute to learning in the university. When students and faculty join such communities, they share the ideas, values, and practices that lead to learning.

Perhaps part of our difficulty in reconceptualizing the college experience is that we still tend to think of the baccalaureate degree as a well-defined learning experience that prepares a student for life, but today learning has become a lifelong activity. Today's students will need to continue to learn, through both formal and informal methods, throughout their lives.

Of course, a college education was never intended to provide all of the knowledge needed for a lifetime. In years past, most of the additional knowledge necessary for a career could be acquired informally, through on-the-job learning or self-study. Today, however, both rapid growth of knowledge and the multiple career transitions facing graduates demand a more strategic approach to lifetime learning. We need to rethink educational goals from this lifetime perspective. We should view undergraduate education as just one step—an important step, to be sure—down the road of a lifetime of learning. This would allow us to better match learning content and experiences with both the intellectual maturation and the needs of the learner.

In a world driven by knowledge, learning can no longer be regarded as a once-is-enough or on-again, off-again experience. People will need to engage in continual learning in order to keep their knowledge base and skills up-to-date. Given this need, the relationship between a student/graduate and the university may similarly change. Just as we have suggested that the word *student* is no longer appropriate to describe an active learner, perhaps the distinction between student and *alumnus* is no longer relevant.

But here we must also add a note of caution, since both the methods of learning and the needs for learning content for the young differ very considerably from those of adult learners. The adult learners served by the growing number of for-profit, on-line schools (University of Phoenix, Jones International University, Unext.com) generally seek both educational experiences and credentials of direct relevance to their careers. Their life experiences have prepared them to learn in a highly directed, pragmatic approach to achieve vocational goals. In contrast, most young college students still have only vaguely formed career goals. Although many seek highly specific educational experiences aimed at particular vocational goals, most will benefit from the far broader educational experience that colleges and universities have traditionally provided through a liberal education, albeit redesigned for the changing learning styles of the digital generation.

Perhaps the relationship between a university and its graduates that is more appropriate for our future is conveyed by the term *lifelong member of a learning community*. Perhaps enrollment should be viewed less as participation in a particular degree program and instead as a lifetime contract with the university, in which the university agrees to provide whatever learning resources are required by its learners or members throughout their life, whatever, whenever, and wherever their educational needs. Clearly, the rapid evolution of distance learning technology will increasingly facilitate this. We also see increasing interest on the part of alumni in remaining connected to their university and to learning opportunities throughout their lives.

Clearly, the classroom will not disappear. Nor will the residential campus experience of undergraduate education for young adults be overwhelmed by virtual universities or "edutainment." These traditional forms of pedagogy will remain valuable opportunities for learning for many in our population at certain formative times of their lives.[14] The university will remain a place where future leaders are shaped and educated. The broader intellectual development of the young, preparing them not simply for careers but for meaningful lives as contributing citizens, will remain a fundamental purpose of undergraduate education.

However, there will be strong pressures on universities to shift away from being faculty-centered institutions in which faculty determine what to teach, whom to teach, how to teach, and where and when to teach. Instead universities will likely evolve into learner-centered institutions, in which learners have far more options and control over what, how, when, where, and with whom they learn. This should not be surprising. In our increasingly egalitarian, market-driven world, the concerns of individuals (or customers or clients) have become the focus of most successful organizations.

In the near term, at least, traditional models of education will coexist with new learning paradigms, providing a broader spectrum of learning opportunities in the years ahead. As students become active learners, they will acquire an increasing ability to select, design, and control their learning environments. Faculty members will be challenged to play a variety of roles as teachers, coaches, consultants, mentors, and designers of experiences to serve the lifelong learning needs of their students. The only real barrier will be the limit of human imagination brought to bear on the ways in which information technology can benefit learning.

RESEARCH AND SCHOLARSHIP

Scholarship in the Digital Age

The earliest applications of information technology in research utilized the computer for solving mathematical problems in science and technology, that is, for number crunching. Digital computers enabled the solution of complex equations resistant to pencil-and-paper mathematical analysis. Computers were used to automate tasks in scientific experimentation such as the control of instrumentation, data collection, and reduction and analysis.

Today, however, research applications that used to require the computational capacity of rooms of supercomputers can be tackled with a contemporary laptop computer. The rapid evolution of digital technology is enabling scholars to address previously unsolvable problems, such as proving the four-color conjecture in mathematics, analyzing molecules that have yet to be synthesized, or simulating the birth of the universe. The humanist or social scientist can rapidly explore the entire literature concerning a subject in a digital library, exploring hypotheses and relationships that would have been lost in the sheer volume of written material.

Beyond solving complex mathematical models or managing large data sets, we are increasingly able to simulate complex phenomena from first principles, for example, solving the equations of motion for millions of atoms representing a material, analyzing the complex dynamics of the global climate, or simulating the crash of an automobile. The use of information technology to simulate natural phenomena has created a third modality of research, on a par with theory and experimentation.

Computer simulation provides a way to probe deeply into the behavior of complex systems, to try out new theories on idealized systems. Scientists still develop hypotheses to be tested in the laboratory or in the field, but a new step has been added to the scientific process. More and more often, the experimental data that emerge are compared to computer simulations. The appearance of new computer-based disciplines such as computational chemistry, computational neuroscience, computational genetics, and bioinformatics suggests that the computer is being used increasingly to augment the scientific mind as it attempts to digest the deluge of data coming from new laboratory instrumentation. In a very real sense, all experimental science is becoming dependent upon computer science, to the extent that computer technology is the common interface between data collection, analysis, and interpretation.

Although the personal computer technology available to researchers continues to advance very rapidly, there will always be scientific problems pushing the limits of the current generation of supercomputers. For example, as we noted earlier, the calculation of protein-folding is considerably beyond the capability of contemporary supercomputers. To perform these calculations, IBM is currently developing Blue Gene, a "petaflop" supercomputer, roughly 100 times faster than existing supercomputers. Such unique machines are generally located at national centers, such as the NSF Supercomputer Centers or the various federal research laboratories, and made available to a consortium of users, much like astronomical observatories.

Some of the most powerful applications of this technology have been in the humanities, social sciences, and the arts. Scholars now can use digital libraries such as JSTOR or ARTSTOR to access, search, and analyze a surprisingly complete collection of scholarly journals or digital images of artistic objects. Archaeologists are developing virtual reality simulations of remote sites and original materials such as papyrus manuscripts that can be accessed by scholars throughout the world. Social scientists are using powerful software tools to analyze massive data sets of verbal and visual materials collected through interviews and field studies. The visual and performing arts are exploring the new power of technologies that merge various media—art, music, dance, theater, architecture—and exploit all the senses—visual, aural, tactile, even olfactory—to create new art forms and artistic experiences.

The emergence of vast data repositories with storage requirements of petabyte magnitude will provide both new opportunities and challenges. Although these are generally associated with experiment-intensive sciences such as high-energy physics, space science, or genomics, such massive data sets will also characterize the humanities and social sciences as they become increasingly involved with video and holographic technologies. New forms of digital archives are evolving such as distributed data grids (e.g., the Grid Physics Network being developed to handle the projected data stream of six petabytes each year collected from the CERN accelerator).[15] Developing the software necessary to access, manipulate, and analyze such vast data sets will be a particular challenge.

These newly emerging areas of research, made possible only by rapidly evolving digital technology, are commonly referred to as "e-science." They demand a sophisticated technology infrastructure, a "cyberinfrastructure" of computers, networks, data repositories, and other digital devices. Much of e-science arises from the vast data collection capability of new facilities such as the Large Hadron Collider in higher-energy physics, the Laser Interferometry Gravity Wave Observatory (LIGO), the system of Earth-observing satellites, and the brain imaging data repositories. E-science also responds to the increasing ability of digital technology to simulate physical phenomena such as global weather patterns or to solve the complex equations characterizing new theories such as the superstring theory of elementary particles.

New types of research organizations are appearing that are based on evolving information technology. An example is the "collaboratory," an advanced, distributed infrastructure that uses multimedia information technology to relax the constraints on distance, time, and even reality.[16] Scholars around the world can now join together to operate remote facilities such as telescopes on Mauna Kea or scientific equipment at the South Pole Station, collaborating in data collection, analysis, and interpretation. A vast array of human team activities in commerce, education, and the arts would be supported by variants of this concept. Perhaps some form of the collaboratory is the appropriate infrastructure ("tooling") for the "learning organization" becoming popular in the business world; perhaps it is the basis for the world universities in the next century. It could well become the generic infrastructure on which to build the workplace of the emerging information age.

Some believe that digital computer and communication technology will allow larger, more efficient interdisciplinary research teams to form that can better tackle complex societal problems. If this is the case, then perhaps researchers will increasingly see it as a duty to participate in team activities. Perhaps digital technology, particularly if we can develop better tools to help distribute human attention, will make it possible for scholars to participate successfully in more different activities simultaneously. A researcher could assume different roles in different teams, as the leader of one, participant in others, occasional consultant in some, and observer/learner in others.

Similarly, technology can enable newcomers to a field to interact with the veterans of the field in new ways that transcend geographic and institutional boundaries. Graduate students can seek mentoring and access to facilities beyond their local advisers and mentors. Technology can also provide pathways for easier interaction across the "tiers" of scholarly activities in a field.

Digital technology also provides the tools to create, from desktop publishing, to digital photography and video, to synthesizing objects atom by atom. We are developing the capacity to create new life-forms through the tools of molecular biology and genetic engineering, and we are now creating new intellectual entities through artificial intelligence and virtual reality. There may even be a shift in knowledge production somewhat away from the *analysis of what has been* to the *creation of what has never been*— drawing rather more on the experience of the artist than upon analytical skills of the scientist.

The Library

The preservation of knowledge is one of the most rapidly changing activities of the university. The computer—or, more precisely, the "digital convergence" of various media from print, to graphics, to sound, to sensory experiences through virtual reality—will likely move beyond the printing press in its impact on knowledge. The library has always been the intellectual heart of the university, collecting and providing access to the written works that represent the knowledge and wisdom of centuries of civilization. Yet digital knowledge comes in many forms in addition to text, including sound and images, multimedia, and virtual reality. Furthermore, digital information is stored not on shelves in physical buildings, but rather on global networks, available to anyone with Internet access.

This poses a particular challenge to the library, shifting it from a focus on collecting and archiving knowledge resources (most commonly in written form), to assisting scholars to navigate a vast array of digital knowledge resources scattered through cyberspace. Just ask colleagues when they last visited a library. Probably years ago. The reason is simple: the library is no longer a place. It is a utility. It is becoming less a collection house and more a center for knowledge navigation, a facilitator of information retrieval and dissemination.[17] The campus library has become less central to most researchers' lives, with digital telecommunications allowing access to primary and secondary materials on-line. Libraries no longer chain their books to the wall; indeed, they no longer require physical visits.

Of course, books are also changing rapidly. We are already beginning to see the early "e-books"—really small laptop computers optimized to display text. New publishing paradigms are appearing, such as the use of the Net to provide downloads for e-books. This technology will evolve very rapidly, with the development of "electronic ink" that allows electronic books to closely resemble conventional books, albeit with the powerful tools of network access to the libraries of the world, hypertext or Web links, the display of nonverbal materials such as video and virtual, and eventually the use of artificial intelligence and software agents. In fact, the key new feature of e-books will be their use of interactive multimedia as a communications medium and their instantaneous access to vast knowledge networks.[18]

Furthermore, creating and managing new forms of archival and support material have become increasingly important to many research fields. Databases of longitudinal economic data, archives of all documents in a particular language or from a particular period, digital video archives of survey interviews, raw data from observatories and nuclear accelerators are increasingly the source material for research, and the management of such vast data sources is stimulating new methods of scholarship. Furthermore, such data archives are typically not physically localized or controlled by a single institution.

Scholarly Communication

Scholarly publication is also changing rapidly. Most scientific results now appear first as preprints on the Web, perhaps authored by a collaborative of scientists. Only many months (or years) later will they appear in refereed journals and then more likely go immediately into the dusty stacks of a library than be read as a physical document. A half century ago Vannevar Bush wrote that "our methods of transmitting and reviewing the results of research are generations old and by now are totally inadequate for their purpose." Yet much remains the same today, except that the volume of literature has increased vastly, with prices soaring to staggering levels driven by a monopolistic publishing industry.[19]

There is a recursive relationship between information technology and scholarly communication, since rapid advances in each depend upon the other. Robert Lucky suggests that "in their influence on how science is transacted, the Internet and World Wide Web have had the greatest impact of any communications medium since possibly the printing press." As with learning, these new electronic media allow the formation of spontaneous communities of unacquainted users, linked together in the many-to-many topology of computer networks. Researchers can now follow the work in their specialization on a day-by-day basis through Web sites. As Lucky notes, "Who could have dreamed even a decade ago that we would have instant access to a billion documents from the comfort and privacy of our office or laptop?"[20]

Even today, science is still characterized by the publication of research results. The current confusion between traditional scholarly publication, in established journals characterized by peer review—and high costs—and less formal Net-based communications, linking together scholars essentially instantaneously, presents an increasing challenge. Here, too, technology is rapidly evolving with the use of Web sites that serve as portals to integrate material of interest to particular scholarly disciplines.

As Lucky predicts, "We are headed technologically to a time when bandwidth and processing speed will be unlimited and free. Latency will approach the speed-of-light delay. Service quality will approach the 'five nines' (99.999 percent) availability of the traditional telephone network. And encryption will finally be freed of its political restraints, assuring security and privacy."

Electronic publication opens vast possibilities, not the least of which is freedom from the monopoly and pricing of commercial publishers, yet important standards of scholarly publication such as critical review and attribution of credit must be retained even as digital technology reshapes scholarly communication. So, too, the access to scientific instrumentation and data and the rapid dissemination of research results allowed by digital media raise complex issues of investigator control and sharing in scholarly investigations. The rising concerns of researchers with protecting intellectual property because of its potential commercial value can also interfere with teamwork and sharing.

The reality is that electronic publishing will become the dominant mechanism for both reading and publishing scholarly materials by the end of this decade. Yet, to achieve this goal, the scholarly community will demand a new paradigm for scholarly communication capable of providing open, on-line access to the work of scholars without payment, on-line repositories of high-quality materials, and a stable economic model to sustain these resources.

ACADEMIC OUTREACH

Public service, the transfer and application of the knowledge of the academy to serve specific needs of society, has long been an important mission of the American university. Service is an extension of the research, teaching, and professional expertise of the faculty and usually triggers images of outreach and extension, of regional systems such as the Cooperative Extension Service, massive medical centers, lifelong learning programs, community economic development, and a host of other activities specifically designed to respond to public needs. In fact, today the concept of public service is increasingly being extended to a form of engagement, of an active partnership, between the university and the communities that it serves.[21]

Digital technology is reshaping the nature of university outreach, extension, and engagement, providing both new opportunities and new challenges.

On-line Education

The simplest conception of computer-mediated distance learning uses multimedia technology via the Internet to provide educational services to distant students. Such instruction can be delivered into either the workplace or the home. In one form, this Internet-mediated instruction would be synchronous—in real time with the instructor and the students interacting together, much like two-way video. The more interesting teaching paradigms of computer-mediated distance learning involve asynchronous interactions, in which students and faculty interact at different times. In a sense, this latter form would resemble a correspondence course, with multimedia computers and networks replacing the mailing of written materials. Since one need not invest in the physical infrastructure of the campus, there is potential for significant cost reductions in the long term. By using an inexpensive delivery mechanism such as the Internet to reach a potentially vast audience, some believe that e-learning can provide instruction at costs far lower than for campus-based instruction.[22]

When implemented through active, inquiry-based learning pedagogies, on-line learning can stimulate students to use higher-order skills such as problem solving, collaboration, and simulation. Some of the early for-profit entrants into this marketplace such as Unext.com and Accenture are using multimedia simulations, case studies, threaded discussions, and real-time collaboration tools to create dynamic learning environments where skills are actively engaged in the learning experience, using a broader array of cognitive tools than in the usual classroom-lecture setting. Of course, the very best universities have long provided such rich educational experiences to a small number of students through seminars or tutorials, but on-line learning has the opportunity to create an experience that combines the rich educational experience offered by elite universities with the global reach of the Internet.

The growth of computer-mediated distance learning has been rapid, increasing at a rate of over 30 percent each year to an estimated 2 million students enrolled in credit-granting courses in 2001. Distance education is now a common activity for most higher education institutions, with over half conducting computer-mediated programs.

Unfortunately, too much of today's use of computer networks to deliver distance learning simply uses the technology to distribute the conventional approaches to pedagogy. In the rush to reduce costs and achieve market share, little attention is usually directed to rethinking the nature of learning or establishing quality standards. Effective distance learning requires more than simply using computer network technology to distribute the conventional classroom experience. We have noted that the most effective form of education involves building communities of learners, interacting in a rich intellectual environment. How can we re-create such learning communities on-line?

Asynchronous Learning Networks

One of the most effective approaches to distance learning is through the use of Asynchronous Learning Networks (ALN). In this approach, computer networks are used to link together an instructor with a distributed community of learners who communicate with one another and access learning materials at any time and from any place. Most of the learning activities in an ALN course do not occur in real time; rather, they can be undertaken at the convenience of each student and the instructor. The key characteristic of the ALN model is the capability of its learners to be part of a community, cooperating asynchronously to perform a common task, learning. Typical implementation of the ALN model is a group of participants (learners, tutors, experts, technicians, and lecturers) supported by a distributed computer system that includes information servers (the Web, FTP, library), their associated clients, and interactive communication software such as electronic mail and conferencing systems.

Here we should recognize the particular character of asynchronous learning.[23] Face-to-face conversation is both geographically local and temporally synchronous. In asynchronous communications, words are not heard as they are spoken but repeated at some later point. This delay allows thought and consideration to mediate the asynchronous communication. Such asynchronous interactions are ideally suited to the Net, since it allows low-cost ways to hold many-to-many conversations among people who are distributed in both space and time. Beyond simple interactions through E-mail and bulletin boards, role-playing games seem ideal for learning. These software constructions provide not only a virtual environment where interactions occur but also common objects for participants to observe, manipulate, and discuss, making the Net a medium both for conversation and for circulating digital objects. Such Net-mediated communities allow open learning in which the student decides when, where, and how to interact with the learning community.[24]

One of the major strengths of ALN is its ability to support networked communication within a community of learners. This feature makes it very different from correspondence courses and other distance education modalities. However, ALN courses must be structured to encourage interaction and collaboration. This is not a trivial educational process; it requires a pedagogical understanding of group dynamics. The faculty need to develop new skills and habits to teach an ALN course. For example, unlike the instructor of a traditional class who may have contact with students two to three times a week, ALN faculty must have a regular (at least daily) online presence and respond to student questions in a timely manner. ALN enables a variety of cooperative activities, enhanced by extended think time. Theoretically, it enables students to acquire benefits that seem to be hard to acquire with other modes of distance learning, such as deep, time-consuming reasoning processes.

Over the past decade, the Alfred P. Sloan Foundation has invested over $35 million in developing the ALN paradigm, sponsoring over 150,000 course units.[25] This experience has established that the ALN approach to distance education can effectively reproduce the classroom over the Internet. The results support the premise that when students are actively involved in collaborative learning on-line, the outcomes can be as good as, or better than, those for traditional classes, but when individuals are simply receiving posted material and sending back individual work, the results are poorer than in traditional classrooms. More specifically, with comparable student-to-faculty ratios, ALN education works as well as conventional classrooms, as measured by student achievement and satisfaction. Some 94 percent of ALN students believe that they learn as much or more than they would in a classroom-based course.[26]

These results reinforce statistics gathered by the National Technological University (NTU) that found that the average grade point average of NTU students (distance learners) is almost half a grade point (on a scale of four) above that of campus-based students taking the same courses. Moreover, Silicon Valley distance learners taking engineering courses via television from Stanford University have traditionally scored about 2 points out of 100 higher than their fellow students based on the Stanford campus.

What about cost? Here it should be stressed again that simply patching technology to a business-as-usual approach is likely to increase costs in the short term.[27] Computer-mediated distance learning, just like computer-enhanced, on-campus education, requires substantial up-front investments. An institution cannot simply dabble in this area at the margins, with incremental investments. Financial success depends upon relatively large enrollments per course, delivered asynchronously, to permit the full amortization of course development costs while still providing net revenues after expenses from tuition. The Sloan Foundation studies have concluded that if the objective is reproducing the interaction experience of the classroom (rather than automating the process through elaborate multimedia productions), the cost to convert a conventional course into ALN format is quite modest, averaging about $10,000 per course.

The caveat is that the ALN approach emphasizes highly interactive learning communities led by an instructor. Some see a potential of distributed learning to actually eliminate the instructor altogether, relying instead on sophisticated multimedia, virtual reality, or simulated environments and perhaps augmented by artificial intelligence software agents. Of course, faculty would still play a role in such automated learning commodities, identifying and preparing content and perhaps even being recorded as a "star" in a multimedia presentation. It is important to note that there are vast differences in the success of on-line courses related not to how much was paid for a star in a videotape but rather to the skill and effort of the professor working with the students. Far from there being "no more costly professors," on-line courses represent an arena of struggle between those who see them as a way of maximizing profit versus those who see them as a way of improving quality as well as access to education. They also represent a new and generally satisfying challenge to faculty members, to change their pedagogy to best take advantage of the fast-changing technology of the Internet, the World Wide Web, and their successors.

As one goes up the learning curve, from community colleges, to regional universities, to research universities, there is less and less activity in e-learning, particularly at the level of research universities. While there are experiments such as Unext.com and Fathom.com, these are "hands-off," without strong participation by the research university faculty. As a result, the research universities do not appear to be learning how to implement this technology as rapidly as others in the postsecondary education enterprise, including, in particular, for-profit organizations.

The Open University

A sharply contrasting approach is that of the open university, in which technology is used to distribute and support a correspondence style of individualized student learning, in contrast to the networked-based interactive learning communities of asynchronous learning networks. This particular approach, successfully pioneered by the British Open University, relies on an "educational scaffolding" of highly sophisticated study materials and decentralized learning facilities where students can seek academic and other forms of educational assistance when they need it. This model has propagated rapidly throughout the world, where such open universities now enroll over 3 million students worldwide.

These institutions are based upon the principle of open learning, in which technology and distance education models are used to break down barriers and provide opportunities for learning to a very broad segment of society. In these models, students becomes more active participants in learning activities, taking charge of their own academic program as much as possible. Many of these open universities are now embracing information technology, particularly the Net, to provide educational opportunities to millions of students unable to attend or afford traditional residential campuses.

The motivation behind open universities involves cost, access, and flex-ibility.[28] The open university paradigm is based not on the extension of the classroom but rather on the one-to-one learning relationship between the tutor and the student. It relies on very high-quality learning materials, such as books, videotapes, and CD-ROM or Net-based software, augmented by facilitators at regional learning centers and by independent examiners. Using this paradigm, for example, the British Open University has been able to provide high-quality learning opportunities (currently ranked among the upper 15 percent of British universities) at only a fraction of a cost of residential education ($4,200 compared to $12,500 per student year in North America).

To date, most open universities rely heavily on self-learning in the home environment, although they do make use of interactive study materials and decentralized learning facilities where students can seek academic assis-tance when they need it. However, with the rapid evolution of virtual dis-tributed environments and learning communities, these institutions will soon be able to offer a mix of educational experiences.

The Virtual University

One of the more provocative approaches to higher education in the in-formation age is the so-called *virtual university*. In cybertalk, "virtual" is an adjective that means existing in function but not in form. A virtual uni-versity exists only in cyberspace, without a campus or perhaps even a fac-ulty. Sophisticated networks and software environments are used to break the learning loose from the constraints of space and time and make it avail-able to anyone, anyplace, anytime.

Already, college directories list over 1,000 virtual colleges, with over 1 million students enrolled in their programs. Yet most of these are simply Internet-based extensions of conventional distance learning, relying upon existing higher education organizations such as extension programs. How-ever, several rapidly emerging virtual organizations do represent radical de-partures from our traditional paradigms for colleges and universities.

The simplest conception of the virtual university uses multimedia tech-nology via the Internet to enable distance learning. Such instruction could be delivered into either the workplace or the home. In one form, this In-ternet-mediated instruction would be synchronous—in real time, with the instructor and the students interacting together. The more interesting teaching paradigms of the virtual university involve asynchronous inter-actions, in which students and faculty interact at different times. In a sense, this latter form would resemble a correspondence course, with multimedia computers and networks replacing the mailing of written materials. As we have noted, there is already sufficient experience with such asynchronous learning to conclude that, at least for many subjects, the learning process is just as effective as in the classroom experience. Furthermore, because one need not invest in the physical infrastructure of the campus, there is opportunity for significant cost reductions in the long term. By using an inexpensive delivery mechanism such as the Internet to reach a potentially vast audience, many hope that a virtual university can provide instruction at costs far lower than those for campus-based instruction. There are presently for-profit entities[29] competing directly with traditional colleges and universities in the higher education marketplace through virtual university structures.

There are many approaches to the virtual university. One possibility would be an organization that simply provides people with access to on-line educational services, linking students and educational providers. Another model is a virtual campus that would offer students a broad array of courses leading toward degrees, perhaps at their home institution. Although such an organization would have a small core faculty, it would rely as well on instructors from other institutions as well as vendors for asynchronous classroom and computer-based training programs. A third model, the "university.com," is aimed primarily at the corporate marketplace. By partnering closely with companies and industry associations, these organizations could develop courses aimed at meeting the workplace skill needs of companies while increasing the competitiveness of a geographical region. Here the university.com would not grant degrees but might instead offer competence-based certificates.[30] The virtual university might even be simply a Web portal, a Web site-based set of linkages to educational providers that collectively distribute services to learners at the time, place, pace, and style that they desire, with quality determined by the client and a variety of approval and accrediting bodies.

A Case Study: The Michigan Virtual University[31]

It is instructive to consider a specific example from our own experience that illustrates these various models. Several years ago we were involved in creating just such a virtual university, both to respond to the changing educational needs of the major industry in our state, the automobile industry, as well as to explore the possibility of new types of learning institutions based upon rapidly emerging digital technology. Through a collaborative effort involving the University of Michigan, Michigan State University, the state of Michigan, the state's other colleges and universities, and the automobile industry, in 1996 we launched the Michigan Virtual Automotive College (MVAC) as a private, not-for-profit, 501(c) 3 corporation aimed at developing and delivering technology-enhanced courses and training programs for the automobile industry. This effort has since evolved into the Michigan Virtual University (MVU), today offering a broad set of educational services to citizens, industry, and the education community in the state of Michigan.

MVAC was designed as a system integrator or broker between colleges and universities, training providers, and the automotive industry. Its goal was to integrate customer needs, available academic/training programs, and development of new materials. It was also designed as a "greenfield" experiment where colleges and universities could come together to test capabilities to deliver their training and educational programs at a distance and asynchronously.

MVAC and its successor, MVU, are universities without campuses or faculties. Courses and programs can be offered from literally any site in the state to any other technologically connected site within the state, the United States, or the world. Although learning technologies are rapidly evolving, MVAC and MVU broker courses that utilize a wide array of technology platforms including satellite, interactive television, Internet, CD-ROM, videotape, and combinations of these. Part of our objective was to develop common technology standards between and among educational service providers and customers for the ongoing delivery of courses. At the outset, MVAC offered courses and training programs at various levels, ranging from the advanced postgraduate education in engineering, computer technology, and business administration to entry-level instruction in communications, mathematics, and computers. The more comprehensive MVU offers a broad range of educational services, more typical of a comprehensive university.

As the previous examples illustrate, there are many different approaches to building virtual universities. Clearly, all depend upon information technology to free themselves from the constraints of campus-based instruction, but they can differ considerably in the way that they are financed, their governance, their markets, and their academic objectives. The sequence of decisions involved in creating the Michigan Virtual Automotive College and the Michigan Virtual University illustrates these considerations.

First, we designed MVAC to be primarily a broker or system integrator, working with the industry to determine its education and training needs and then, in turn, working with established educational institutions to respond to these needs through the use of information technology. In this sense, MVAC would have no campus, no faculty, and a very limited administrative staff. Its primary function would be to open up new channels for the delivery of educational services.

At the outset, we also decided that MVAC would not grant degrees. Although there had been some early thought given to chartering MVAC as a state educational institution similar to the Western Governors University, in the end we decided against this. We wanted MVAC to be clearly perceived by Michigan's existing colleges and universities as value-adding, not competitive. Rather than creating an independent, degree-granting capability—and facing the rather considerable challenges of accreditation—we instead decided to rely upon the established degree programs and cooperative agreements with existing institutions.

Second, we initially focused MVAC on a brokering role among institutions. That is, we viewed our initial market as companies, not individual employees or citizens. Furthermore, we viewed our suppliers as academic institutions, not individual faculty or staff. We realized that at some future point, as we developed capacity to deliver high-quality, cost-effective educational services beyond the workplace and onto the desktop and into the home, the possibility of offering programs to individual clients might become of interest. However, at the outset, by confining our efforts to working with companies and academic institutions, we greatly simplified our marketing and support activities.

Third, we decided to form MVAC as a not-for-profit, independent corporation. While a for-profit organization would probably have been capable of faster growth because of access to capital markets, we believed that the not-for-profit character would better allow us to form relationships with other colleges and universities. While some state support ($10 million) was provided to capitalize and launch MVAC, it was our intent that the operation be self-supporting based on educational fees and contracts within three years.

Finally, we believed that the governance structure of MVAC should clearly reflect the three key participants: Michigan's colleges and universities, the automotive industry, and the state of Michigan. Although the University of Michigan, Michigan State University, and the state of Michigan were founding members of the 501(c) 3 membership corporation, we formed an executive committee structure containing representatives from Michigan's other universities and community colleges, the Big Three, the supplier industry, and the United Automobile Workers (UAW).

Within a short time after its founding, strong pressures developed within the state to establish similar industry-specific virtual colleges to respond to the needs of the states' other economic sectors. The MVAC model was used as the template for virtual colleges focused on industries such as health care products, furniture, tourism, and plastics. These were developed as "mirror sites," making extensive use of the experience of MVAC, including administration, contracting, technology platforms, and academic services.

There was considerable interest expressed in extending the concept to include the delivery of educational services directly to individuals. Clearly, with digital convergence—the merging of television and the network computer—it should soon be possible to deliver sophisticated educational services directly into the home. The goal of making the vast resources of Michigan's educational infrastructure—its colleges and universities and cultural organizations—available to all of the state's citizens, wherever they are and whenever they desire them, at high quality and at a cost they can afford is a dream that may soon be within reach. To this end, a second institution, the Michigan Virtual University, was formed not only to coordinate the various industry-specific virtual colleges such as MVAC but also to assist the state's colleges and universities in providing a broader array of educational services based on information technology.

Adult students are seeking quality and convenience in educational products. Given the growing number of education and training providers on the Internet, the challenge will be to create an environment that attracts and retains students. From our experience, we believe that there are several keys to getting and keeping students connected on-line to virtual universities.

Obviously, a solid marketing strategy is important to ensure that prospective students at least visit the virtual university's Web site or Web portal. Once students reach the site, they should be assisted by a career guidance system that will allow them to learn on-line about jobs and careers associated with different educational programs. A third ingredient to a successful program is visitor access to job profiles to learn about the skills and competencies needed to qualify for different jobs and careers. Other services of considerable value are competence and skills assessment tools. Finally, it is important to package individual courses into curricula that help students acquire the skills and competencies to reach their goals.

Of course, beyond structural and program issues, there are important pedagogical issues to consider. Gone are the days when utilizing passive telecommunications technology is acceptable. Learners gravitate to more interesting teaching formats in which the subject matter fits the delivery medium and the medium fits the learner. A well-planned evaluation program is important to assess which learning packages and strategies work best for different groups of learners under different circumstances.

Distance learning based on computer-network-mediation allows virtual universities to push their campus boundaries out to serve learners anywhere, anytime. Those institutions willing to build such learning networks could see their learning communities expand by an order of magnitude.

The current concept of distance learning, even if implemented via the Internet through virtual universities, is still bound to traditional ideas and approaches,[32] but as true learning communities are constructed in cyberspace, traditional educational institutions will feel increasing competition and pressure to change. The university will continue to be the primary source of "content" for educational programs, but other organizations more experienced in "packaging" content, for example, entertainment companies, may compete with universities to provide educational services to the mass market. In a similar sense, it could well be that the role of the faculty member will shift rapidly from that of organizing and teaching individual courses. As higher education shifts from a cottage industry to mass production, faculty may become members of design teams developing content for broader markets.

THE FACULTY CHALLENGE

We suggested earlier that the changing nature of learning in the digital age will likely demand major changes in the role of the faculty. It is imperative that academic institutions provide the resources and support necessary to enable faculty members to adapt to the changing learning and scholarly paradigms of the digital age. Increasingly powerful computers allow scholars to solve complex problems and simulate natural phenomena, while networks provide access to scientific literature and data and help one communicate and collaborate with colleagues. The impact of information technology on teaching can be equally profound, linking students and faculty through networks, allowing access to original materials, and supporting new forms of pedagogy such as distributed virtual environments. The array of tools for productivity—electronic mail, word processors, spreadsheets, contact managers, symbolic mathematical tools, presentation software, Web browsers and search engines, data warehouses, and multimedia—continues to expand.

Failing to keep pace with the rapid evolution of these tools can put one at a considerable disadvantage. While it is not necessary to be an early adopter of each wave of new technology, some facility with mainstream technology such as the Internet and personal productivity tools has become essential for keeping pace with the scholarly community. Recent surveys suggest that many scholars worry that they are falling behind their colleagues in their use of information technology. They fear the resulting isolation from their research colleagues and an inability to take advantage of the emerging tools for teaching and scholarship necessary for the classroom and laboratory. Institutions must provide sufficient resources to enable faculty members to keep pace with developments in information technology through robust technology environments, staff support, and training opportunities. Today's faculty members must make the personal commitment to take advantage of these opportunities—to keep pace with technology just as they try to keep pace with research advances in their fields.

Unlike other sectors of our society where turnover is high and the focus can be on hiring new people, in the university, tenure and other practices result in timescales characterizing faculty replacement on the order of a generation. In earlier times, universities would wait for a generation of professors to retire before an academic unit could evolve. In today's high-paced world, when the doubling time for technology evolution has collapsed to a year or less, institutions simply must look for effective ways to reskill our faculties or risk rapid obsolescence. Information technology provides important tools for the conduct of research and teaching, communication, administration, and personal productivity.

In the very near term, colleges and universities will be challenged to meet the technology and support staff infrastructure needs for both "early adopter" and "early follower" faculty who choose to implement information technology in their instruction and research. Propagating these tools to the faculty at large and then meeting the corresponding needs for support will be an even more significant financial as well as cultural challenge.

Applications of information technology can improve the quality and productivity of one's scholarship, teaching, and administrative activities. As a result, technology early adopters and pathfinders should be rewarded through compensation, promotion, and perhaps even tenure. However, in most colleges and universities, faculty evaluations are based on more traditional criteria such as peer assessment, scholarly publications, grantsmanship, graduate student supervision, and teaching. Junior faculty and research staff should keep pace with information technology to the extent that it improves their professional performance, but they should be realistic in expecting rewards for doing so.

Spending too much time developing information technology for the classroom or laboratory has harmed the careers of many junior faculty. Promotion reviews often fail to weigh properly achievements such as software and hardware development. Publishing in on-line journals or through sophisticated Web sites is usually discounted in favor of traditional, peer-reviewed articles in well-established scholarly journals. An elegantly coded subroutine developed to solve a research problem or novel application of multimedia in the classroom will almost always go unappreciated or unnoticed by senior colleagues more accustomed to evaluating scholarly publications in peer-reviewed journals.

However, perhaps even more challenging will be the longer-term needs of the faculty as they shift from their traditional roles as classroom lecturers to the new skills required to manage an active learning process. For example, one might characterize the faculty time spent today on instructional activities in the current classroom paradigm as roughly 60 percent in research, content development, and organization and perhaps 40 percent in classroom presentation and student interactions (assisted heavily by graduate teaching assistants). As students become active learners, and the content of the classroom becomes increasingly a commodity (developed and presented by leading faculty at leading institutions), the faculty role will shift to one predominantly concerned with mentoring activities, guiding, shaping, and coaching the active learning process of students.

The active learning environment that we suggest as the paradigm for learning in the digital age is remarkably closer to the historical ways of early learning than is the lecture format of today's university classroom, for example, the scholar surrounded by disciples. It could also be a new and possibly threatening experience to most of today's faculty, accustomed to the detached role of "the sage on the stage" characterizing large lecture courses.

Like any tool, digital technology can be perceived as either a threat to the status quo or an opportunity to improve and enhance one's activities. Today faculty members have the primary responsibility for designing and supervising learning environments. They determine course character and content. They design the curriculum. They manage the learning activities of their students. Information technology is likely to change these roles.

The content of courses will increasingly be provided by digital objects— Web sites, simulations, environments—designed, produced, and distributed by others, much as textbooks are today. While the rich and engaging content of well-produced multimedia learningware may threaten and even displace the sage on the stage, it can also make great teachers even greater by providing them with the opportunity to extend and leverage their efforts far beyond the traditional classroom, but they can do so only if their efforts to utilize technology are well supported, encouraged, and rewarded.

Faculty will play a variety of roles: researcher, synthesizer, mentor, evaluator and certifier of mastery, architect, and navigator. These roles will not be played in equal measures by all faculty. The digital age university will enable greater role differentiation and specialization. Part of the challenge will be not only to identify and provide training and support for the new faculty roles of the digital age but also to agree upon new standards for professional practice. These must be reflected both in the nature of graduate education as well as in the evolving relationship between the university and its faculty.

CONCLUDING REMARKS

The university is a complex institution, evolving over centuries to serve our civilization in myriad ways, albeit based upon ancient and time-honored values. It serves as a custodian not simply of the knowledge but also of the values, traditions, and culture of our society. It not only educates and discovers but also challenges the existing order and drives change. It remains essential to produce the educated citizens necessary for a democratic society. It affirms the fundamental values, principles, and integrity of learning and reason. It not only honors the past, serves the present, and creates the future but does so with the aim of transforming knowledge into wisdom.

Information technology is rapidly transforming each of the many activities of the university, from teaching, to scholarship, to outreach. Cynics sometimes point to television as a technology once believed to have transforming implications for education, but today it is largely dominated by the commercial entertainment industry. However, television is a broadcast technology, enabling one-to-many distribution, without opportunity for the feedback and interaction so necessary for an active learning environment. Information technology enables many-to-many communications, unconstrained by space and time, that can be used to build and sustain learning communities.

It is important that we view information technology not as simply a threat to the status quo but rather as an opportunity to enhance and enrich those activities most essential to the role and mission of the university. Today it is clear that in most cases information technology is underutilized in higher education. Technology is primarily used at the margins, serving as extensions rather than transformations of the way that we learn and teach,[33] yet the evolution of this technology continues to accelerate at superexponential rates, promising to deliver, in effect, infinite processing speed and infinite bandwidth in the not too distant future (at least compared to current technology). Hence, the fundamental activities of the university, education and research, will continue to be reshaped in increasingly profound ways by evolving information technology. Rather than adapting our traditional activities of teaching and scholarship to the technology of the moment, we should instead challenge those developing and implementing digital technology to shape it so that it helps our students to learn, our faculty to teach, our scholars to conduct research, and our institutions to serve. Our faculties must make demands upon the technology and not be driven by it. They must insist that this technology be used to strengthen the enduring values of the university and its capacity to serve our changing world.

NOTES

1. Kellogg Commission on the Future of the State and Land-Grant Universities, *Renewing the Covenant: Learning, Discovery and Engagement in a New Age and Different World* (Washington, DC: National Association of State Universities and Land-Grant Colleges, 2000); James J. Duderstadt, "New Roles for the 21st Century University," *Issues in Science and Technology* 16, no. 2 (2000), 37–44.

2. John Perry Barlow, "The Economy of Ideas: A Framework for Rethinking Patents and Copyrights in the Digital Age," *Wired* 2, no. 3 (March 1994).

3. Martin R. Stytz, "Distributed Virtual Environments," *IEEE Computer Graphics and Applications* 16 (May 1996), 19–31.

4. For an excellent example of such virtual universities, see the Web site for the Michigan Virtual Automotive College at <http://www.mvac.org> and the article by Scott Bernato, "Big 3 U," *University Business* (September–October 1998), 20–27.

5. John Seely Brown and Paul Duguid, *The Social Life of Information* (Cambridge: Harvard Business School Press, 2000).

6. David Shenk, *Datasmog: Surviving the Information Glut* (New York: Harper, 1998); Katie Hafner, "Teenage Overload, or Digital Dexterity?" *New York Times*, Circuits, D1 (April 12, 2001).

7. Committee on Developments in the Science of Learning, National Research Council, *How People Learn: Brain, Mind, Experience, and School* (Washington, DC: National Academy Press, 2000).

8. Brown and Duguid, *The Social Life of Information.*

9. Don Tapscott, *Growing Up Digital: The Rise of the Net Generation* (New York: McGraw-Hill, 1999).

10. Richard Lanham, *The Electronic Word: Democracy, Technology, and the Arts* (Chicago: University of Chicago Press, 1993).

11. Michael T. Moe, *The Knowledge Web* (New York: Merrill-Lynch, 2000).

12. Lewis J. Perelman, *School's Out* (New York: Avon, 1993).

13. John Seely Brown and Paul Duguid, "Universities in the Digital Age," *Change* (July 1996), 11–19.

14. Gregory C. Farrington, "The New Technology and the Future of Residential Undergraduate Education," in *Dancing with the Devil: Information Technology and the New Competition in Higher Education*, ed. Richard N. Katz (San Francisco: Educause and Jossey-Bass, 1998), 73–94.

15. Ian Foster, "The Grid: A New Infrastructure for 21st Century Science," *Physics Today* (February 2002), 42–47.

16. "All the World's a Lab," *New Scientist* 2077 (April 12, 1997), 24–27; T. A. Finholt and G. M. Olson, "From Laboratories to Collaboratories: A New Social Organizational Form for Scientific Collaboration," *Psychological Science* 9, no. 1 (1997), 28–36.

17. "Books, Bricks, and Bytes," *Daedelus* 125, no. 4 (1996), v–vii.

18. William Stephenson, *The Diamond Age* (New York: Bantam Spectrum Books, 2000).

19. Vannevar Bush, "As We May Think," *The Atlantic Monthly* 176, no. 1 (1945) 101–108; <http://www.theatlanticmonthly.com/unbound/flashbks/computer/bushf.htm>.

20. Robert Lucky, "The Quickening of Science Communication," *Science* 289 (July 14, 2000), 259–264.

21. *Renewing the Covenant.*

22. Ted Marchese, "Not-So-Distant Competitors: How New Providers Are Remaking the Postsecondary Marketplace," *AAHE Bulletin* (May 1998), <http://www.aahe.org/bulletin/bull_1/May 98 html>.

23. "On-Line Education: Learning Effectiveness and Faculty Satisfaction," *Proceedings of the 1999 Sloan Summer Workshop on Asynchronous Learning Networks*, John Bourne, ed. (Nashville: Center for Asynchronous Learning Networks, 2000).

24. Carol A. Twigg, "The Need for a National Learning Infrastructure," *Educom Review* (September–October 1994), 17–24; Carol Twigg, "Toward a National Learning Infrastructure: Navigating the Transition," National Learning Infrastructure, part 3, *Educom Review* (November–December 1994), 3. Posted on the Internet to the Horizon List, courtesy of Dr. Twigg.

25. "On-Line Education."

26. Ibid.

27. Richard Larson, "MIT Learning Networks: An Example of Technology-Enabled Education," *Forum Futures* (1999), 59–74.

28. John S. Daniel, "Why Universities Need Technology Strategies," *Change* (July 1997), 10–17.

29. Marchese, "Not-So-Distant Competitors."

30. Diane Oblinger, Carole A. Barone, and Brian L. Hawkins, *Distributed Education and Its Challenges: An Overview* (Washington, DC: American Council on Education, 2001).

31. The Web site of the Michigan Virtual University can be found at <http://www.mivu.org/>.

32. Myles Brand, "The Wise Use of Technology," *Educational Record* (Fall 1995), 39–46.

33. Richard N. Katz, ed., *Dancing with the Devil: Information Technology and the New Competition in Higher Education* (San Francisco: Educause and Jossey-Bass, 1998).

CHAPTER 4

The Impact of Information Technology on the Form, Function, and Financing of the University

Each of the many activities of the university involves knowledge, and as such, each is being transformed by information technology. History suggests that fundamental technological change also drives corresponding structural changes in social institutions. Although the university has managed to adapt to the technological changes of earlier times with its structure and function largely intact, information technology will pose somewhat different challenges, both because of its extraordinary pace of evolution and because of the way that it reshapes the most fundamental activities of the university as a knowledge-based institution.

For example, information technology could lead to the disaggregation of some university activities, not only separating teaching from research but also spinning off key functions such as the production of learning resources, the assessment of student learning, and even the granting of degrees. Technology could also enable the aggregation of other activities, such as alliances among universities in the use of major scholarly resources such as astronomical observatories or research libraries or joining together the learning-intensive approach to undergraduate education of the liberal arts college with the vast intellectual resources of the research university.

Information technology is likely to reshape the relationship between the university and its students and faculty. We have already suggested that this technology may transform some students into consumers of educational services, allowing them to mix and match various elements of their education from an array of providers, including not only traditional colleges and universities but also on-line, for-profit universities and publishers. Faculty members, already accustomed to using technology to collaborate with colleagues around the world, may exploit the increasingly ubiquitous telecommunications and transportation resources to develop teaching and research relationships with multiple institutions.

The traditional models for financing higher education are likely to be threatened by emerging information technology. Most colleges and universities will be challenged to develop sustainable financial schemes for building and supporting the technology infrastructure necessary for quality teaching and research—not to mention attracting and retaining high-quality students and faculty members. Although this technology is unlikely to reduce the cost of the traditional, classroom-based curriculum, experience from industry suggests that significant improvements in quality, productivity, and cost can be achieved by reengineering both process and management. Many colleges and universities will feel strong market forces from emerging for-profit competitors in high profit-margin areas such as general education and professional education. These new competitors will also threaten the cross-subsidies that research and graduate-intensive universities utilize to support advanced education and scholarship.

Clearly, a wide range of policy issues is being raised by the new technologies. For example, while the ownership of intellectual property such as research data is well established, the ownership of instructional content—perhaps even the course itself—is less clear, particularly in view of the long tradition of faculty authors owning the rights to textbooks. The certification and awarding of degrees will become increasingly complex for students enrolling in a diverse array of institutions, some campus-based, others on-line.

There are other challenges. Many universities are simply unprepared for the new plug-and-play generation, already experienced in using computers and Net-savvy, who will expect—indeed, demand—sophisticated computing environments in their college experience. More broadly, information technology is rapidly becoming a strategic asset for universities, critical to their academic mission and their administrative services, that must be provided on a robust basis to the entire faculty, staff, and student body.

Beyond this, we are likely to see entirely new types of educational institutions evolve with the appearance of new learning life-forms such as "e-learning," "virtual universities," and "I-campuses." Driven by information technology, the network will be more than a web that links together learning resources. It is becoming the architecture of advanced learning organizations.[1] Information, knowledge, and learning opportunities can now be distributed across robust computer networks to hundreds of millions of people. The knowledge, the learning, the cultural resources that used to be the prerogative of a privileged few are rapidly becoming available to a much vaster audience.

One can imagine the learning networks evolving into a seamless continuum of educational opportunities and services, in which the degree becomes less and less important, and what a person has learned becomes far more significant. Learning communities will be more extended and diverse with a network architecture. Since they will evolve unconstrained by space and time, the number of off-campus learners will vastly outnumber on-campus students. Beyond that, the distinction between learner, teacher, and researcher may become blurred. All will be able to make contributions to learning, teaching, and scholarship.

Conventional mechanisms for university planning and decision making are likely to be seriously challenged by the rapid and disruptive nature of information technology. It will require that institutions reconsider even the most fundamental questions regarding their values and their roles. For example, how do we define a student in a society of increasingly pervasive educational needs? What is the appropriate role for the faculty as students assume more responsibility for their education in an active and collaborative learning environment? How do we define and value university autonomy in an increasingly interdependent world? As the timescale for decisions and actions compresses, during an era of ever more rapid change, authority will tend to concentrate so that the institution can become more flexible and responsive. The academic tradition of extensive consultation, debate, and consensus building before any substantive decision is made or action taken will be one of our greatest challenges, since this process may be incapable of keeping pace with the profound changes swirling about higher education.

A century ago, the steam engine, electrification, the telephone, and the automobile changed our society in ways that were then unimaginable. Today digital technology, computers, networks, and software are once again transforming our economy, our institutions, and our lives. Universities can no more escape the transformative character of the digital age than they could the Industrial Revolution. Universities must anticipate these forces, develop appropriate strategies, and make adequate investments if they are to prosper during this period.

THE ORGANIZATION OF THE UNIVERSITY

Colleges and universities are organized along the lines of academic and professional disciplines, grouped into larger units such as a college of arts and sciences or a school of engineering, as well as into smaller subunits such as a department of history or an institute of biotechnology research. Since academic degrees are associated with such academic units and since faculty appointments (including tenure) reside within them, they tend to endure over many decades. The university also has a parallel structure reflecting both its administrative activities and its relationship with external constituencies. For example, most universities have plant departments to care for physical facilities, development offices to raise private gifts, police departments for campus security, and athletics departments to entertain the public. In contrast to academic units, these administrative units tend to be organized along functional lines and are occasionally redefined or reshuffled as needs change.

Yet another way to understand the organization of the contemporary university is to compare it to a city, comprising a bewildering array of neighborhoods and communities. To the faculty, it is highly Balkanized, divided up into highly specialized academic units, frequently with little interaction even with disciplinary neighbors, much less with the rest of the campus. To the student body, the university is an exciting, confusing, and sometimes frustrating maelstrom of challenges and opportunities, rules and regulations, which draws students together only for cosmic events such as football games or campus protests. To the staff, all too frequently invisible to, or ignored by, the students and faculty, the university has a more subtle character, with parts woven together by policies, procedures, and practices that have evolved over decades.[2]

In some ways, the modern university is so complex, so multifaceted that it seems that the closer that one is to it and the more intimately that one is involved with its activities, the harder it is to understand in its entirety. It is easy to lose sight of the forest for the trees. Students see the university as classes, assignments, and exams associated with their academic programs. To undergraduates enrolled on a residential campus, the university becomes a home, a place where they are fed, sheltered, and entertained. For many others, commuting to campus from work or family, the university's image is all too frequently a parking lot. All students feel at times that they are only tourists, traveling through the many adventures—or hurdles—of their university education, entering as raw material and being stamped and molded into graduates during their brief experience on campus.

Faculty members also see the university in their own terms, as a place to teach and learn, conduct research and write, to be sure, but also as a way station in their career. Their academic duties rarely extend beyond their departments. Their view of the university is all too frequently bounded by their disciplines or professional colleagues, by physics and physiology, English and engineering.

Staff see the university somewhat more broadly than faculty and students, since they must serve not only each of these internal constituencies but also those external to the university. To most staff the university is a corporation (with a high calling, to be sure) but operating within the same administrative, financial, and legal constraints as any other corporate organization in business or government.

The university administration and governing board also see the university more broadly. Not only must they provide leadership for its various internal constituencies, but they also manage its relationships with those beyond the campus: state and federal governments, business and industry, alumni and foundations, the public and the press, and other colleges and universities.

Beyond the campus, each of these external constituencies also has a view of the university. Sometimes this perspective is shaped by the services that they receive from the university (e.g., research or economic development). State and federal governments all too frequently see the university as an outstretched hand, requesting support. The public sees the university primarily through the news media—and all too frequently on the sports pages.

Universities are various physical places: classrooms, libraries, and laboratories; theatres and football stadiums; campus walks and arboretums. They are activities, numerous and diverse, such as teaching, research, athletics, and financial operations. Most of all, they are people. The faculty, students, and staff are the university's most important asset. The character, role, and interaction of these important communities are key in defining the nature of the university, and through these communities and the relationships that they reflect among people and concerning their use of knowledge, information technology is having its most profound impact on the organization of the university.

Academic Structures

Although the basic academic organization of the university appears relatively static, at least in comparison to that of corporations or governments, it does evolve and change over time as knowledge evolves. Typically, the formation of new academic and professional disciplines reflects the ever-increasing fragmentation and specialization of knowledge. Departments become splintered, made up, in some cases, of loose confederations of faculty in rarefied subfields who have more in common with peers in their disciplines at other universities than with campus colleagues, sometimes breaking away to form new academic units. Since this organizational evolution is driven by the growth and fragmentation of knowledge itself, it is understandable why it would be influenced by information technology.

Academic disciplines continue to dominate the modern university, developing the curriculum, marshaling resources, administering programs, and doling out rewards. Not surprisingly, faculty members tend to focus their loyalty on their disciplines instead of their home institutions. The formation of virtual communities of scholars using rapidly evolving information technology has accelerated this trend. Some fear the loss of cohesiveness of a broad community of scholars. As universities have built stronger and stronger disciplinary programs, they have also created powerful centrifugal forces that threaten to tear their intellectual communities apart.

Concerns about the fragmentary nature of knowledge are not new. Calls for more fluidity in intellectual inquiry arose as soon as the disciplines began to form at the end of the nineteenth century. So why has today's effort to break down the barriers between the disciplines taken on special importance? In part, the new emphasis comes with the shifting nature of knowledge production. Never before has the speed of change itself become the central issue of intellectual life. Disciplinary configurations are changing so rapidly that departments have difficulty coping with new ways of seeing. Biology has evolved from the macroscopic to the microscopic, becoming more dependent upon fields such as physics, chemistry, and computer science. Physics and astronomy have become more dependent upon engineering fields such as electronics and computers in acquiring and interpreting data. Literary criticism depends more heavily on fields such as anthropology and history.

At the same time, we can no longer ignore the importance of the knowledge that we produce for the wider society. We began to realize the social impact of knowledge in the 1950s, but today information is replacing material objects as a primary economic and social force. We have made the transition from atoms to bits, from material goods to knowledge. In our increasingly complex, interdependent world, narrow answers will not succeed. The "interdisciplinary momentum" is not a fad but a fundamental and long-term restructuring of the nature of scholarly activity.

The intellectual character of the university is dynamic. Achieving the appropriate balance between the disciplines and interdisciplinary teaching and scholarship, between basic and applied research, between analysis and creativity is just one of the many intellectual challenges before the modern university, yet these are not new. The birth of, competition among, and disappearance of scholarly areas have always been a critical part of the university's history.

The academic structure of the university is of critical importance, since whoever controls that structure determines the rules and means for acquiring knowledge, for legitimating it, and for passing it on to new generations. Although in recent times this authority and responsibility rested with the research university, information technology has enabled the rapid growth of research activity in other sectors of society such as industry and government. It is important to think about the research enterprise as being more than just a research university. We need to find better ways to engage multiple disciplines, no matter where they are, in universities or industry.

The Internet is creating new types of scholarly communities, free from the constraints of traditional academic disciplines, structures, and institutions just as they are from space and time. The defining feature of an academic conference on the Internet is precisely "a sense of collegiality, the nurturing experience of conversing with those who have similar interests."[3] There is no intrinsic reason that the prediction that scholarship will increasingly be conducted by teams assembled opportunistically to solve particular problems has to be a bleak one. True, it threatens to turn the university into a more chaotic place in which academics may have to abandon expectations of uniform pay, stable employment, and a steady career, but it also promises to break down the joint tyranny of the department and the discipline, which have done so much to erode the unity of the university in the past. A trend in many universities has been to create problem-oriented research centers with no permanent staff or departmental allegiance at all.

We might even question whether we may be nearing the end of the current paradigm of research and should consider the exploration of different approaches, particularly if we take seriously the creation of "human sciences" that truly bridge the two cultures. We may be at an inflection point in recasting the current paradigm for research and in finding new tools and methods for tackling major problems. Again we come back to the challenge of better training researchers to be willing to pick up fundamentally new tools and developing new ways to look at problems.

Unbundling and Disaggregation of Functions

The modern university has evolved into a monolithic institution encompassing all aspects of learning and, indeed, student life. These institutions have become highly vertically integrated over the past several decades. They provide courses at the undergraduate, graduate, and professional levels. They support residential colleges, professional schools, lifelong learning, athletics, libraries, museums, and entertainment. Many colleges and universities have become comparable to a small city in both complexity and range of services provided: housing and food services, health care and entertainment, personal and environmental safety, and even electricity and telephone service.

Today's comprehensive universities, at least as full-service organizations, are at considerable risk. We are already beginning to see a growing number of differentiated competitors for many of these activities. Universities will experience increasing pressure to spin off or sell off or close down parts of their traditional operations in the face of this new competition. They may well find it necessary to unbundle their many functions, ranging from admissions and counseling, to instruction and certification.

An example might be useful here. We discussed earlier the concept of a virtual university, a university without a campus or faculty that provides computer-mediated distance education. The virtual university develops and focuses on the core competencies of marketing and delivery. It works with the marketplace to understand needs, and then it outsources courses, curriculum, and other educational services from established colleges and universities—or perhaps individual faculty—and delivers them through sophisticated information technology.

Capitalizing on one's strengths and outsourcing the rest are commonplace in many industries. Consider, for example, the computer industry, in which webs of alliances exist among hardware developers, manufacturers, software developers, and marketers of hardware and software. These are constantly being created and modified in response to competitive dynamics.

This idea can be applied to academe. While we are very good at producing intellectual content for education, there may be others who are far better at packaging and delivering that content. While in the past universities have had a monopoly on certifying learning, there may be others, whether they are accreditation agencies or other kinds of providers, more capable of assessing and certifying that learning has occurred. Many of our other activities, for example, financial management and facilities management, are activities that might be outsourced and better handled by specialists.

Other types of disaggregation may occur. As for-profit competitors increasingly position themselves to go after low-hanging fruit, cherry-picking high-profit, low-cost programs such as business education, universities will find themselves less able to use these programs to subsidize other academic programs such as the liberal arts. It could well be that the economics of the competitive marketplace could fragment the university, pulling away lucrative professional education and leaving an impoverished and highly fragmented core of traditional academic disciplines in many institutions.

Even the very intellectual organization of the university might fragment, as narrowly focused communities of scholars, linked together by electronic technology rather than campus proximity, pull apart from the broader faculty structures such as departments and schools. Although information technology enables scholarly communication across vast distances, it may well further disaggregate the intellectual life of the campus.

DIGITAL INFRASTRUCTURE

One of the great challenges to college and university leaders is to determine, implement, and sustain the information technology infrastructure necessary for successful teaching and research in the digital age. As the use of this technology becomes more pervasive in both the academic and administrative activities of the contemporary university, investment in IT infrastructure becomes less a luxury and more an absolute requirement of learning and scholarship, not to mention the operation and management of the institution. Beyond that, however, this infrastructure becomes key to the attraction and retention of high-quality students and faculty. After all, rarely will the best faculty attempt to pressure the university into investing in an adequate infrastructure for their teaching and research activities. They will simply leave, attracted to other institutions with more supportive environments. The same is true for students, who are increasingly attracted to colleges and universities with demonstrable commitments to state-of-the-art digital environments.

Colleges and universities traditionally tend to look at technology from the cost perspective, much like capital facilities. However, information and communications technology should be viewed instead as a strategic asset, critical to the fundamental academic mission and quality of the institution. Moreover, today's digital generation will demand sophisticated computing environments with the same convenience they have experienced at home or at play. Similarly, many faculty members will base their decision to come, stay, or depart based on the quality of the technology environment.[4]

Hence, the "why" of digital infrastructure is obvious. How about the "what"? What kind of infrastructure is necessary? Where should one make the investments? In networking? In computer hardware? In support staff? In special-purpose facilities such as virtual reality laboratories and digital libraries? What about the trade-off with other, more traditional investments in physical infrastructure? Put another way, should one invest in "bricks" or "clicks"? This is yet another important strategic question that we attempt to address in this and later chapters, but with the caveat that like all observations concerning this subject, the goals are likely to change with the evolution of the technology.

The final question is, of course, "how?" High on the list of most university administrators is the concern about the costs of acquiring and supporting the infrastructure demanded by the digital age. All universities face major challenges in keeping pace with the profound evolution of information and its implications for their activities. Not the least of these challenges is financial, since as a rule of thumb most organizations have found that staying abreast of this technology requires an annual investment comparable to that of other capital expenditures. For a very large campus, this can amount to hundreds of millions of dollars per year! Since the life cycle of much of this technology is only a few years, these will be recurring costs demanding a sustainable financial plan.

Elements of the Necessary Infrastructure

Here one is not only concerned with the IT infrastructure such as computer and networking hardware, applications software, and the corresponding services such as telecommunications, on-line resources, and financial operations. Equally critical are the human resources, the IT professionals, the hardware and software engineers, the training and support staff necessary to maintain and operate these complex systems. So, too, are the myriad policies and practices necessary for such IT-intensive systems such as access, authentication, authorization, encryption, and directory services.

While the processing power of computers continues to increase, of far more importance to universities is the increasing bandwidth of communications technology, both through copper/fiber wire plants as well as via wireless technology. In today's distributed technology environment, connectivity is the key objective. Students, faculty, and staff need to connect with knowledge resources and with one another with the greatest possible convenience, anytime, anyplace. Both Internet access to off-campus resources and "intranet" capability to link students, faculty, and staff together are the highest priority. The key theme will be transparent and ubiquitous connectivity, essential to the formation and support of digitally mediated communities.

Universities are straining to keep up with the connectivity demands of students. Today's undergraduates are already spending hours every day on the Net interacting with faculty, students, and home while accessing knowledge distributed about the world. Simply keeping pace with the demands of off-campus students for access to campus-based resources and the Internet is overloading many universities. Installing a modern on-campus network—a "wire plant"—has become one of the most critical capital investments faced by the university. Of comparable importance is persuading community telecommunications and cable television companies to provide robust Internet access to the homes of faculty, students, and staff.

The Internet itself is evolving rapidly. University research initiatives such as the Internet2 project and broader federal efforts such as the Next Generation Internet or the National Information Infrastructure projects are contributing to this growth. This will compel universities to move rapidly to keep pace with the bandwidth of available backbone networks.[5]

As digital technology becomes increasingly ubiquitous, universities will have to make intelligent decisions as to just what components they will provide and which should be the personal responsibility of members of the community. While networks and specialized computing resources will continue to be the responsibility of the university, the purchase of personal computers, personal digital appliance (PDAs), and other digital devices such as personal communicators will almost certainly be left to the student, faculty, or staff member. In many cases these individual decisions will be made in an environment of financial subsidy from the institution.

Universities will need to strive for synergies in the integration of various technologies. Beyond the merging of voice, data, and video networks, there will be possibilities as well to merge applications across areas such as instruction, administration, and research. The issue of financing will become significant as institutions seek a balance between institution-supported central services and point-of-access payments through technologies such as smart cards.

Historically, technology has been seen as a capital expenditure for universities or as an experimental tool to be made available to only a few. Today, higher education should conceive of information technology both as an investment and as a strategic asset that will be used by the entire faculty, staff, and student body to sustain and enhance the mission of the university.

University Operations

The university is a school. It is a city. It is also a business, and, like all large, complex businesses, it relies increasingly on information technology to implement and manage its activities. For example, the financial operations of the university such as payroll, investment management, and accounting require state-of-the-art business information systems. Beyond that, there is an array of other businesslike functions, including governance (trustees, faculty senate), employee relations (unions, tenure meetings), procurement, customer relationship management (counseling, careers, scholarships, alumni), and marketing (products, services, students). The university is also a vendor, providing educational services, course materials, credentials, hotel (e.g., residence halls), medical services, telecommunications, entertainment (football?), and an increasing number of Web-based products and services. It furthermore has a large and diverse service business, providing student and staff services, counseling, alumni services, and consulting and contract research.

We don't generally think of the university in business terms, for example, students as customers and faculty recruiting as marketing. Reporting lines, budgets, and cost accountability are all too frequently foreign concepts, yet in terms of operations, the university is very much a business, with financial and public accountability comparable to that of other public corporations. Furthermore, we find it necessary to function in an increasingly e-business world both with other organizations (universities or businesses or government agencies) and with clients (students, faculty, alumni).

High on the lists of concerns of most colleges and universities these days is the development and/or reengineering of enterprise administrative systems, those massive software applications that link together management and business operations such as enrollment data, revenues, purchasing, accounts payable, and so on. During the past few years, the looming threat of the Y2K bug stimulated many institutions to spend millions of dollars reengineering enterprise systems into more sophisticated enterprise resource planning (ERP) systems. Here the intent was in part to recognize that a broader context was needed to describe the contemporary university, capable of capturing new organizational configurations, more complex student participation patterns, changing faculty roles, and new revenue and expenditure flows. The goal was to integrate student, financial, and human resources systems, in preparation for yet a further transition to network-based e-business applications.

Although there has been a history of "homegrown" software development in higher education, most institutions have sought the assistance of established software vendors such as PeopleSoft and Accenture for such mission-critical applications as ERP, yet even "off-the-shelf" software applications required very substantial modification to meet the complex needs of universities, as both vendors and academic institutions have learned through sometimes bitter experience. All too frequently, vendors underestimated the complexity of these tasks, just as universities underestimated the true costs of building workable ERP systems. The promises of reengineering remain largely unrealized for many institutions. In many instances, large, expensive applications programs designed to institute change have been only partially implemented (or even abandoned), often with less than anticipated results. The IT professional landscape is currently littered with the bodies of many a chief information officer (CIO) who was blown up stepping on an ERP land mine.

There are two other areas where we come up short compared to the commercial sector. One, ironically, is human resource development. Although as educational institutions, universities should be leaders in the development of human potential, in reality our education activities tend to focus more on selecting—or filtering—out talent than developing it, either among our students or faculty. Unfortunately, we usually tend to ignore this important function with staff altogether. This is particularly critical when new technologies require that we continually invest in the education and training of our people, reskilling them for new roles in an ever-changing environment.

The second shortcoming of universities is again ironic: we seriously underinvest in "corporate research and development" compared to most other organizations. For example, most corporations invest from 3 percent to as much as 10 percent of their gross revenues in research aimed at improving their products and services, yet universities invest almost nothing in improving pedagogy and scholarship. To be sure, research universities spend hundreds of millions of dollars on research performed for others, but they spent almost nothing to improve the quality of their own activities.

Financing IT Systems and Software

The evolving e-learning environment requires a reconsideration of the financial management of the university, with new organizations of both expenditures and revenues. There will be a need for new kinds of financial information to support management and administrative functions. For example, costs might include:

Infrastructure (bandwidth, facilities)
Equipment (computers, routers)
Software (operating systems, applications)
Student-faculty support (training, help desks)
Content (courseware development or acquisition)

Although the college campus may look much the same in the decade ahead as it does today, it is clear that it will be managed and financed in much different ways. For example, because IT equipment, infrastructure, outsourced course materials, and support staff are likely to constitute more of the expenditure budget, faculty compensation (hence, faculty numbers) will probably decline. While the conventional wisdom of today suggests that universities will use IT investment to improve quality (and perhaps competitiveness), the shift in expenditure mix from faculty human resources to technology will eventually demand productivity increases. Of course, the lesson learned time and time again from industry is that IT improves technology only if the work process is reengineered, that is, if IT productivity goes hand in hand with process transformation. Fortunately, there is ample evidence from distance learning (e.g., the Open University) that technology coupled with process reengineering can break the widely perceived linkage between expenditure per student (or student-to-faculty ratios) and educational quality.

There is another financial consideration far more threatening to research and graduate-intensive universities. These institutions operate with financial models based on cross-subsidies among various university activities. For example, low-cost, high-profit instruction in large, introductory courses or classroom-based programs in lucrative professional schools such as business and law generates the resources to support high-cost instruction in advanced undergraduate and graduate programs as well as faculty scholarship. The emergence of for-profit, technology-inventive competitors will threaten the revenue stream from these high-margin programs, forcing institutions to develop new financial models.

Information technology will change the relative cost of producing and delivering educational services in various ways, driving some costs up and others down. We might conjecture about what will happen to the current monopolies characterizing colleges and universities—particularly the research universities—when the price of transactions and the exchange of data drops very significantly because of digital communications. What happens when distance diminishes as a consideration? What happens when globalization and decentralization become economically beneficial? What happens, of course, is that the barriers to competitors to enter the higher education marketplace are lowered. In fact, technology now allows competitors to use a university's own faculty and students to compete with it through current policies governing the intellectual products associated with research and instruction.

One might counter this concern by noting that many high-cost university programs have operated successfully for many years. Consider, for example, medical education, one of the most costly professional disciplines. A century ago we "academized the barbershop" (as one of our colleagues put it), and it has not only been running well but grown to the point where it has overshadowed much of the rest of the university. Today, not only do we find medical education healthy and well financed, but with the largesse of federal funding agencies such as the National Institutes of Health, it now constitutes the bulk of the teaching, research, and professional services budget of the contemporary university. Yet, despite the success of the current financial model for medical education, our current health care delivery system is dysfunctional, and the United States lags behind much of the rest of the world in various health indices.

The message from this case study is that simply reshaping the business model for financing higher education in a digital world is not enough. We must do so within the context of the social mission of the university.

The "P Word": Productivity

What about productivity? Information technology can certainly enhance the quality of academic programs, but extensive experience in the private sector has suggested that this technology is able to improve productivity and lower costs only if the fundamental process of work itself is reengineered. Before we can achieve an economic benefit from this technology, we must first reexamine our current paradigms for teaching and learning, as we discussed in the previous chapter.

Experience has shown that the opportunities presented by new technologies can be exploited only by developing new methods for accomplishing work and new organizations for managing activities. We frequently hear about companies "restructuring" or "reengineering" themselves to respond to technology-driven change. Government is also challenged to transform itself to be more responsive and accountable to the society that supports it. Transformation for the university is necessarily more challenging, since our various missions and our diverse array of constituencies give us a complexity far beyond that encountered in business or government.

To date, most transformation efforts in higher education have focused upon administrative processes, for example, rebuilding administrative systems for enterprise resource planning or preparing for e-business. The more important transformations necessary to unleash the power of information technology will involve the core activities of the university, teaching and scholarship. They will shift the institutional culture from being provider-driven (i.e., faculty-centered) to learner-centered. They will cut across disciplinary or administrative boundaries to better link together people and their activities. Neither the deification of the disciplines nor the command-control-communication hierarchy of the administration will likely survive the crosscutting character of digital technology. Nor will the current glacial pace of decision making and change long survive a world in which the technological event horizon has become a few years.

As we have argued, these past approaches will not be adequate to address the major paradigm shifts in learning and scholarship driven by technology in the years ahead. From the experience of other organizations in both the private and public sector, we can identify several features of the transformation processes that are applicable as well to the university. First it is essential to recognize that the real challenge lies in transforming the culture of an institution. Financial or political difficulties can be overcome if the organization can let go of rigid habits of thought, organization, and practices that are incapable of responding rapidly or radically enough. To this end, those most directly involved in "production" must be involved in the design and implementation of the transformation process. Clearly, in the case of a university, this means that the faculty must play a key role.

The shift toward on-line courses to serve new educational markets will also drive new financial models. Although simply repurposing the traditional classroom interactive experience into an on-line form such as asynchronous learning is relatively inexpensive (estimated at $10,000 per course), sophisticated efforts to automate and distribute college courses are considerably more costly. For example, the Open University estimates the production costs of a one-year course at $1.5 million, although this investment can be recouped if the product is utilized for thousands of students. These models suggest that, increasingly, educational investments will be made in the front end, in course production, rather than at the application point, in the classroom, through the support of faculty. In such a commodity environment, the "amateur" professor operating in the traditional "handicraft" mode will be at a distinct disadvantage.

Finally, experience in other sectors has shown the critical importance of leadership. Major institutional transformation does not occur by sitting far from the front lines and issuing orders. Rather, leaders—in our case, university presidents—must pick up the flag and lead the transformation effort. Here we face the particular challenge of the limited personal experience with digital technology of the current generation of senior university leaders. Most utilize commonplace tools such as word processing, electronic mail, the Web, and e-commerce. However, unlike the plug-and-play generation, most of today's generation of leaders have spent their lives as scholars, teachers, and administrators in the world prior to networked PCs. They tend to lack the intuitive understanding of this technology, its mercurial character, and the power of the tools that it currently or will soon provide. They tend to underestimate the pace of its evolution and its transforming character. They sometimes keep their institutions in a state of denial, clinging to a vision of the past that not only is no longer relevant but probably never existed in the first place. Hence, the first task of academic institutions is to engage their leadership, both administrative and academic, in an intellectually honest and vigorous exercise of understanding the implications of technology for their institutions.

POLICIES AND PRACTICES

As information technology blurs the traditional boundaries between the campus, the workplace, the home, and the marketplace, the need for a cohesive and consistent set of policies to guide the use of information technology becomes ever more imperative. For example, universities need to determine under what conditions and for what members of the community access to the network, network-based services, and networked information is a basic right of the campus community.

Clearly, these policies must be consistent with other university policies, practices, and values. For example, the commitment to academic freedom, critical debate, and free dissemination of information and ideas should always transcend the changes driven by technology, yet information technology raises many new issues such as the ownership of course materials and the potential for, and meaning of, franchising campus programs for distribution via distance learning technology, whether by the university or other agents. Because conventional copyright law protects not ideas but their expression, it is particularly vulnerable to technological change. Academic institutions have a strong and vested interest in achieving a balance between proprietary rights and exemptions for educational use or libraries.

In a sense, just as information technology has brought us to an inflection point in the nature of education and scholarship, it could also force us to redefine the relationship between the university and its teachers and students. The university will face a major challenge in retaining instructional "mind-share" among its best-known faculty. Although we have long since adapted to the reality of those faculty members' negotiating release time and very substantial freedom with regard to research activities, there will be new challenges as instructional content becomes a valuable commodity in a for-profit postsecondary education marketplace. Do we need new policies that restrict the faculty's ability to contract with outside organizations for instructional learningware? Can these policies be enforced in the highly competitive marketplace that exists for our best faculty? Is it possible that we will see an unbundling of students and faculty from the university, with students acting more as mobile consumers, able to procure educational services from a highly competitive marketplace, and faculty members acting more as freelance consultants, selling their services and their knowledge to the highest bidder?

The challenge of developing university policies appropriate for the digital age is compounded by the degree to which information technology is changing the roles of all of the participants in the university, as students evolve into active learners (and consumers of educational services), as faculty members evolve into mentors, guides, and designers of learning environments, and as staff assume increasingly complex roles in building and maintaining sophisticated IT infrastructure.

Although information technology today is used primarily to augment and enrich traditional instructional offerings, over the longer term it will likely change the learning paradigm. It will likely change the paradigms of scholarship, and it will certainly change the relationship between faculty and staff and the university. For example, as the university is viewed increasingly as a "content provider," with the evolution of the commodity classroom, learningware, and the like, we will need to rethink issues such as ownership of faculty course materials.

CULTURAL ISSUES

Although making the necessary investment in the technology infrastructure and support services will strain university budgets, the most critical challenges may involve the culture of the university. We have already noted that there will be great diversity in the technology needs of various disciplines and programs, and these needs will likely not be aligned with financial resources. An important strategic issue faces most universities: should the evolution of information technology be carefully coordinated and centralized or allowed to flourish in a relatively unconstrained manner in various units?

Another cultural issue involves just who within the university community will drive change. Our experience suggests that it will not be the faculty or staff but rather the students themselves who will lead in the adoption of new technology. Many of our entering students have computing skills far beyond those of our faculty. As members of the digital generation, they are far more comfortable with this emerging technology. They are a fault-tolerant population, willing to work with the inevitable bugs in "Version 1.0" of new hardware and software. They not only accept but relish the uncertainty associated with innovation.

Unfortunately, the same cannot be said of most faculty members, who function most comfortably in a stable, unchanging environment. There is great diversity among the faculty. Some are highly entrepreneurial and market-driven. Others are staunch defenders of the status quo and solidly anchored to their campus surroundings. With respect to technology, some people are early adopters, some are determined followers, some are "wait and see," and some are simply ostriches.

THE UNIVERSITY AS A PLACE

Will the campus continue to exist as a place where learning and scholarship occur? Information technology is rapidly breaking the bonds of space and time, allowing educational services to be provided to anyone, anytime, anyplace. Students are already distributing their educations among multiple institutions in an open learning environment. The activities of faculty members increasingly are identified with disciplinary groups linked across institutions and even continents by robust computer networks. Scholarly communication is increasingly sustained by electronic mail, collaboration technology, and perhaps distributed virtual environments rather than face-to-face on campus or at conferences. The work of students and faculty no longer is confined to the campus but rather is determined by convenience and need, sometimes in the office, sometimes at home, sometimes on the road, and usually linked to knowledge resources in cyberspace.

Some aspects of higher education will continue to be campus-based. For example, the socialization of young students is highly campus-dependent, although perhaps poorly understood. So, too, some forms of professional training that require direct interaction between individual students and faculty members such as medicine and artistic performance will be difficult to displace from the campus (although one of the early applications of Internet2 is to use telepresence technology to bring a master class from faculty at one university to musicians at another). However, many other activities such as those general education or professional education curricula based primarily on classroom lectures (e.g., business administration, education, and law) are already being redesigned for technology-based learning. As we have mentioned, research and scholarship long ago broke loose from the campus and now have become global activities, heavily dependent upon information technology, and, of course, most university service activities already extend far beyond the campus, even being characterized by the term "extension services."

The relative importance of the campus to the university will change, but the campus will not disappear. Rather, it will be transformed. The traditional cycles of academic life will continue for many learners, but time, place, and content boundaries will all become negotiable. Higher education will provide a variety of choices.

The most profound changes may be those made in institutional arrangements rather than the physical infrastructure that makes up what people think of as a university.[6] Our view of what the university of the next millennium should be is based on our sense of what universities do, what roles they play in society, and why people think them worth the often huge sums of money invested in an education; most important of all, it is based on our understanding of how people learn. Reaching back for a historical precedent, we argue that, just as education has not been built around isolated individuals, so it has not always been built around individual campuses. Past administrative arrangements allowed flexible, small, distal communities to develop at a variety of sites, allowing scholars to congregate in dispersed, peripheral learning groups, for which a university provided both cover and support.

UNIVERSITY PLANNING AND DECISION MAKING

A rapidly evolving world has demanded profound and permanent change in most, if not all, social institutions. Corporations have undergone restructuring and reengineering. Governments and other public bodies are being overhauled, streamlined, and made more responsive. Individuals are increasingly facing a future of impermanence in their employment, in their homes, and even in their families. The nation-state itself has become less relevant and permanent in an ever more interconnected world.

The contemporary university is one of the most complex social institutions of our times. The importance of this institution to our society, its myriad activities and stakeholders, and the changing nature of the society that it serves all suggest the importance of experienced, responsible, and enlightened university leadership, governance, and management. American universities have long embraced the concept of *shared governance* involving public oversight and trusteeship, collegial faculty governance, and experienced but generally short-term administrative and usually amateur leadership. While this system of shared governance engages a variety of stakeholders in the decisions concerning the university, it does so with an awkwardness that tends to inhibit change and responsiveness.

Both the pace and nature of the changes occurring in our world today have become so rapid and so profound that our present social institutions—in government, education, and the private sector—are having increasing difficulty in even sensing the changes (although they certainly feel the consequences), much less understanding them sufficiently to respond and adapt. The impact of information technology on the university will likely be profound, rapid, and discontinuous—just as it has been and will continue to be for the economy, our society, and our social institutions (e.g., corporations, governments, and learning institutions). It will affect our activities (teaching, research, outreach), our organization (academic structure, faculty culture, financing and management), and the broader higher education enterprise as it evolves into a global knowledge and learning industry.

The glacial pace of university decision making and academic change simply may not be sufficiently responsive to allow the university to control its own destiny. There is a risk that the tidal wave of societal forces could sweep over the academy, both transforming higher education in unforeseen and unacceptable ways and creating new institutional forms to challenge both our experience and our concept of the university.

As many leaders in higher education have come to realize, our changing environment requires a far more strategic approach to the evolution of our institutions. It is critical for higher education to give thoughtful attention to the design of institutional processes for planning, decision making, management, and governance. The ability of universities to adapt successfully to the profound changes occurring in our society will depend a great deal on the institutions' collective ability to develop and execute appropriate strategies. Key is the recognition that in a rapidly changing environment, it is important to develop a planning process that is not only capable of *adapting* to changing conditions but to some degree capable of *modifying* the environment in which the university will find itself in the decades ahead. We must seek a progressive, flexible, and adaptive process, capable of responding to a dynamic environment and an uncertain—indeed, unknowable—future.

Traditional planning processes are frequently found to be inadequate during times of rapid or even discontinuous change.[7] Tactical efforts such as total quality management, process reengineering, and planning techniques such as preparing mission and vision statements, while important for refining status quo operations, may actually distract an institution from more substantive issues during more volatile periods. Furthermore, incremental change based on traditional, well-understood paradigms may be the most dangerous course of all, because those paradigms may simply not be adequate to adapt to a future of change. If the status quo is no longer an option, if the existing paradigms are no longer viable, then more radical transformation becomes the wisest course. Furthermore, during times of very rapid change and uncertainty, it is sometimes necessary to launch the actions associated with a preliminary strategy long before it is carefully thought through and completely developed.

An excellent example of the kind of unanticipated challenges enabled by information technology is peer-to-peer computing, best represented by the explosion of the Internet-based software Napster, which allowed students to exchange digital music files, bringing the recording industry to its knees (and overwhelming the networks of many university campuses). Beyond the surprises triggered by a "killer app," this example also illustrates that information technology is triggering a true revolution in which the traditional thought leaders and administrators are no longer in charge. In the Napster world, the plug-and-play, rather than the "go-and-grab" generation, will embrace and exploit this technology in ways that we cannot even imagine, much less control.

In this sense, we must recognize that decision making and planning will increasingly occur in a world of great uncertainty. In attempting to navigate white water rather than a golden pond, we should sometimes forget about ambitious, long-term goals and simply focus on how we can steer to shore!

A DIVERSE FUTURE FOR DIVERSE INSTITUTIONS

As true learning communities evolve in cyberspace, traditional educational institutions will feel increasing competition and pressure to change. The university will continue to be the primary source of "content" for educational programs, but other organizations more experienced in "packaging" content, for example, entertainment companies, may compete with universities to provide educational services to the mass market. In a similar sense, it could well be that the role of the faculty member will shift rapidly from that of organizing and teaching individual courses. As higher education shifts from a cottage industry to mass customization, faculty may become members of design teams developing content for broader markets. The traditional lecture system, intrinsically inefficient in knowledge transmission, could decline in importance as robust, electronically mediated technology becomes available. This technology may enable an expansion of other activities requiring direct human contact, such as guidance, tutorials, and hands-on mentoring.

It is ironic that the cyberspace paradigm of learning communities is a mechanism that may return higher learning to the older tradition of the scholar surrounded by disciples in an intense interrelationship. In a sense, it recognizes that the true advantage of universities is in the educational process, in the array of social interactions, counseling, tutorial, and hands-on mentoring activities that require human interaction. In this sense, information technology will not so much transform higher education—at least in the early phases—as enrich the educational opportunities available to learners.

Liberal arts colleges that continue to stress such mentoring, hands-on, tutorial-based education will be least challenged by the emerging knowledge media. It is the large, comprehensive universities that rely heavily on impersonal mass education that are at great risk. A significant share of this conventional mass education can be offered commercially and electronically. After all, a large part of the function of large universities is mass information transfer, which can be performed quite effectively and efficiently via information technology. Virtual universities, even when constructed along the conventional distance learning paradigm, may well provide formidable competition to large universities in terms of both quality and price.

Those universities that understand their strengths in building learning communities, providing students with the capacity to interact and learn within these communities, and then certifying the learning process may well find the coming digital revolution an extraordinary opportunity. Universities that understand both their unique role and the profound nature of the new technology could well evolve into truly global institutions, using the Net to provide educational services to an increasingly knowledge-dependent world.

In the near term it seems likely that the university as a physical place, a community of scholars, and a center of culture will remain. Information technology will be used to augment and enrich the traditional activities of the university, in much their traditional forms. The current arrangements of higher education may shift. For example, students may choose to distribute their college education among residential campuses, commuter colleges, and on-line or virtual universities. They may also assume more responsibility for, and control over, their education. Colleges and universities should consider such emerging possibilities as they develop strategies for the future.

While it is certainly true that the university is different from a corporation or a branch of government, it is naive to believe that information technology will not have an eventually even greater impact on both the quality and productivity of academic activities. If universities demand that the basic character of teaching and scholarship remain unchanged, then technology is likely to add costs, albeit with some increase in quality. Just as in industry or government, transforming the basic nature of "work," in this case, learning and scholarship, will likely enable dramatic increases in both quality and productivity. If universities are unwilling to consider these changes, they will rapidly fall behind other emerging institutions that adopt new learning paradigms more suited to the digital age. If the leadership in higher education does not chart a course for their institutions into the digital age, others such as government or the marketplace will attempt to chart that course for them, or they will navigate around those institutions that moor themselves to the past, finding other learning institutions capable of seizing the opportunities offered by information technology.

We have entered a period of significant change in higher education as our universities attempt to respond to the challenges, opportunities, and responsibilities before them.[8] This time of great change and of shifting paradigms provides the context in which we must consider the changing nature of the university.

NOTES

1. Michael G. Dolence and Donald M. Norris, *Transforming Higher Education: A Vision for Learning in the 21st Century* (Ann Arbor, MI: Society for College and University Planning, 1995).

2. James J. Duderstadt, *A University for the 21st Century* (Ann Arbor, MI: University of Michigan Press, 2000), 147–64.

3. Richard Lanham, *The Electronic Word: Democracy, Technology, and the Arts* (Chicago: University of Chicago Press, 1993), 127.

4. Michael A. McRobbie and Judith G. Palmer, "Strategic and Financial Planning for Information Technology in Higher Education," in *Forum Futures 2000*, ed. Maureen E. Devlin and Joel W. Meyerson (San Francisco: Jossey-Bass, 2001), 127–40.

5. For information concerning the Internet2 project, see the Web site for the University Corporation for the Advancement of Internet Development at <http://www.internet2.edu>.

6. John Seely Brown and Paul Duguid, *The Social Life of Information* (Cambridge: Harvard Business School Press, 2000).

7. Michael E. Porter, *Competitive Strategy: Techniques for Analyzing Industries and Competitiveness* (Boston: Free Press, 1998).

8. "The Glion Declaration: The University at the Millennium," *The Presidency*, (Fall 1998), 27–31.

CHAPTER 5

The Impact of Information Technology on the Higher Education Enterprise

Today the U.S. higher education enterprise consists of roughly 3,800 colleges and universities serving the diverse educational needs of our nation. In addition, there is a complex infrastructure of publishers, accreditation agencies, and testing services and an increasing array of technology hardware, software, and services providers serving the higher education marketplace. Although our discussion thus far has been concerned primarily with the impact of information technology on the individual college and university, we must also consider its impact on the higher education enterprise and the environment of postsecondary education.

Information technology has already created a rapidly growing "e-economy," characterized by instantaneous electronic transactions between business and customers (B2C, or "e-commerce") and between business and business (B2B, or "e-business") that will demand that the contemporary university function in an increasingly digital world, in the way that it manages its resources, relates to its clients and suppliers, and conducts its affairs. As we have seen, this technology is also transforming the academic functions of the university, adding "e-learning" to the acronyms of the digital age.

There is a more serious challenge. In the past, American colleges and universities enjoyed a monopoly over advanced education because of regional influence and their control of credentialing through the awarding of degrees. However, today all of these market constraints are being challenged. The traditional handicraft approach of higher education curriculum development is challenged by the emerging edutainment industry. Although students continue to seek the credential of a college degree and the brand name of established institutions, the increasing interest in measuring learning outcomes could well transform the measures of the quality of a college education away from inputs such as faculty reputation, endowment, or admissions selectivity, to outcomes such as learning effectiveness. Higher education is breaking loose from the moorings of physical campuses, even as its credentialing monopoly begins to break apart.

The growth in the size and complexity of the postsecondary enterprise is creating an expanding array of students and educational providers. Traditional colleges and universities are losing their monopolies for students, faculty, and public and private resources. They are likely to experience increasing difficulty in retaining market share, although their absolute market size may well increase due to the increasing educational needs of our society.

Today, the total education market in the United States, including preschool, K–12, college, and workplace training, is estimated to be over $700 billion per year. The postsecondary education market itself (including adult education) approaches $300 billion. Little wonder that as the educational needs of our society intensify and as information technology eliminates traditional barriers to market entry such as campus infrastructure and certification, there is likely to be an explosion in the appearance of new competitors. This highly competitive market will selectively drive very severe price competition, particularly for high profit-margin educational programs in areas such as business education and general education.

With the emergence of new competitive forces and the weakening influence of traditional regulations, the higher education enterprise is likely to undergo a massive restructuring similar to that of other "deregulated" sectors such as health care, telecommunications, transportation, and banking. As a result, higher education will evolve from a loosely federated system of colleges and universities serving traditional students from local communities, to, in effect, a *global knowledge and learning industry*. This industry, currently estimated at almost $2.2 trillion in the United States alone, consists of an increasingly interrelated web of institutions, corporations, and organizations whose principal products and services involve knowledge—its creation, transfer, and application.[1] Beyond schools, colleges, and universities, it includes companies providing information technology, telecommunications, information services, entertainment, and a host of other knowledge-intensive products.

As our society becomes ever more dependent upon new knowledge and educated people, upon knowledge workers, this global knowledge business must be viewed clearly as one of the most active growth industries of our times. Colleges and universities will have to learn to cope with the realities of this emerging sector of our economy—the incredible pace of its technology-driven evolution and its intense competitiveness—even as they struggle to preserve their most important traditional values and character. They will have great opportunities—and obligations—for leadership, but if they remain moored to past practices and perspectives, they may well see others move into the role of market leaders.

THE FORCES OF THE MARKETPLACE

Powerful economic, social, and technological forces are driving change at a rapid pace in the marketplace for postsecondary education. These forces are far more powerful than many within the higher education establishment realize. There are increasing signs that our current paradigms for higher education, the nature of our academic programs, the organization of our colleges and universities, and the way that we finance, conduct, and distribute the services of higher education may simply not be able to adapt to the demands and realities of our times. Let us first consider these forces of the marketplace in more detail.

Economic Forces

Since the late 1970s, higher education in America has been caught in a financial vise.[2] On the one hand, the magnitude of the services demanded of our colleges and universities by society has increased considerably. Enrollments have increased steadily as the growing educational needs of adult learners have compensated for the temporary dip in the number of high school graduates associated with the postwar baby boom/bust cycle of the 1980s and 1990s. University research, graduate education, and professional education have all grown in response to societal demand. Professional services provided by colleges and universities also continue to increase in areas such as health care, technology transfer, and extension—all in response to growing needs.

The costs per unit of activity of providing education, research, and service have increased at an even faster rate, since these university activities are dependent upon a highly skilled, professional workforce (faculty and staff); they require expensive new facilities and equipment; and they are driven by an ever-expanding knowledge base. Higher education has yet to take the bold steps to constrain cost increases that have been required in other sectors of our society such as business and industry, in part because of the way that our colleges and universities are organized, managed, and governed and in part because of the people- and knowledge-intensive nature of the enterprise.

As the demand for educational services has grown and as the operating costs to provide these services have risen, public support for higher education flattened and then declined over the past two decades.[3] The growth in state support of public higher education peaked in the 1980s and then fell during the 1990s as many states faced limited tax resources and the competition of other priorities such as entitlement programs and corrections. Although there was some recovery in the late 1990s, state funding began another decline as we entered the new century. While the federal government has sustained its support of research, growth has been modest in recent years and highly skewed toward the biomedical sciences. Federal student financial aid programs have shifted from grants, to loans, to tax incentives, no longer benefiting those whom they were originally designed to serve, namely, those students with the most need.

To meet growing societal demand for higher education at a time when costs are increasing and public support is stagnant or declining, most institutions have been forced to increase tuition and fees sharply. More specifically, tuition costs for both public and private colleges and universities have grown at 3.3 times the consumer price index since 1980, triggering strong public concern about the costs and availability of a college education, along with accelerating forces to constrain or reduce tuition levels at both public and private universities.[4] As a result, most colleges and universities are now looking for ways to control costs and increase productivity, but most are also finding that their current organization and governance make this very difficult.

Today it is clear that the higher education enterprise in America must change dramatically if it is to restore a balance between the costs and availability of educational services needed by our society and the resources available to support these services.

Changing Societal Needs

The needs of our society for the services provided by our colleges and universities are continuing to grow. Significant expansion will be necessary just to respond to the needs of a growing population that will create a 30 percent growth in the number of college-age students over the next two decades. These traditional students are only part of the picture; we must recognize the impact of the changing nature of the educational services sought by our society.

Today's undergraduate student body is no longer dominated by 18–22-year-old high school graduates from affluent backgrounds. It comprises as well increasing numbers of adults from diverse socioeconomic backgrounds, already in the workplace, perhaps with families, seeking the education and skills necessary for their careers. When it is recognized that this demand for higher education may be significantly larger than that for traditional undergraduate education, it seems clear that either existing institutions will have to change significantly or new types of institutions will have to be formed.

Many adults sense the demands of the high-performance workplace for continual learning and updating of skills. The percentage of jobs in the United States requiring knowledge skills increased from 20 percent in 1950, to 65 percent in 2000, and the level of these skills continues to rise. As former University of Phoenix president Jorge De Salva notes,

> In a world where technology expenditures dominate capital spending and the skills that accompany it have half-lives measured in months, not years; where knowledge is accumulating at an exponential rate; where information technology has come to affect nearly every aspect of one's life; where the acquisition, management, and deployment of information are the key competitive advantages; where electronic commerce already accounts for more than 23 million jobs and nearly $500 billion in revenue; education can no longer be seen as a discrete phenomenon, an option exercised only at a particular stage in life or a process following a linear course.[5]

Little wonder that most of today's workers recognize education as the key to good jobs, fulfilling careers, and economic security. They fear that without further education, they may be only months from the unemployment line. Furthermore, the expectations and needs of these adults for high-quality, cost- and time-effective, and convenient educational services will place additional pressure on higher education.

The transitions from student, to learner, to consumer, from faculty-centered, to learner-centered institutions, from teaching, to the design and management of active learning experiences, and from student, to a life-long member of a learning community all suggest great changes ahead for our institutions. We already see the early stages of a major transformation in the educational activities of the university, driven in part by the changing character of our students. Today's college students require a different form of education in which interactive and collaborative learning will increasingly replace the passive lecture and classroom experience. The student has become a more demanding consumer of educational services, although frequently this is directed at obtaining the skills needed for more immediate career goals.

The needs for other higher education services are also changing dramatically. The relationship between the federal government and the research university is shifting from a partnership in which the government is primarily a patron of discovery-oriented research, to a process of procurement of research aimed at addressing specific national priorities. The academic health center has come under great financial pressure as it has been forced to deal with a highly competitive health care marketplace and the entry of new paradigms for health care delivery such as managed care. While the public appetite for the entertainment provided by intercollegiate athletics continues to grow, our colleges also feel increasing pressures to align these activities better with academic priorities and national imperatives (such as the Title IX requirements for gender equity).

Even as the nature of traditional activities in education, research, and service changes, society is seeking new services from higher education, for example, revitalizing K–12 education, securing economic competitiveness, providing models for multicultural societies, rebuilding our cities and national infrastructure. All of this is occurring at a time when public criticism of higher education is high, and trust and confidence in will or ability of the university to address social needs are relatively low.

Technological Change

As knowledge-driven organizations, colleges and universities are greatly affected by the rapid advances in information technology—computers, telecommunications, networks. This technology has already had a dramatic impact on campus research activities, enabling the computer simulation of complex phenomena, linking scholars together in networked communities such as collaboratories, and providing them access to the vast resources of digital libraries and knowledge networks. Many of our administrative processes have become heavily dependent upon information technology. This new technology is likely to have an even more profound impact on the educational activities of the university and how we deliver our services. To be sure, there have been earlier technology changes such as television, but never before has there been such a rapid and sustained period of technological change with such broad social applications.

Most significant here is the way in which emerging information technology has relaxed the constraints of space and time. We can now use powerful computers and networks to deliver educational services to anyone at anyplace and anytime, confined no longer to the campus or the academic schedule. The market for university services is expanding rapidly, but so is competition, as new organizations such as virtual universities and learningware providers enter this marketplace to compete with traditional institutions.

New technologies are making possible innovative learning environments for students that will likely lead to enhanced and more efficient learning at less expense. Furthermore, the Internet has reduced the marginal costs of the distribution of both educational content and educational services to near zero, although there remains a relatively high start-up cost for content development.[6]

Market Forces

The weakening influence of traditional regulations and the emergence of new competitive forces, driven by economic realities, changing societal needs, and emerging technology, are likely to drive a massive restructuring of the higher education enterprise. From the experience with other restructured sectors of our economy such as health care, transportation, communications, and energy, we could expect to see a significant reorganization of higher education, complete with the mergers, acquisitions, new competitors, and new products and services that have characterized other economic transformations. More generally, we may well be seeing the early stages of the appearance of a global knowledge and learning industry, in which the activities of traditional academic institutions converge with those of other organizations such as telecommunications, entertainment, and information service companies.

As we have noted, even today the size of the market for postsecondary education is formidable, amounting to over $300 billion per year and constituting nearly one-third of U.S. education spending. Both the size of this market and the fraction associated with technology-intensive delivery such as on-line and asynchronous networks will grow rapidly.

A Broader Perspective

From a broader perspective, it is clear that these strong market forces are arising because of the imbalance among supply, demand, and distribution created by an array of economic, social, and technological forces. An increasing population, the growth in the needs of adults for advanced education, and a growing recognition that education is directly correlated with income are driving demand beyond the capacity of the existing postsecondary education enterprise. This situation is aggravated by the fact that colleges and universities have traditionally been rather insensitive to market demand—they tend to do what they want to do. Furthermore, the high cost of traditional forms of education and the tradition-bound nature of the academy are constraining supply. There is also a distribution problem, since much of the growth in demand for higher education is at levels (adult education) or in regions (the South and Southwest in the United States) where capacity is quite limited.

These are the forces driving a restructuring of the postsecondary education enterprise. A demand that exceeds current supply will draw new providers into the marketplace. New technologies and delivery paradigms will evolve to better distribute educational opportunities to those who need advanced education. There will be strong pressures to shift national priorities from high-end knowledge creation to mass or even universal education. The current methods of financing the "intellectual supply chain" will need to be replaced by new financial schemes appropriate for the digital age and a knowledge-driven society.

The perspective of a market-driven restructuring of higher education as an industry is frequently both alien and distasteful to the academy, yet it is nevertheless an important framework for considering the future of the university. While the postsecondary marketplace may have complex public and private cross-subsidies and numerous public misconceptions, it is nevertheless very real and demanding. Universities will have to learn to cope with the competitive pressures of this rapidly evolving marketplace while preserving their most important values and roles.

THE NEW COMPETITORS

Although the potential of information technology for enhancing and distributing education has been known for many years, its penetration into the curriculum has been relatively modest, in large part because of resistance by the faculty. Although ability of the faculty to control the university has eroded in recent decades, they still control its educational activities. Faculties serve as the gatekeepers not only defining the academic disciplines and membership in the academy but also controlling entry to the professions that so dominate contemporary society. While there is competition among institutions for students, faculty, and resources—at least in the United States—the extent to which institutions control the awarding of degrees has led to a tightly controlled competitive market. Furthermore, most colleges and universities serve primarily local or regional areas, where they have particularly strong market positions. As with most monopoly organizations, today's university is provider-centered, functioning primarily to serve the needs and desires of the faculty rather than the students whom they teach or the broader society that supports them.

This carefully regulated and controlled enterprise could be eroded by several factors. First, the great demand for advanced education and training cannot be met by such a carefully rationed and controlled enterprise. The traditional higher education enterprise cannot constrain the growth of knowledge or the educational needs of a society. Students are increasingly viewing education as a system rather than as a collection of the courses offered by individual faculty members. Second, the expanding marketplace will attract new competitors, exploiting new learning paradigms and increasingly threatening traditional providers. Perhaps most important of all, newly emerging information technology will not only relax the constraints of space and time but also transform students into learners and consumers. Open learning environments will provide learners with choice in the marketplace—access to learning opportunities, knowledge-rich networks and digital libraries, collections of scholars and expert consultants, and other mechanisms for the delivery of learning.

As the need for advanced education becomes more intense, there are already signs that some institutions are responding to market forces and moving far beyond their traditional geographical areas to compete for students and resources. Hundreds of colleges and universities increasingly view themselves as competing in a national or even international marketplace. Even within regions such as local communities, colleges and universities that used to enjoy a geographical monopoly now find that other institutions are establishing beachheads through extension services, distance learning, or even branch campuses. With advances in communication, transportation, and global commerce, several universities in the United States and abroad increasingly view themselves as international institutions, competing in the global marketplace.

Today colleges and universities have become the most technology-intensive, the most wired communities in our society. In the United States over 90 percent of college students currently access the Net, with 52 percent doing so daily. Over 2 million students are enrolled in distributed learning courses, up from 710,000 in 1998. Over 80 percent of four-year colleges now offer some form of distance learning. Nearly 40 percent of college classes use Internet resources as part of their syllabus, with over 25 percent having a Web site and 50 percent using E-mail. Technology has become an important element of the competition among colleges and universities for students, faculty, and resources.

Faculty have long been accustomed to dictating what they wish to teach, how they will teach it, and where and when the learning will occur. Students must travel to the campus to learn. They must work their way through the bureaucracy of university admissions, counseling, scheduling, and residential living, and they must pay for the privilege, with little of the power of traditional consumers. If they manage to navigate the maze of requirements, they are finally awarded a certificate to recognize their experience—a college degree. This process is sustained by accrediting associations, professional societies, and state and federal governments.

Although traditional colleges and universities enjoy competitive advantages based upon long-standing reputation and control of accreditation and credentialing, these could be eroded quite rapidly by the vast resources that the commercial sector is capable of focusing on these efforts. Furthermore, the higher comfort level of industry with technological innovation, intensely competitive marketplaces, strategic alliances, and rapid decision making could prove to be decisive advantages. Finally, with access to the vast resources of capital markets and unhindered by other social commitments or public governance, for-profit providers could cherry-pick the best faculty and most attractive products (learning software, courses, or programs) from traditional educational institutions. The competitive threat is very real.

The evolution from faculty-centered and -controlled teaching and credentialing institutions to distributed, open learning environments is already happening. The new learning services are increasingly available among many providers, learning agents, and intermediary organizations. Such an open, network-based learning enterprise seems more capable of responding to the staggering demand for advanced education, learning, and knowledge. It also seems certain not only to provide learners with more choices but also to create more competition for the provision of knowledge and learning services.

For-Profit Universities

Beyond competition among existing colleges and universities, there are new educational providers entering the marketplace with the aim of providing cost-competitive, high-quality education to selected markets.[7] Already more than 1,000 virtual universities are listed in college directories with over 1 million students enrolled in their programs. It has been estimated that today there are over 1,600 corporate training schools in the United States providing both education and training to employees at the college level. Industry currently spends over $60 billion per year on corporate training. It is only a matter of time before some of these competitors enter the marketplace to provide educational services more broadly.

Furthermore, there is likely to be a shift in higher education from public tax support, to exploitation of private capital markets. The potential is enormous, since although education contributes more than 10 percent of the gross domestic product (GDP), it accesses less than 1 percent of the capital markets (compared to 14 percent for health care). In recent years we have seen the emergence of new aggressive for-profit education providers that are able to access the private capital markets (over $4 billion in the last year). Sophisticated for-profit entities such as the University of Phoenix and Unext.com are moving into markets throughout the United States, Europe, and Asia. It is estimated that in 1998 the revenues of for-profit and proprietary educational providers were in excess of $3.5 billion and growing rapidly.

An excellent example of the emerging commercial market is provided by the University of Phoenix, which already operates over 100 learning centers in 32 states. Phoenix targets the educational needs of adult learners whose career and family responsibilities make access to traditional colleges and universities difficult. By relying on highly structured courses formatted for the students' convenience and taught by practitioners as part-time instructors, Phoenix has developed a highly competitive paradigm.

Most Phoenix instruction is provided by part-time faculty members drawn from the business world and other professions, although all have a master's or doctorate and are provided extensive training by Phoenix. As one put it, "We're not professional teachers; we're professionals who teach. We come, we teach, we go." Phoenix builds its classroom-based curriculum through highly structured courses, taken one at a time with an average of 14 students per class (9 in on-line courses), lasting five or six weeks, with four-hour workshops. In addition, Phoenix is moving aggressively into distance education, with numerous on-line offerings. In 2002, roughly 18 percent of Phoenix's 100,000 students were enrolled in on-line courses. Student enrollments (and profits) at Phoenix are increasing at a rate of over 20 percent per year.

The Phoenix paradigm both targets and responds very effectively to the needs of adult learners in the workplace. Since these students seek to complete their education while working full-time, they want all necessary classes to be available in the sequence that they need and at times that do not conflict with their work hours. For this to become a reality, the current practice that permits faculty to decide what and when they will teach must be modified. This is not an easy matter, especially when it comes to tenured faculty. Furthermore, adult students seek a curriculum and faculty that are relevant to the workplace. They expect faculty to stay abreast of the most recent knowledge and most up-to-date practices in their field.

Phoenix students seek a time-efficient education. They want to learn what they need to learn, not what the professor may desire to teach that day; they want it in the structure that will maximize their learning. They also want their education to be cost-effective. They do not want to subsidize what they do not consume (e.g., student centers, football stadiums), and they do not want to pay much overhead for the education that they seek. They expect a high level of customer service. They want convenience: campuses that are convenient and safe, with well-lit parking lots and with all administrative and student services provided where the teaching takes place. In summary, these adult students are approaching their education as aggressive consumers of educational services, and early-entry competitors such as the University of Phoenix are learning how to respond to this market.

Yet another interesting model is Unext.com, which aims at creating a globally recognized, brand-name, virtual academic institution, Cardean University, to provide both corporations and individuals with expert-rich content from a set of prestigious university partners (currently, Columbia University, Stanford University, the University of Chicago, Carnegie-Mellon University, and the London School of Economics). Unext.com has chosen to disaggregate the learning experience by using top research universities to identify what is important to know, hiring cognitive scientists to develop problem-based, on-line courses, hiring instructors to guide students in the use of these tools, and developing assessment methods to measure learning progress. Unext.com's growth strategy first envisions providing Fortune 1000 corporations with courses critical to their employees' professional and financial success. Longer-term, it sees its growth potential dependent on international markets, since unlike the United States, where postsecondary education is readily available, content from world-class universities in many parts of the world is limited. Unext.com hopes to serve this demand with its best-in-class content, superior learning network, and universal curriculum.

Many other for-profit, industry-based educational institutions are also evolving rapidly, such as Jones International University (the first purely on-line university to become accredited), Sylvan Learning Systems and its subsidiaries, Athena University, Computer Learning Centers, and the World Learning Network. These join an existing array of proprietary institutions such as the DeVry Institute of Technology and ITT Educational Services. Not far behind is an array of sophisticated corporate training programs, such as Motorola University and the Disney Institute, originally formed to meet internal corporate training needs but now exploring offering educational services to broader markets. Of particular note here are the efforts of information services companies such as Accenture and McKinsey that are increasingly viewing education as just another information service.

It is important to recognize that while many of these new competitors are quite different from traditional academic institutions, they are also quite sophisticated in their pedagogy, their instructional materials, and their production and marketing of educational services. Most of these new entrants such as the University of Phoenix and Jones International University are focusing on the adult education market. Some, such as Unext.com, have aggressive growth strategies beginning first with addressing the needs for business education of corporate employees. Using on-line education, they are able to offer cost reductions of 60 percent or more over conventional corporate training programs since they avoid travel and employee time off. They are investing heavily (over $100 million in 2000) in developing sophisticated instructional content, pedagogy, and assessment measures. For example, Caliber Learning and the Open University invest heavily in the production of sophisticated learning materials and environments, utilizing state-of-the-art knowledge concerning learning methods from cognitive sciences and psychology. They develop alliances with well-known academic institutions to take advantage of their brand names (e.g., Wharton in business and MIT in technology). They approach the market in a highly sophisticated manner, as we noted earlier, first moving into areas with limited competition, unmet needs, and relatively low production costs such as large undergraduate survey courses amenable to mass production and commoditization but then moving rapidly up the value chain to more lucrative, highly customized professional education.

Hence, it is likely that some of these for-profit competitors will move up the learning curve to offer broader educational programs, both at the undergraduate level and in professional areas such as engineering and law. The initial focus of new for-profit entrants on low-end adult education is misleading, since in a few years their capacity to compete with traditional colleges and universities could become formidable indeed.

The Open University

For many years, the educational needs of many nations have been addressed by open universities, institutions relying on both televised courses and correspondence education to enable students to study and earn degrees at home. Perhaps most notable has been the British Open University, but this is only one of many such institutions that now enroll over 3 million students worldwide.

The British Open University (OU) utilizes a very sophisticated correspondence school model, using faculty to produce very sophisticated learning packages consisting initially of broadcast tapes and books but evolving rapidly to Net-based technologies. Roughly 40 percent of its expenditures are spent on course development, with the typical course costing $1.5 million to produce. Key in the OU model is the use of facilitators at sites convenient to students who act as tutors, preserving in a sense the tutorial experience so characteristic of the British educational system.

Today the Open University enrolls more than 164,000 students, with an average age of 37. More than 20,000 of these students are enrolled outside the United Kingdom, with more than 130,000 of its students employed. A network of over 300 regional centers provides tutoring and support services. The Open University was recently ranked 10th among 77 English universities in quality of teaching. It regularly receives ratings of "excellent" in its courses, and its graduates are sought by graduate programs in leading British research universities such as Oxford and Cambridge.[8]

The Open University and other similar "mega" institutions are based upon the principle of open learning, in which technology and distance education models are used to break down barriers and provide opportunities for learning to a very broad segment of society. In these models, students become more active participants in learning activities, taking charge of their own academic program as much as possible. Many of these open universities are now embracing information technology, particularly the Net, to provide educational opportunities to millions of students unable to attend or afford traditional residential campuses.

The motivation behind open universities involves cost, access, and flexibility.[9] The open university paradigm is based not on the extension of the classroom but rather on the one-to-one learning relationship between the tutor and the student. It relies on very high quality learning materials such as, books, videotapes, and CD-ROM or Net-based software, augmented by facilitators at regional learning centers and by independent examiners. Using this paradigm, for example, the British Open University has been able to provide high-quality learning opportunities (currently ranked among the upper 15 percent of British universities) at only a fraction of a cost of residential education ($4,200 compared to $12,500 per student year in North America).

To date, most open universities rely heavily on self-learning in the home environment, although they do make use of interactive study materials and decentralized learning facilities where students can seek academic assistance when they need it. However, with the rapid evolution of virtual distributed environments and learning communities, these institutions will soon be able to offer a mix of educational experiences.

Clearly, the open university will become an increasingly important player in higher education at the global level. The interesting question is whether these institutions might also gain a foothold in the United States. After all, newly emerging institutions such as the Western Governors University and the University of Phoenix are exploiting many of the concepts pioneered by the Open University. In 1998, the British Open University launched a new venture known as the Open University of the United States. It signed cooperative agreements with Florida State University, the California State University, and the Western Governors University as it prepared to enter the North American marketplace.[10] After these initial steps, the Open University concluded that its financial model, the high start-up costs, and the difficulties in achieving accreditation through cooperative agreements were insufficient to compete effectively with highly subsidized American colleges and universities, and the effort was abandoned in 2002.

University Consortia

In the face of such competition, traditional colleges and universities are also responding with an array of new activities. Most university extension programs are moving rapidly to provide Internet-based instruction in their portfolios. University collaboratives such as the National Technological University and the Midwest University Consortium for International Activities have become quite formidable competitors. They are being joined by a number of new organizations such as the Western Governors University, the Michigan Virtual University, and an array of university-stimulated dot-coms such as UNext.com and Fathom.com that aim to exploit both new technology and new paradigms of learning.

One of the earliest of these efforts was the National Technological University (NTU), launched in the 1980s by Lionel Baldwin, dean of engineering at Colorado State University, as a consortium of universities offering graduate education courses to engineers in industry via first videotape, then satellite transmission, and today increasingly Internet-based technology. Since there is great diversity in the nature of the various universities offering courses through the NTU paradigm, there is also great diversity in content and pricing. To date, NTU has awarded more than 1,400 M.S. degrees in engineering and management to fully employed professionals and managers. In 2002, NTU was acquired by Sylvan Learning Systems as part of its Online Higher Education division.

One of the great challenges of nonprofit academic institutions is the acquisition of sufficient capital to allow growth. NTU has recently formed a privately held, for-profit subsidiary, the NTU Corporation, which has completed two rounds of financing at levels of $15 million and $30 million. It has also merged with the Public Broadcasting Systems Business Channel to gain a premier brand in educational media.[11]

Perhaps the most publicized of the recent virtual university initiatives is the Western Governors University (WGU). Formed as a private, nonprofit corporation in 1997 by the governors of the western United States, WGU is a competence-based and degree-granting virtual university. Twenty-one colleges and corporations from 16 western states and Guam deliver courses through the Internet and other advanced telecommunications and networking technologies. WGU does not hire its own faculty but relies instead on faculty from the providing institutions and organizations. WGU also plans to act as a clearinghouse to electronically market distance learning courses and to deliver training to corporate employees.

With California enrollments expected to grow by approximately 500,000 over the next 10 years, a similar effort known as the California Virtual University (CVU) was developed to offer residents the education that they need without adding additional students to its campuses. The CVU, launched by Governor Pete Wilson in April 1997, aimed to bring together all distance independent education offerings of California's 301 accredited colleges and universities into an interactive on-line catalog. However a change in governor removed political support, and CVU was forced to close its doors in 1999.

Industry Infrastructure

The difficulty in some of the early efforts such as the Western Governors University and the California Virtual University, coupled with the high start-up costs associated with on-line offerings, has led many colleges and universities to seek the assistance of a growing array of e-learning companies to better leverage their assets. A diverse array of new products, services, and providers is entering the e-learning marketplace, from curriculum and content development (On-lineLearning, NYR Onlines, educational publishers), to software learning environments (Lotus, Convene, WebCT, Blackboard.com, Eduprise.com), to teleconferencing (Caliber, One-Touch), and to educational management organizations (Unext.com, University of Phoenix). Of particular interest is the rapid evolution of higher education Web portals that bring for-profit companies into direct contact with students, through Web sites that link useful information for students with advertising and e-commerce.

While much of the early attention focused on creating on-line curricula offerings, there has also been a transformation in the administrative use of information technology on the campuses. Universities are rapidly changing the way that they operate, bringing everything from student recruiting, to alumni relations onto the Internet. Increasingly, they are choosing to outsource the technology and the solutions from experienced, for-profit companies. A list of recent examples of the rapidly evolving e-learning infrastructure includes:

- On-line admission (Embark, CollegeNet, XAP)
- On-line student services (Campus Pipeline, MyBytes.com, Jenzabar)
- On-line textbooks (varsitybooks.com, textbooks.com, ecampus.com, efollet.com)
- On-line procurement (CommerceOne, Ariba)
- On-line alumni (Harris Publications)
- On-line delivery and management (Blackboard, WebCT, eCollege.com, Convene)
- On-line content distributors (Caliber, UNEXT.com, Pensare)
- Learning portals (Asymetrix, HungryMinds.com, SmartPlanet.com, Blackboard.com)

Some Future Possibilities

The joining of computers and communications has only begun, and it has already redefined the entire value chain in many industries. As it emerges, the megaindustry created by the union of computers, communications, entertainment, media, and publishing will likely challenge and in some instances even displace schools as the major deliverer of learning.

Although the early attention of the new competitors has been providing educational services to the corporate marketplace and adult learners, clearly, the 800-pound gorilla in the distributed learning marketplace will be providing learning opportunities directly to individuals, whether on the job, in their home, or even on the road. This would seriously challenge the traditional monopoly that colleges and universities have had in postsecondary education. It would also challenge the faculty control of the higher education curriculum.

The e-learning marketplace is continuing to evolve very rapidly. Content is becoming more important, placing a premium on Web portals, on-line enablers, marketing channels, and information-organizing schemes. On-line enablers, the outsourcers who create virtual campuses within brick-and-mortar colleges, can provide potentially unlimited access to seemingly unlimited content sources. The channels that they establish for marketing education can easily be used to market other products to that very important consumer group. On-line information portals can provide remote proprietary and nonproprietary educational content, and, more importantly, they can integrate themselves into the traditional institutions. Traditional institutions that begin with outsourcing educational functions to the portals could eventually find it cost-effective to outsource other academic, administrative, financial, and student services to the technologically savvy portals.

The importance of the role that Web portals and on-line enablers will play in the transformation of the traditional academy cannot be overestimated. Students may find it possible to replace or supplement their alma mater's courses with courses or learning experiences derived from any other accredited institution, corporate university, or relevant database. Fear of this possibility has spurred traditional institutions to undermine innovations such as the ill-fated California Virtual University, to slow the efforts of the Western Governors University, and to force the United Kingdom's Open University to abandon its ambitious plans for the United States. The resistance of the entrenched faculty will make it difficult for traditional institutions to take advantage of new technology and adapt to the evolving needs of students.

From a broader perspective, we might view the rapid evolution of a global knowledge and learning industry as a continuation of an ever-expanding role and presence of the university during the past century. From the Land Grant Acts of the nineteenth century, to the commitment to universal access to higher education after World War II, to the concern about cost and efficiency in the 1980s, to the role of the university in a knowledge-driven society, there have been both a growth in the number and complexity of the missions of the university and the entry into postsecondary education of new players and competitors. Today we might think of the postsecondary education industry as consisting of a core of research, doctoral, and comprehensive educational institutions; four-year colleges; two-year colleges; proprietary institutions; and professional and specialized institutions. This core is supported, sustained, and augmented by an array of external players, including state and federal government, business and industry, and foundations. The traditional postsecondary institutions will be joined at the core of the emerging knowledge and learning industry by new players: telecommunications companies, entertainment companies, information technology companies, information service providers, and corporate and governmental education providers.[12]

THE RESTRUCTURING OF THE HIGHER EDUCATION ENTERPRISE

We have discussed the powerful economic, social, and technological forces reshaping the postsecondary education marketplace and stimulating the emergence of myriad new competitors in both the public and commercial sectors. In spite of the growing awareness of these social forces, many within the academy still believe that change will occur only at the margins of higher education. They see the waves of change lapping on the beach as just the tide coming in, as it has so often before. They stress the role of the university in stabilizing society during a period of change rather than leading those changes. This, too, shall pass, they suggest, and they demand that the university hold fast to its traditional roles and character. They will do everything within their power to prevent change from occurring.

Over the horizon there may well be a tsunami of forces that could drive a rapid and profound restructure of the higher education enterprise, similar to what has happened in many other industries in recent years. As a recent Merrill Lynch report notes, although the education sector represents nearly 10 percent of U.S. gross national product (GNP), it receives less than 0.2 percent of private capital formation. Higher education alone represents a market of $237 billion, of which only $5 billion is served by the for-profit sector. In the past, the primary barriers to private sector entry into higher education, apart from philosophical objections to the profit motive in higher education, have been the large sunk costs and the unprofitability of the traditional campus-based university. Today, however,

technology and changing societal needs enable the entrance of now focused, low-cost, and profitable private sector competitors.

A recent prospectus on possible venture capital investments in education noted, "We believe education represents the most fertile new market for investors in many years. It has a combination of large size (approximately the same size as health care), disgruntled users, lower utilization of
technology, and the highest strategic importance of any activity in which
this country engages. . . . Finally, existing managements are sleepy after
years of monopoly."[13]

Will this restructuring of the higher education enterprise really happen?
If you doubt it, just consider the health care industry. While Washington
debated federal programs to control health care costs, the marketplace took
over with new paradigms such as managed care and for-profit health centers. In less than a decade the health care industry was totally changed and
continues to change rapidly today. Today the higher education enterprise
consists of a constellation of traditional institutions, for example, research
universities, four-year colleges and universities, two-year colleges, proprietary institutions, and professional and specialized institutions. The postsecondary enterprise of tomorrow, the global knowledge and learning industry, will also contain computer hardware and software companies,
telecommunications carriers, information services companies, entertainment companies, information resource organizations, and corporate and
governmental educational organizations.

Who will drive the restructuring of higher education? State or federal
governments? Not likely. Traditional institutions such as colleges and universities working through statewide systems or national alliances such as
the American Association of Universities or the American Council on Education? Also unlikely. The marketplace itself, as it did in health care,
spawning new players such as virtual universities and for-profit educational
organizations? Perhaps. Regardless of who or what drives change, the
higher education enterprise is likely to be dramatically transformed over
the next decade.[14] It could happen from within, in an effort to respond to
growing societal needs and limited resources. But it is more likely to be
transformed by new markets, new technologies, and new competition. In
this rapidly evolving knowledge business, the institutions most at risk will
not be of any particular type or size but rather those most constrained by
tradition, culture, or governance.

In a sense, education today is one of the last remaining sectors of our
economy dominated by public control that have failed to achieve the standards of quality, cost-effectiveness, and technological innovation de-

manded by our knowledge-driven society. Furthermore, compared to other sectors that have been subject to massive restructuring, ranging from utilities, to telecommunications, to transportation, to health care, the education industry represents the largest market opportunity for the private sector since health care in the 1970s.

The Current Higher Education "System"

We have noted that the higher education enterprise in America consists of over 3,800 institutions of postsecondary education, ranging from small colleges, to gigantic state university systems; from religious, to secular institutions; from single-sex, to coeducational colleges; from vocational schools, to liberal arts colleges; from land-grant, to urban, to national research universities. One might also include in this enterprise a number of other organizations and institutions, including textbook publishers, accreditation agencies, coordination bodies, and an increasing array of technology companies.

The growth in the higher education enterprise over the last several decades has been exceptional. From an enrollment of 3 million students and a $7 billion expenditure in 1960, higher education in the United States today enrolls over 15 million students and spends over $237 billion per year.[15] The majority of this growth has been due to public colleges and universities, which today enroll over 80 percent of all college students.

Traditionally, the higher education enterprise has been pictured as a learning pyramid, with the community colleges at the base, the accredited public and private four-year colleges at the next level, the institutions offering graduate degrees next in the pyramid, and the research universities at the pinnacle. In some states these roles are dictated by a master plan. In others, the role and mission of educational institutions are not constrained by public policy but rather determined by available resources or political influence.

In reality, however, institutional roles are far more mixed. It is true that community colleges serve primarily local communities, but they provide quite a broad range of educational services, ranging from two-year associate degrees to highly specialized training. They also provide an increasing amount of postgraduate education to individuals currently holding baccalaureate degrees who wish to return to a college in their community for later specialized education in areas such as computers or foreign languages.

Many small liberal arts colleges strongly encourage—in some case, even pressure—their faculty to be active scholars, seeking research grants and publishing research papers in addition to teaching. Certainly, too, many four-year colleges have added graduate programs and adopted the title "university" in an effort both to serve regional interests and to acquire visibility and prestige. At the other end of the spectrum, many research universities have been forced to take on significant responsibilities in remedial education at the entry level, particularly in areas such as language skills and mathematics, as a result of the deterioration of K–12 education. Many have even moved directly into the K–12 education arena, creating and managing charter schools or even entire school systems. These trends will only increase an already significant blurring of roles among various types of institutions.

Higher education scholar Martin Trow notes that in discussing the impact of information technology on the traditional higher education enterprise, it is important to make a distinction between the elite, mass, and universal access to education. Elite forms of higher education aim at a kind of adult socialization, the shaping of mind, character, and sensibility. This requires a relatively prolonged association between students and teachers, a high ratio of teachers to students, a rigorous and demanding curriculum, and an opportunity for study without the distractions of family, responsibilities, outside work, or other competitive involvements. This form of higher education is found in both small liberal arts colleges and the undergraduate programs of richly endowed private universities.

Mass higher education centers on the transmission of knowledge rather than the shaping of character. Studies are less intense and are compatible with part-time employment during the school year. Postsecondary education marked by universal access is not oriented primarily toward gaining certificates or credit toward degrees. This is growing rapidly, and today's students study all sorts of things for all sorts of reasons that escape categorization. While it is sometimes convenient to give whole institutions one of these labels—for example, the University of California as elite, the California State University System as mass, and community colleges as universal access—the real situation is more complex, since each type of institution is involved in all three.

Some suggest that we need to think of higher education in the decades ahead as a mature industry.[16] After all, most states are already providing postsecondary education to 60 percent or more of high school graduates. Public support of higher education for traditional purposes, whether from state or from federal governments, is unlikely to increase. As is happening with other mature industries such as health care, both the public sector and private sector are asking hard questions about the cost, efficiency, productivity, and effectiveness of our colleges and universities.

To view higher education only from the perspective of its traditional constituencies, however, is to miss the point of the transformation that must occur as we enter an age of knowledge. For example, if lifetime education becomes a necessity for job security—as it has already for many careers—the needs for college-level education and training will grow enormously. So, too, American higher education could well be one of this nation's most significant export commodities, particularly if we can take advantage of emerging technologies to deliver high-quality educational services on a global scale. Higher education could be—should be—one of the most exciting growth industries of our times, but this will depend on the development of new models of higher education that utilize far more effective systems for financing and delivering learning services.

Core Competencies

As we have noted, the modern university's Achilles' heel is its overextension, its attempt to engage in, and control, all aspects of learning. Universities provide courses at the undergraduate, graduate, and professional level, and they support residential colleges, professional schools, lifelong learning, athletics, libraries, museums, and entertainment. Today's monolithic universities, at least as full-service organizations, are at considerable risk. These institutions have become highly vertically integrated over the past several decades. Today we are already beginning to see a growing number of differentiated competitors for many of these activities. Universities are under increasing pressure to spin off, sell off, or close down parts of their traditional operations in the face of this new competition and to examine the contributions and cost-effectiveness of other heretofore integral components.

The most significant impact of a deregulated higher education "industry" may be to break apart this monolith, much as other industries have been broken apart through deregulation. As universities are forced to evolve from "faculty-centered" to "learner-centered," they may well find it necessary to unbundle their many functions, ranging from admissions and counseling, to instruction and certification. An example might be useful here. We discussed earlier the concept of a virtual university, a university without a campus or faculty that provides computer-mediated distance education. The virtual university might be viewed as the "Nike approach" to higher education. Nike, a major supplier of athletic shoes in the United States and worldwide, does not manufacture the shoes that it markets. It has decided that its strength is marketing and that it should outsource shoe manufacturing to those who do it better and more cheaply. In a sense, the virtual university similarly stresses marketing and delivery. It works with the marketplace to understand needs; then it outsources courses, curriculum, and other educational services from established colleges and universities—or perhaps individual faculty—and delivers them through sophisticated information technology.

Capitalizing on one's strengths and outsourcing the rest are commonplace in many industries. Consider, for example, the computer industry, in which webs of alliances exist among hardware developers, manufacturers, software developers, and marketers of hardware and software. These are constantly being created and modified in response to competitive dynamics.

This idea can be applied to academe. While our faculties are very good at producing intellectual content for education, others may be far better at packaging and delivering that content. While in the past universities have had a monopoly on certifying learning, others, whether they are accreditation agencies or other kinds of providers, may be more capable of assessing and certifying that learning has occurred. Many of our other activities (e.g., financial management and facilities management) are activities that might be outsourced and better handled by specialists.

Higher education is an industry ripe for the unbundling of activities. Universities, like other institutions in our society, will have to come to terms with what their true strengths are and how those strengths support their strategies—and then be willing to outsource needed capabilities in areas where they do not have a unique advantage.

The Emergence of a Commodity Market

Throughout most of its history, higher education has been a cottage industry. Individual courses are a handicraft, made-to-order product. Faculty members design from scratch the courses that they teach, whether they are for a dozen or several hundred students. They may use standard textbooks from time to time—although many do not—but their organization, their lectures, their assignments, and their exams are developed for the particular course at the time that it is taught. Students would be surprised to know that their tuition dollars per hour of lecture at our more elite universities amount to over $50—the price of a ticket to a Broadway show.

In a very real sense, the industrial age bypassed the university. So, too, our social institutions for learning—schools, colleges, and universities—continue to favor programs and practices based more on past traditions than on contemporary needs, yet it may be quite wrong, however, to suggest that higher education needs to evolve into a mass production or broadcasting mode to keep pace with our civilization. In a sense, this was the evolutionary path taken by K–12 education, with disastrous consequences. Besides, even industry is rapidly discarding the mass production approach of the twentieth century and moving toward products more customized to particular markets.

Our ability to introduce new, more effective avenues for learning, not merely new media in which to convey information, will change the nature of higher education. This will bring with it new modes of organization, new relationships among universities and between universities and the private sector. The individual handicraft model for course development may give way to a much more complex method of creating instructional materials. Even the standard packaging of an undergraduate education into "courses," in the past required by the need to have all the students in the same place at the same time, may no longer be necessary with new forms of asynchronous learning. Of course, it will be a challenge to break the handicraft model while still protecting the traditional independence of the faculty to determine curricular content. Beyond that, there is also a long-standing culture in which most faculty members assume that they own the intellectual content of their courses and are free to market these to others for personal gain (e.g., through textbooks or off-campus consulting services). Universities may have to restructure these paradigms and renegotiate ownership of the intellectual products represented by classroom courses if they are to constrain costs and respond to the needs of society.

Let us return to our earlier example of content preparation. As we have noted, universities—more correctly, faculty—are skilled at creating the content for educational programs. Indeed, we might identify this as one of their core competencies. However, most faculty have not been particularly adept at "packaging" this content for mass audiences. Many faculty have written best-selling textbooks, but these have been produced and distributed by textbook publishers. In the future of multimedia and Net-distributed educational services, perhaps the university will have to outsource both production and distribution to those most experienced in reaching mass audiences—the entertainment industry.

As distributed virtual environments become more common, there may come a time when the classroom experience itself becomes a "commodity," provided to anyone, anywhere, anytime—for a price.

In such a commodity market, the role of the faculty member would change substantially. Rather than spending most of his or her time developing content and transmitting it in a classroom environment, a faculty member might instead have to manage a learning process in which students use an educational commodity (e.g., the Microsoft Virtual Biology Course). Clearly, this would require a shift from the skills of intellectual analysis and classroom presentation, to those of motivation, consultation, and inspiration.

Information Technology as a "Disruptive Technology"

The past several decades have revealed the raw power of information technology to reshape markets and put at risk even the most successful companies. Clayton Christensen has coined the term "disruptive technologies" to refer to those innovations that disrupt the normal flow of events, that change all the rules.[17] Although most technologies (in Christensen's terms, "sustaining technologies") can be discontinuous or radical in character at times, they tend to operate within the status quo and rarely precipitate the failure of leading firms. Disruptive technologies, however, tend to evolve apart from the marketplace, sometimes overshooting demands or undercutting the traditional core competencies of successful firms. Although successful organizations learn to stay at the crest of wave after wave of sustaining technologies, they can stumble and fail over the unanticipated impact of disruptive technologies. The same is clearly true for other types of social institutions in other sectors of our society, such as colleges and universities.

In many cases, disruptive technologies first appear rather innocuous and nonthreatening. Only later, after they have become established, does their disruptive impact on the status quo and competitive stance become apparent. An excellent example here is distributed learning. The early forms of distance learning curricula certainly do not appear to threaten the rich educational experience available to students at brand-name universities. However, several of the for-profit competitors are investing heavily in learning how to develop and conduct on-line education. Furthermore, the technology itself is evolving according to Moore's law or faster, with the rapid increases in processing power, display technology, bandwidth, and connectivity likely to transform the on-line learning into a far richer, immersive experience. This will soon pose formidable competition to traditional, campus-based education and to those institutions that have failed to develop the capability to deliver technology-based instruction.

Mergers, Acquisitions, Hostile Takeovers

Experience in other sectors of our society suggests that one of the most significant impacts of information technology is eroding or obliterating the boundaries that define organizations. For example, the Internet has re-shaped the boundaries of the business firm by restructuring the economics characterizing transactions. The Internet has reduced key determinants of transaction and production costs such as capital and labor requirements and information flow, leading to both aggregation and disaggregation of industrial sectors. Clearly, we might expect the same process to occur in higher education, as the traditional boundaries are reshaped or eroded. Examples here would be the boundaries between different types of institutions (e.g., community colleges, regional universities, and research universities), levels of education (K–12, undergraduate, graduate, professional, workplace), economic sectors (higher education, business, government), roles (student, faculty, staff, alumni), and so forth.

Not only are we likely to see the appearance of new educational entities in the years ahead, but, as in other deregulated industries, there could well be a period of fundamental restructuring of the enterprise itself. Some colleges and universities might disappear. Others might merge. Some might actually acquire other institutions. One might even imagine Darwinian "hostile takeovers," where some institutions devour their competitors and eliminate their obsolete practices. Such events have occurred in deregulated industries in the past, and all are possible in the future that we envision for higher education.

One might also imagine affiliations between comprehensive research universities and liberal arts colleges. This might allow the students enrolling at large research universities to enjoy the intense, highly personal experience of a liberal arts education at a small college while allowing the faculty members at these colleges to participate in the type of research activities occurring only on a large research campus.

Actually, this has happened before. As the population of college-age students swelled during the decades following World War II, many of our public universities evolved into complex systems, spawning regional campuses, absorbing formerly normal schools and technical colleges, and attempting to dominate statewide or regional markets. This expansion was driven by strong growth of public tax support to respond to the education needs of a growing population. Today we see the possibility of market competition and private dollars driving a rearrangement of higher education.

As much as some resist thinking about education in these terms, taking the perspective of higher education as a postsecondary knowledge industry is an important viewpoint that will require a new paradigm for how we think about what we have to offer. Internally, it suggests the possibility of radical changes in the academic structure of the university, its educational processes such as teaching and research. Externally, it suggests both competing and collaborating with an array of noneducational organizations such as the telecommunications and entertainment industry. As our society becomes ever more dependent upon new knowledge and educated people, this global knowledge business must be viewed as one of the most active growth industries of our times.

There is another concern here. The emerging for-profit, on-line education providers are moving up the technology learning curve very rapidly. Their stress on learning assessment, student perspectives, and cost-efficiency contrasts sharply with the "take it or leave it" approach of most traditional educators. Although these competitors are currently focusing their efforts on providing learning opportunities to those currently underserved or unserved by traditional higher education such as working adults seeking their first college degree, they could develop a competence for quality instruction for advanced degrees, particularly in professional education. Universities may soon find their most lucrative professional and graduate programs under considerable competitive pressure from for-profit educational companies characterized by both higher productivity and demonstrable quality advantages.

The research university will face particular challenges in this regard. Although rarely acknowledged, most research universities rely upon cross-subsidies from low-cost, high profit-margin instruction in general education (e.g., large lecture courses) and relatively low instructional-cost professional education (e.g., business administration and law) to support graduate education and research. These high-margin programs are just the low-hanging fruit most attractive to technology-based, for-profit competitors. In this sense, the emergence of a significant technology-based commercial sector in the postsecondary education marketplace could undermine the current business model of the research university and threaten its core activities in research and graduate education.

A GLOBAL KNOWLEDGE AND LEARNING INDUSTRY

The forces driving change in higher education, both from within and without, may be far more powerful than most people realize. It could well be that both the pace and nature of change characterizing the higher education enterprise both in America and worldwide will be considerably beyond what can be accommodated by business-as-usual evolution. As one of our colleagues put it, while there is certainly a good deal of exaggeration and hype about the changes in higher education for the short term—

meaning five years or less—it is difficult to overstress the profound nature of the changes likely to occur in most of our institutions and in our enterprise over the longer term—a decade and beyond.

While some colleges and universities may be able to maintain their current form and market niche, others are likely to change beyond recognition. Some will disappear entirely. New types of institutions—perhaps even entirely new social learning structures—will probably evolve to meet educational needs. In contrast to the last several decades, when colleges and universities attempted to become more similar, the years ahead will demand greater differentiation. There will be many different paths to the future.

Products

We have considered the higher education enterprise from the perspective of conventional classifications of colleges and universities, but suppose instead we were to consider our colleges and universities as elements of a far broader global knowledge and learning industry. The key products of the university are three in number, whether articulated as teaching, research, and service; or learning, discovery, and engagement; or people, ideas, and tools. Put in business terms, the core competencies of the university are educated people, intellectual content, and knowledge services.

Content Models

If content is a key market niche of the university, it does present some unusual challenges. Unlike other products, the intellectual content of the university is not kept in warehouses or on shelves—or even in libraries, for that matter. Instead, it resides in the minds of its faculty, students, and staff, and like its faculty, students, and staff, it can walk out the door.

The difficulty in controlling the knowledge produced in a university is best illustrated by the current paradigm for scholarly communication. The university pays its faculty and provides them with expensive laboratories and libraries in order for them to conduct original research. They, in turn, give most of this knowledge away to publishers of scholarly journals, who, in turn, charge their host universities exorbitant fees just to put the knowledge back in their libraries in journal form. Even beyond this, most publishers also charge authors or institutions page charges to further subsidize the cost of this form of scholarly communication.

A similarly strange practice occurs in the transfer of technical knowledge into the marketplace. Since the early 1980s, the Bayh-Dole Act has allowed universities to retain ownership of the intellectual property generated by government-sponsored research. Hence, they establish technology transfer organizations capable of developing and marketing this research-generated intellectual property in the hopes of reaping income based on licensing or equity interest in spin-off companies. Here again, we find the interesting situation that the taxpayer is asked to pay twice for this knowledge, first in the tax dollars undergirding government-sponsored research on the campuses and then once again to purchase the products or services based on this knowledge in the marketplace.

Furthermore, as a knowledge-driven economy becomes ever more dependent upon new ideas and innovation, there will be growing pressures to commercialize intellectual assets of the university—its faculty and students, its capacity for basic and applied research, and the knowledge generated through its scholarship and instruction become ever more valuable. Public policy, through federal actions such as the Bayh-Dole Act and state investment in research and technology transfer, has encouraged the transfer of knowledge from the campus to the marketplace, but since knowledge can be transferred not only through formal technology transfer mechanisms such as patents and licensing but also through the migration of faculty and students, there is also a risk that the rich intellectual assets of the university will be "clear-cut" by its own faculty, even as support for graduate education and research erodes.

Thus far we have been primarily discussing the intellectual content resulting from research, but what about that generated by the instructional activities of the faculty? Here the assumption has long been that course content belongs to the professor. It can be assembled into publishable form (e.g., textbooks or CD-ROMs), that can be marketed to benefit the faculty member (but rarely the institution). It will accompany a faculty member who jumps from one institution to another, thereby benefiting a competitor. Put another way, there are few rules or practices governing the intellectual content associated with instruction, at just that time when such learningware is becoming increasingly valuable.

MARKET REALITIES AND CIVIC PURPOSE

The market forces unleashed by technology and driven by increasing demand for higher education are very powerful. If allowed to dominate and reshape the higher education enterprise, we could well find ourselves facing a brave new world in which some of the most important values and traditions of the university fall by the wayside. Although traditional colleges and universities play a role in this future, they are both threatened and reshaped by shifting societal needs, rapidly evolving technology, and aggressive, for-profit entities and commercial forces. Together these could drive the higher education enterprise toward the mediocrity that has characterized other mass media markets such as television and journalism. As we assess these market-driven emerging learning institutions, we must bear in mind the importance of preserving the ability of the university to serve a broader public purpose. While universities teach skills and convey knowledge, they also preserve and convey our cultural heritage from one generation to the next, perform the research necessary to generate new knowledge, serve as constructive social critics, and provide a broad array of knowledge-based services to our society, ranging from health care to technology transfer.

If higher education refuses to change, if it insists on clinging to its traditional culture and practices, it could well find its role diminished in a rapidly changing society. Limited in resources and under assault by its stakeholders, universities could find their intellectual resources picked off by more nimble knowledge-networking organizations. Intense market competition quickly reveals all the flaws in monopoly enterprises. All colleges and universities will be affected, since many of even the most elite institutions do a poor job at undergraduate education. To be sure, brand names will continue to carry significant value, but these will be determined by increasingly diverse criteria, responding to an increasingly diverse marketplace. No longer will university endowment and student selectivity be sole determinants of market competitiveness.

The great power of marketplace competition lies in establishing high quality as well as cost-effectiveness as the determinants of survival. In this sense, the student marketplace, not academic committees or USN&WR, determines the winners. The most serious threat of the emerging competitive marketplace for knowledge and education is the danger that it will not only erode but also distort the most important values and purposes of the university. In a highly competitive market economy, short-term pressing issues usually win out over long-term societal investments. It is essential to strive for a balance between quite different goals and values, between the university as a source of intellectual property and a force driving the universal access to learning, between commercial value and a public good.

NOTES

1. Michael T. Moe, *The Knowledge Web* (New York: Merrill-Lynch, 2000).

2. Joseph L. Dionne and Thomas Kean, *Breaking the Social Contract: The Fiscal Crisis in Higher Education*, report of the Commission on National Investment in Higher Education (New York: Council for Aid to Education, 1997).

3. David W. Breneman, Joni E. Finney, and Brian M. Roherty, *Shaping the Future: Higher Education Finance in the 1990s* (San Jose: California Higher Education Policy Center, April 1997).

4. Patricia J. Gumport and Brian Pusser, *Academic Restructuring in Public Higher Education: A Framework and Research Agenda* (Stanford, CA: National Center for Postsecondary Improvement, 1998), 111.

5. Jorge Klor De Alva, "Remaking the Academy in the Age of Information," in *Issues in Science and Technology* (Washington, DC: National Academy Press, 1999).

6. Richard Larson, "MIT Learning Networks: An Example of Technology-Enabled Education," *Forum Futures* (1999), 59–74.

7. William H. Graves, "Free Trade in Higher Education: The Meta University," *Journal on Asynchronous Learning Networks* 1, no. 1 (1997).

8. John S. Daniels, *Megauniversities and Knowledge Media* (London: Kogan-Page, 1998).

9. John S. Daniel, "Why Universities Need Technology Strategies," *Change* (July 1997), 10–17.

10. John Palattella, "The British Are Coming; the British Are Coming," *University Business* (July/August 1998), 25–30.

11. Richard D. R. Hoffman, "National Technological University," *Greentree Gazette* (July 2000), 10–12.

12. Marvin W. Peterson and David Dill, "Understanding the Competitive Environment of the Postsecondary Knowledge Industry," in *Planning and Management for a Changing Environment: A Handbook on Redesigning Post-secondary Institutions*, ed. M. Peterson, D. Dill, and L. Mets (San Francisco: Jossey-Bass, 1997).

13. Nations Bank Montgomery Securities, *Communications Market Quarterly Update* (December 1996).

14. Donald N. Langenberg, "Taking Control of Change: Reinventing the Public University for the 21st Century," *Reinventing the Research University*, Kumar Patel, ed. (Los Angeles: University of California Press, 1994).

15. Dionne and Kean, *Breaking the Social Contract*.

16. Arthur Levine, "Higher Education's New Status as a Mature Industry," *Chronicle of Higher Education* (January 31, 1997), A48.

17. Clayton M. Christensen, *The Innovator's Dilemma: When New Technologies Cause Great Firms to Fail* (Cambridge: Harvard Business School Press, 1997).

CHAPTER 6

Visions for the Future of the University

I n the previous chapters we suggested that information technology is likely to drive rapid, significant, discontinuous, and unpredictable change in all aspects of the university: its activities of teaching, research, and service; its organization, management, and financing; and the nature of the higher education enterprise and its environment. Although technology-driven change can lead to an uncertain future, it is possible to prepare institutions for change by imagining and understanding possible future scenarios.

Beyond considering what *could* happen to our colleges and universities because of technology-driven change, it is important also to determine what *should* happen. What form of university will be necessary to serve a knowledge-intensive global society? How can we assure that our universities will evolve into forms that will be supportive of quality learning and scholarship? How can we protect and preserve our most important values, traditions, and roles for future generations?

In this chapter we explore various visions for the future of the university in the digital age. Here our aim is not to propose any particular scenario but rather to lay out a range of possibilities to provide a context for planning and decision making.

TECHNOLOGY TRENDS

It is useful at the outset to identify those technology trends that we believe to be most significant for higher education.

Trend 1: The pace of evolution of information technology (e.g., Moore's law) will continue to be characterized by rapid exponential growth.

First, we believe that the extraordinary evolutionary pace of information technology not only is likely to continue for the next several decades but could even accelerate on a superexponential slope. Photonic technology is evolving at twice the rate of silicon chip technology (e.g., Moore's law), with miniaturization and wireless technology advancing even faster, implying that the rate of growth of network appliances will be incredible. For planning purposes, we can assume that within the decade we will have bandwidth and processing power a thousand times greater than current capabilities.

Trend 2: The Net will be ubiquitous and pervasive.

During the next decade a combination of increasing bandwidth, robust and mobile connectivity, and miniaturization will lead to a pervasive, global network environment linking a substantial fraction of the world's population as well as most of our economic, social, and cultural activities.

Trend 3: Information technology will relax (or obliterate) conventional constraints such as space, time, and monopoly, thereby disrupting the status quo.

The rapid information-processing speeds of digital devices and the essentially instantaneous character of digital communications networks allow knowledge and knowledge services to be set free from the constraints of space and time. Information technology is a disruptive technology, operating outside the status quo and traditional market constraints. As such, it tends to drive rapid, profound, and discontinuous change. It brings event horizons for major change ever closer. The future is becoming less certain.

Trend 4: Information technology will equalize access to information, education, and research.

Information technology provides unusual access to knowledge and knowledge services (such as education) hitherto restricted to the privileged few. Like the printing press, this technology not only enhances and broadly distributes access to knowledge but in the process shifts power away from institutions to individuals who are educated and trained in the use of the new knowledge media.

Trend 5: Digital technology will change dramatically the ways we handle data, information, and knowledge.

Digital networks permit voice, image, and data to be made instantaneously available across the world to wide audiences at low costs. The creation of virtual environments where human senses are exposed to artificially created sights, sounds, and feelings liberates us from restrictions set by the physical forces of the world in which we live. Close, empathic, multiparty relationships mediated by visual and aural digital communications systems will become common. They lead to the formation of closely bonded, widely dispersed communities of people interested in sharing new experiences and intellectual pursuits created within the human mind via sensory stimuli.

Trend 6: Information technology will elevate the importance of intellectual capital relative to physical or financial capital.

Information technology is driving a social transformation into a new age in which the key resource necessary for prosperity, security, and social well-being has become knowledge itself. Intellectual capital (i.e., educated people and their ideas) has become more important than physical or financial capital to a knowledge-intensive society.

SCENARIOS FOR THE NEAR TERM

Let Them Eat Cake

One possibility would be a market-driven future in which commercial, convenience store models such as the University of Phoenix and Net-based cyber universities such as Unext.com become the predominant form of higher education available to most people. While these are certainly not forms of higher education that fulfill the broader public purpose of the university, these models have proven quite effective in meeting the workplace skills of many adults. Furthermore, while these technology-based, for-profit institutions do not provide the rich intellectual experience of the residential campus, they could provide increasingly strong competition to the commuter-based education available to a significant fraction of college students at community colleges and regional public universities.

However, our experience with such market-driven, media-based enterprises has not been altogether positive. The broadcasting and publication industries suggest that commercial forces can lead to mediocrity, an intellectual wasteland in which the lowest common denominator of quality dominates. For example, although the campus will not disappear, the escalating costs of residential education could price this form of education beyond the range of all but the affluent, relegating much, if not most, of the population to low-cost (and perhaps low-quality) education via shopping mall learning centers or computer-mediated distance learning. In this dark, market-driven future, the residential college campus could well become the gated community of the higher education enterprise, available only to the rich and privileged.

This dark future is the great fear of those who deplore and resist the widespread deployment of information technology in higher education, yet the potential of this technology and the educational needs of our society are too great to ignore. Hiding our heads in the sand will not slow the pace of technological change. Nor should we feel comfortable if some elite colleges and universities long concerned with educating only the best and brightest decide to sit this one out, using their vast wealth to continue to sustain the status quo in teaching and scholarship while ignoring the needs of a nation (not to mention a world) for advanced education. Such is particularly the case for our nation's research universities.

It would be both unrealistic and inappropriate for our research universities to abandon their critical roles in elite education and scholarship to become heavily involved in the universal education needed by our society. Furthermore, the market for educational services will be broad and diverse, and the brand name for exceptional quality characterizing these institutions will still carry considerable value.

Throughout most of history of higher education in America, these same institutions have been the leaders for the broader enterprise. They have provided the faculty, the pedagogy, the textbooks and scholarly materials, and the standards for all of higher education. They have maintained a strong relationship and relevance to the rest of the enterprise, even though they were set apart in role and mission. As the rest of the enterprise changes, there is a risk that if the research university becomes too reactionary and tenacious in its defense of the status quo, it could well find itself increasingly withdrawn and perhaps even irrelevant to the rest of higher education in America and throughout the world.

Perhaps a more constructive approach would be to apply the extraordinary intellectual resources of the research university to assist the broader higher education enterprise in its evolution to new learning forms. Although it may not be appropriate for most research universities to become directly involved in mass or universal education, they certainly are capable of providing the templates or paradigms that others could use. They have done this before in other areas such as health care, national defense, and the Internet. To play this role, the research university must be prepared to participate in experiments in creating possible futures for higher education.

Break It Down

Some time ago, a leading information services company visited our university to share with us their perspective on the higher education market. They suggested that the size of the higher education enterprise in the United States during the next decade could be as large as $300 billion per year ($635 billion if K–12 is included), with 30 million students, roughly half today's traditional students and the rest adult learners in the workplace. (Incidentally, they also put the size of the world market at $3 trillion.) Their operational model of the brave new world of market-driven higher education suggested that this emerging domestic market for educational services could be served by a radically restructured enterprise consisting of 50,000 faculty "content providers," 200,000 faculty learning "facilitators," and 1,000 faculty "celebrities," who would be the stars in commodity learningware products. The learner would be linked to these faculty resources by an array of for-profit services companies, handling the production and packaging of learningware, the distribution and delivery of these services to learners, and the assessment and certification of learning outcomes. Quite a contrast with the current enterprise!

An even bolder arrangement of the elements of the future higher education enterprise was suggested by Brown and Duguid.[1] In their model, students would not be constrained to a particular college or university but rather would become active learners with many options. They would first select a suitable "degree-granting body," which would determine degree requirements, develop appropriate assessment measures, and provide the appropriate credentials when evidence of learning has been achieved. Working with the degree-granting body, students would have the opportunity to design their education, drawing upon the services of various faculty and learning environments.

In this enterprise, faculty would behave as independent contractors, first becoming associated with various degree-granting bodies and perhaps campus environments. Although some learning environments would very much resemble today's college campuses, others would be virtual, distributed over powerful knowledge networks. This model would allow the student/learner's educational program to be assembled from a variety of learning providers and experiments, which might change as an individual's educational needs change throughout his or her life.

Stan Davis and Jim Botkin propose an even more market-dominated future in their provocative book on the knowledge business, *The Monster under the Bed*.[2] They suggest that we may be approaching the end of schooling as we know it. They begin by noting that the marketplace for learning is being redefined dramatically from K–12 to K–80, or lifelong learning, whose major segments are customers, employees, and students, in that order. A new meaning of education and learning is bursting onto the scene in America, shifting from just-in-case education early in one's life to just-in-time education provided as continual updates throughout our working lives.

A new generation of people-centric technologies could revolutionize learning by employees and customers in business before it affects students and teachers in schools. Davis and Botkin suggest that the evolutionary stages of digital technology, first centered on providing data, then information, and now knowledge, parallel the three major learning markets—students, employers, and consumers. Student education, in a holdover from the rote learning of the industrial period, focuses more on the mastery of data than does employee and customer learning. Employee education, experiencing an explosive period of growth that parallels the postdata information period of the last 20 years, concentrates on information. Customer learning and education, on the other hand, are just now beginning their growth phase, and these will emphasize knowledge.

Business is coming to bear the major responsibility for the kind of education that is necessary for any country to remain competitive in the new economy. Business-driven learning will be organized according to the values of today's information age: service, productivity, customization, networking, and the need to be fast, flexible, and global. Education is moving more toward the certification of competence with a focus on demonstrated skills and knowledge—on "what you know" rather than "what you have taken" in school. As education becomes more a continuous process of certification of new skills, institutional success for any higher education enterprise will depend more on successful marketing, solid quality assurance and control systems, and effective use of the new media, not solely on the production and communication of knowledge.

Davis and Botkin conclude by noting that although our education system has been a public one for over a century, only the means of delivery, the schools, have been public. Other links in the education value chain have always been for profit (e.g., publishers). Business is evolving new ways that will revolutionize learning and ultimately free education from the failed hegemony of public schools and the dominance of government. Business, more than government, may drive the changes in education that are required for the emerging knowledge-based economy.

The Core-in-Cloud University

Many research universities are already evolving into so-called core-in-cloud organizations,[3] in which academic departments or schools conducting elite education and basic research are surrounded by a constellation of quasi-university organizations—research institutes, think tanks, corporate research and development (R&D) centers—that draw intellectual strength from the core university and provide important financial, human, and physical resources in return. Such a structure reflects the blurring of basic and applied research, education and training, and the university and broader society.[4]

More specifically, while the academic units at the core retain the traditional university culture of faculty appointments (e.g., tenure), and intellectual traditions (e.g., disciplinary focus), those quasi-academic organizations evolving in the cloud can be far more flexible and adaptive. They can be multidisciplinary and project-focused. They can be driven by entrepreneurial cultures and values. Unlike academic programs, they can come and go as the need and opportunity arise. Although it is common to think of the cloud being situated quite close to the university core, in today's world of emerging electronic and virtual communities, there is no reason that the cloud might not be widely distributed, involving organizations located far from the campus. In fact, as virtual universities become more common, there is no reason that the core itself has to have a geographical focus.

To some degree, the core-in-cloud model could revitalize core academic programs by stimulating new ideas and interactions. It could provide a bridge that allows the university to better serve society without compromising its core academic values. However, like the entrepreneurial university, it could also scatter and diffuse the activities of the university, creating a shopping mall character with little coherence.

A Case Study in Experimentation: The University of Michigan Media Union[5]

Experimentation plays a key role in understanding possible futures for the university in the digital age. Sometimes they require considerable investment. To illustrate, it is useful to consider a major experiment launched by the University of Michigan in the 1990s known as the Media Union (Figure 6.1). This technology-intensive facility was designed to be a test bed for developing, studying, and implementing the new paradigms of the university enabled by information technology. It gave the university the chance to try out different possibilities before they become widespread realities, helping us avoid potentially expensive or even dangerous mistakes while maximizing the extraordinary capacities of our new tools.

The Media Union created an environment where students and faculty could join colleagues beyond the campus, developing and testing new visions of the university, exploring teaching, research, service, extension, and other areas. Even more importantly, the Media Union fostered a new spirit of excitement and adventure. It provided the foundation for a risk-tolerant culture, where students and faculty are strongly encouraged to "go for it," accepting failure as a part of the learning process as they reach for ambitious goals. Organized around dynamic, integrative themes, the Media Union worked to break down the compartmentalized nature of the larger university.

Figure 6.1
The University of Michigan Media Union

Originally, we envisioned the Media Union as a common connecting point between the four schools on the university's North Campus: Engineering, Architecture and Urban Planning, Music, and Art, all of which are intimately concerned with the act of creation. Although all four schools operated within close proximity of each other, in the past there had been little collaboration between them. This made little sense. Increasingly, society demands designs that combine aesthetics, efficiency, and durability. As engineers become more like artists, artists and musicians have become more interested in new environments for their creations; and architects are increasingly concerned with the structural integrity and beauty of their designs.

We soon realized, however, that the Media Union must be a resource for the entire university. The need for interdisciplinary collaboration extends beyond the creative disciplines, and as a facility designed in part to bridge the limitations of time and distance, what better place to bring the various campuses of the university together? The Media Union acted as a catalyst, helping faculty and students from different fields realize their similarities while capitalizing on their differences.

More specifically, this 250,000-square-foot facility, looking like a modern version of the Temple of Karnak, contains almost 1,000 workstations for student use. It has thousands of network jacks for students to plug in their laptops and wireless modems if they wish to work in its surrounding plazas and gardens during the summer. The facility contains a 1.5-million volume library for art, science, and engineering, but perhaps more significantly, it is the site of our major digital library projects. There are a sophisticated teleconferencing facility, design studios, visualization laboratories, and a major virtual reality complex. Since art, architecture, and music students work side by side with engineering students, the Media Union contains sophisticated recording studios and electronic music studios. It also has a state-of-the-art sound stage for "digitizing" performances, as well as numerous galleries for displaying the results of student creative efforts. Consequently, the Media Union is open 24 hours a day, seven days a week, so that students have round-the-clock access to its facilities.

The "virtual" nature of the research teams in the Media Union entices not only campus scholars but exciting thinkers around the world to participate. While groups may meet physically from time to time, many of the members of these project teams participate through interactive technology. Members need not leave their home institution or even their homes to join in close collaboration with other scholars who are thousands of miles away.

For the Media Union to succeed, we realized that we had to take risks, accepting that we might stumble before we could walk. When we began the planning for this project in the 1980s, our challenge was to envision a building that could become a campus "commons," both physically and virtually. We struggled with designing a place that would allow colleagues from very different disciplines and across great distances to collaborate with each other. Ultimately, we had no final answers—just ideas. We knew that we probably would not get it all right from the beginning. In fact, it was clear that stagnation would have arrived if the Media Union ever settled comfortably into any single form.

One of the problems in experimental centers like the Media Union at other universities has been that projects often move in when the facility is built—and then never leave. Limited paradigms take hold and then can't be shaken loose. Instead of propagating flexibility within the larger university, the reverse often happens; and these centers find themselves infected by the stolid, incremental "disease" of large institutions. Creating a fluid structure that continually embraces new ideas was a great struggle. A related challenge was learning to sustain spaces that are truly neutral in their academic orientation.

Another challenge involved finding ways to let the energy and enthusiasm from the center's cutting-edge research projects trickle out into the common areas of the building and ultimately to the entire university. The facility's interactive library was open to all members of the Michigan community, but much of the rest of the building was reserved for a wide spectrum of research projects and groups. Researchers and scholars needed space of their own to work together, but we worried that if they remained isolated behind closed doors (even glass doors), we would lose the opportunity for our students and colleagues to experience their excitement. Even allowing the outside world "virtual" access to the union's projects might not be enough. As our architecture dean, Robert Beckley, noted, "There are ways in which we would like the building to have the messy, intriguing look of a house for mad scientists." If we expected the Media Union to be a catalyst, changing the common practices of our community, we were challenged to find ways for these new practices to move beyond the building's studios.

The New University

Experience has revealed the difficulty of approaching university transformation by changing existing programs and activities. While such a direct approach may suffice for incremental changes at the margin, an effort to achieve more dramatic change usually creates so much resistance that little progress is possible. It is sometimes more effective to take a "greenfield" approach by building separately a model of the new paradigm, developing the necessary experience with it, and then propagating successful elements of the model to modify or perhaps replace existing programs.

One possible approach to major university transformation taken in earlier and more affluent times was to build a separate campus. The efforts of the University of California (UC) in the 1960s to explore academic colleges built around research themes at UC-San Diego and residential learning at UC-Santa Cruz are examples of this approach. However, today's resource-limited environments are substantially different from the population boom-driven 1960s, and it is difficult to justify such separate new campuses to explore new educational paradigms—not to mention finding sites comparable to the bluffs overlooking the Pacific. There is a more important reason to consider an alternative approach: we believe that it is far more effective to develop and explore such new paradigms of the university directly, within an existing university community, and better to prototype and rapidly propagate successful efforts.

To this end, at Michigan we considered a concept known as the *New University*, an environment in which creative students and faculty could join colleagues from beyond the campus to develop and test new paradigms of the university. In some ways, the New University would be a laboratory where the fundamental missions of the university—teaching, research, service, and extension—could be redeveloped and tested. But it would also be aimed at developing a new culture, a new spirit of excitement and adventure that would propagate to the university at large. In such an academic enterprise, we would hope to build a risk-tolerant culture in which students and faculty were strongly encouraged to "go for it," in which failure is accepted as part of the learning process and is associated with ambitious goals rather than poor performance.

Although we took only the early steps in designing and creating the New University during 1990s, the concept did guide many of our actions. More specifically, we saw this laboratory university as allowing us to experiment with the various paradigms of the twenty-first-century university.

We envisioned the New University as having both a physical and a virtual presence. For example, we developed new physical facilities, such as the Media Union described in the previous section, to serve as environments for these experiments. These exciting new centers were designed both to explore and to test many of the more exciting innovations that might well determine the character of the university in the years to come.

This includes integrating the use of information technology to provide students and faculty with access to the world, collective and interactive learning, and immersion in the cultural artifacts of our civilization.

These physical facilities were augmented by a virtual environment based on information technology and networks that would extend across and beyond the campus. The role of the university in the Internet2 project provided a particular opportunity. We launched other activities, such as an array of digital library projects, a university-wide interactive video system with over 100 broadcasting channels available to students and faculty, collaboration-technology projects, and a set of broad linkages to hundreds of institutions, both in this country and abroad.

In terms of structure, we saw the New University not as organized along conventional disciplinary lines but, rather, as stressing integrative themes. Further, while it would offer academic degrees, such programs would stress far stronger linkages among undergraduate, graduate, professional, and lifetime education programs than those offered by the traditional university. We also envisioned the New University as more effectively integrating the various activities of the university by engaging its students in an array of teaching, research, service, and extension activities. Further, the New University would almost certainly involve an array of outreach activities, for example, linking alumni to the on-campus activities of the university or providing richer and more meaningful international experiences for students. While the New University would enroll a significant number of students, it would not have a large, permanent faculty or staff. Rather, it would draw faculty members from across the university and throughout the world who would become associated with the New University for specific programs. This would allow it far greater flexibility, since it could avoid the constraints posed by faculty appointments and tenure.

During the 1990s this vision served to guide the University of Michigan's transformation effort, to help reinvent the institution so that it could better serve a rapidly changing world. We created a campus culture in which both excellence and innovation were our highest priorities. We restructured our finances so that we became, in effect, a privately supported public university. We dramatically increased the diversity of our campus community. We launched major efforts to build a modern environment for teaching and research using the powerful tools of information technology. Yet with each transformation step that we took, with every project that we launched, we became increasingly uneasy. We realized that the forces driving change in our society were stronger and more profound than we had

first thought. Change was occurring far more rapidly than we had anticipated. The future was becoming less certain as the range of possibilities expanded to include more radical options.

We concluded that in a world of such dynamic change, as we faced a
future of such uncertainty, the most realistic near-term approach was to
explore possible futures of the university through experimentation and
discovery. Rather than continue to contemplate possibilities for the future through abstract study and debate, it seemed a more productive
course to build several prototypes of future learning institutions as working experiments. In this way we could actively explore possible paths to
the future.

Through a major strategic effort known as the Michigan Mandate, we
significantly enhanced the racial diversity of our students and faculty, providing a laboratory for exploring the themes of the "diverse university." We
established campuses in Europe, Asia, and Latin America, linking them
with information technology, to understand better the implications of becoming a "world university." We launched major initiatives such as the
Media Union (a sophisticated multimedia environment) and a virtual university (the Michigan Virtual University), and we played a key role in the
management of the Internet to explore the "cyberspace university" theme.
We launched new cross-disciplinary programs and built new community
spaces that would draw students and faculty together as a model of the "di-
visionless university." We placed a high priority on the visual and performing arts, integrating them with disciplines such as engineering and architecture to better understand the challenges of the "creative university."
We launched an array of other initiatives, programs, and ventures, all designed to explore the future.

All of these efforts were driven by the grassroots interests, abilities, and
enthusiasm of faculty and students. Our approach as leaders of the institution was to encourage a "let every flower bloom" philosophy, to respond
to faculty and student proposals with "Wow! That sounds great! Let's see
if we can work together to make it happen! And don't worry about the risk.
If you don't fail from time to time, it is because you aren't aiming high
enough!" We tried to ban the word "no" from our administrative vocabu-
lary.

To be sure, some of these experiments were costly. Some were poorly understood and harshly criticized by those defending the status quo. All ran
a very high risk of failure, and some crashed in flames—albeit spectacu-
larly. While such an exploratory approach was disconcerting to some and

frustrating to others, many on our campus and beyond viewed this phase as an exciting adventure, and all of these initiatives were important in understanding better the possible futures facing our university. All have had influence on the evolution of our university.

With increasing differentiation, there will be many "new" universities as institutions attempt to define themselves in the marketplace both by core competencies and by differences. Some colleges and universities may continue to focus on the traditional educational paradigms discussed in earlier chapters, but many will undergo or exploit significant transformations to explore an array of themes:

- From teaching, to learning organizations
- From students, to active learners
- From faculty-centered, to learner-centered
- From solitary learning, to interactive, collaborative learning
- From classroom learning, to learning communities
- From linear, sequential curricula, to hyperlearning experiences
- From credit-hour or seat-time credentialing, to learning assessment
- From just-in-case learning, to just-in-time learning, to just-for-you learning
- From student or alumnus, to lifelong member of a learning community
- From campus-based, to asynchronous, to ubiquitous learning opportunities

Furthermore, there will be many paradigms to explore, some coming from within the higher education community but many coming from other sectors of our society.

SCENARIOS FOR THE LONGER TERM

Knowledge and Learning Networks

Driven by information technology, the network has become more than a web that links together learning resources. It has become the architecture of advanced learning organizations.[6] Information, knowledge, and learning opportunities are now distributed across robust computer networks to hundreds of millions of people. The knowledge, the learning, the cultural resources that used to be the prerogative of a privileged few are rapidly becoming available anyplace, anytime, to anyone.

The implications of a networked learning architecture are manifold. First, it makes less and less sense for institutions to attempt to be comprehensive, to go it alone. Rather, the key will be forming alliances, sharing resources, specializing in what they can be really good at, and relying on other focused institutions to provide the rest. The fact learned through painful experience in business and industry is that only world-class, competitively priced products will succeed in a global marketplace. This does not mean that the largest, most prestigious institutions will necessarily be the most successful. Indeed, smaller, more focused, and more nimble institutions may be able to develop world-class learning services that could compete very effectively with traditional offerings.

In fact, the powerful tools for learning provided by information technology, when coupled to the changing educational needs of our society and the changing character of our students, suggest that it may be time to explore an entirely new architecture for learning in a society with ubiquitous digital technology. Perhaps it is time to consider a blank sheet approach to learning, by setting aside existing educational systems, policies, and practices and instead first focusing on what knowledge, skills, and abilities a person will need to lead a productive and satisfying life in the century ahead and then, by considering the diversity of ways in which people learn and the rich array of knowledge resources emerging in our society, designing a new ecology of learning for the twenty-first century.

Some interesting trends in technology suggest that new types of "community knowledge structures" may, in fact, appear, ones that will not be derivative of traditional institutions such as schools or libraries. To illustrate, consider the concept of a knowledge and learning network that links together an array of public and private knowledge resources to serve a diverse population. Such an infrastructure, comprising not only technological but also organizational and social components, would link together the people of the region and their social institutions with a vast array of knowledge and learning resources.

Here, it is important to realize that infrastructures are not just technology. They are profoundly human constructs, facilitating the formation and growth of networks of people who interact, share information, learn together, and create virtual communities on-line based upon their shared interests rather than any shared geography.

More specifically, we see the knowledge and learning network infrastructure is likely to consist of three components:

1. A state-of-the-art Internet knowledge network, linking the people and their institutions with knowledge and learning resources within the region and beyond as illustrated in Figure 6.2. This technology infrastructure, developed and funded through a public–private sector partnership, would link homes, businesses, and industry with public re-

Figure 6.2
A Knowledge and Learning Network

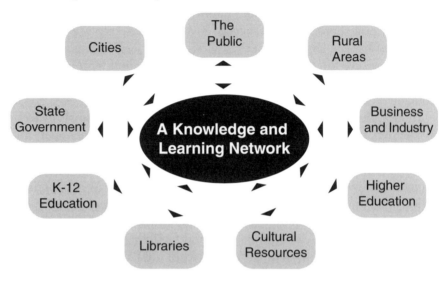

sources such as schools, college, universities, libraries, cultural centers, and government agencies. It would provide the community infrastructure with a range of functions such as learning, access to knowledge and cultural resources, public services, and electronic commerce.

2. Organizations, policies, and programs designed to dramatically accelerate the transfer of knowledge—technology, education, training—to the private sector, including the formation of new structures such as virtual schools and colleges, enhanced state support of efforts to attract major federal R&D grants and contracts, private funds for seed and venture capital, technology parks, and programs to assist in the transfer of technology from universities and corporate research laboratories to business and industry.

3. Organizations capable of managing the network infrastructure and knowledge transfer process, providing the strategic vision necessary to exploit emerging technologies, and benchmarking a region's climate for economic growth. In addition, new nonprofit structures might be formed to manage the evolving knowledge and learning infrastructures, drawing on strong partnerships with state and local government, higher education, nonprofit foundations, and business and labor.

The challenge will be linking these extraordinary assets in a manner that responds to the rapid evolution in information technology and achieves leadership in the emerging global knowledge industry.

Quins University

Lee and Messerschmitt have suggested yet another provocative vision for the future of the university, which they have labeled Quins University, as in "Quins University Is Not Stanford."[7] Their model is global in extent, with many geographical sites, linked together in cyberspace. They further suggest that the slogan of Quins is "a university without gates" ... or Gates, for that matter!

In a sense, they attempt to use information technology to combine the social structure of the Oxbridge (or Yale/Harvard) residential colleges with the educational imperatives of a knowledge society, for example, lifelong, anyplace-anytime, affordable learning. Quins attempts to address the need for higher education to grapple with factors such as the expanding number of years that people spend in education, delaying family and "real life," followed by a career marked by rapid obsolescence and declining employment prospects brought on by the rapid expansion of knowledge. They also note that lengthening life expectancy and possibly mandated increases in retirement age result in longer careers accentuating these difficulties. Finally, their paradigm attempts to address the loss of community and adverse psychological effects that come from rapid job and occupational changes and geographical mobility.

The Quins design is intended to respond not only to the needs for ubiquitous lifelong educational opportunities but as well to a social need for belonging and community in a world increasingly characterized by job and home mobility. To create this social structure, Quins divides participants into distinct global villages. Villagers are admitted to a specific village and develop a camaraderie with fellow villagers that lasts a lifetime. Even with twenty-first-century telepresence, a purely electronic village fails to completely address the human need for personal interaction and companionship. Consequently, each village is associated with a set of globally scattered geographical sites for face-to-face interactions.

The Quins model extends education to an entire lifetime—extending even to quality of life-enhancing activities in retirement. It seeks a full integration of education and work that dramatically shortens the initial, full-time, college-level education to a mere two years. A continuing education process perpetuates the educational experience throughout a lifetime, tracking the expanding knowledge base and changing life and career needs. Quins provides a lifelong relationship to the Quins village to provide a sense of community even as workers change jobs and locations frequently. Although much of education can be provided through on-line pedagogy, Quins recognizes that in-residence programs, configured as sabbaticals, are necessary to allow renewal and more intensive educational experiences within a social context.

To this end, the Quins paradigm is based on a lifelong education model that discards the notion that a certain body of knowledge defines an educated person, as well as the antiquated idea of educating only the young and the concept of "graduation." Lee and Messerschmitt imagine that an important epistemic change is the abandonment of the notion that any single human mind can bear any significant fraction of what is knowable and that there is a static body of information that can be conveyed. Even the Renaissance notion of an "educated person" has been discarded—there is no longer a canonical body of basic knowledge that defines this notion. Instead, the assimilation and synthesis of established knowledge are combined with the discovery of new knowledge in an environment in which learning and scholarship merge. An infrastructure of digital libraries, information search agents, immersive exploratory environments, and visualization of information spaces supports these intellectual activities.

The University à la *Neuromancer*

Ray Kurzweil's book, *The Age of Spiritual Machines*, predicts that over the next decade intelligent courseware will emerge as a common means of learning, with schools increasingly relying on software approaches, leaving human teachers to attend primarily to issues of motivation, psychological well-being, and socialization.[8] Eventually, in two or three decades, Kurzweil sees human learning accomplished primarily by using virtual teachers and enhanced by widely available neural transplants. More specifically, he speculates that learning will evolve as follows. By 2009 (one decade after his book appeared) he speculates that although schools will not be on the cutting edge, the profound importance of the computer as a knowledge tool will be widely recognized. Many children will learn to read on their own using their personal computers before entering grade school.

By 2019, most learning will be accomplished using intelligent software-based simulated teachers. To the extent that teaching is done by human teachers, they often will not be in the local vicinity of the student. The teachers will be viewed more as mentors and counselors than as sources of learning and knowledge. By a decade further out, 2029, human learning will be primarily accomplished using virtual teachers and enhanced by the widely available neural implants. The implants will improve memory and perception, but it will not yet be possible to download knowledge directly. Although enhanced through virtual experiences, intelligent interactive instruction, and neural implants, learning still will require time-consuming human experience and study. This activity will constitute the primary focus of the human species, and education will become the largest profession, as human and nonhuman intelligences are primarily focused on the creation of knowledge in its myriad forms. There will be almost no human employment in production, agriculture, and transportation.

Finally, a century hence, in 2099, learning will no longer the struggle it once was; rather, the struggle will be in discovering new knowledge to learn.

While many would argue (indeed, many *have* argued) with Kurzweil's view of the future, it does illustrate just how profoundly our world might be changed by the exponential evolution of information technology.

PATHS TO THE FUTURE

Of course, these scenarios are likely to be regarded by many of our colleagues in higher education as simply unrealistic speculation. Despite all evidence to the contrary, many still believe that change will occur only at the margins of higher education. After all, they note, the university remains one of the few social institutions that has survived for a millennium with its fundamental purpose and values largely intact. It has gathered and preserved the most important knowledge and traditions of our civilization, passing them on from one generation to the next. While the faculty itself creates the new knowledge that can drive social change, it prefers to do so in an institutional environment that is largely static.

History suggests that the university must change and adapt in part to preserve these traditional roles. Many others, both within and outside the academy, believe that significant change will occur throughout the higher education enterprise, in each and every one of our institutions, yet even these people see change as an evolutionary, incremental, long-term process, compatible with the values, cultures, and structure of the contemporary university.

A few voices, however, primarily outside the academy, believe that both the dramatic nature and compressed timescale characterizing the changes of our times will drive not evolution but revolution. They have serious doubts about whether the challenges of our times will allow such gradual change and adaptation. They point out that there are really no precedents to follow. Some suggest that long before reform of the educational system comes to any conclusion, the system itself will collapse.[9]

Some colleges and universities may be able to maintain their current form and market niche. Others will change beyond recognition. Still others will disappear entirely. New types of institutions—perhaps even entirely new social learning structures—will evolve to meet educational needs. In contrast to the last several decades, when colleges and universities endeavored to become more similar, the years ahead will demand greater differentiation. There will be many different paths to the future.

Hence, we believe it inappropriate to suggest a particular "end state" for the university in the digital age. Indeed, there will be many possible end states, and they are likely to be only transitory. Instead, we believe that most leaders of our colleges and universities would prefer a direction or a path rather than a specific goal. In fact, for many college and university leaders facing the challenge of navigating the white-water rapids of a period of intense change, simply knowing how to keep the boat moving ahead without capsizing may be sufficient. Drifting with the current is the most dangerous tack of all.

Of course, most institutions seek to make wise investments and launch strategic initiatives today within a framework for the longer term, but there also needs to be an awareness that profoundly nonlinear and discontinuous things could happen. We will likely be encountering many tipping points in the years ahead. Hence, we might best conclude this section of the book by identifying several of the key questions—rather, tensions—that will influence the paths to the future taken by colleges and universities.

First, we must acknowledge the growing tension between rapid technological change and the need to preserve the ancient values and roles of the university that have served our civilization for a millennium. The timescales of change in the university are necessarily different from those characterizing digital technology. This must be both recognized and accommodated. In this regard, while most universities are facing very near-term imperatives such as identifying, building, and supporting the necessary technology infrastructure for quality education and research, not to mention university operations, we must also keep in mind the possibility of technological surprise.

Second, in a knowledge-driven society the unique roles of the university in research and advanced education become even more critical to our society. However, in a marketplace being disrupted by technology-intensive competitors, the old business models for supporting such activities through subsidy from high-margin activities such as general education may no longer be adequate.

Third, it is ironic that even as the unique roles of the university become ever more valuable, information technology is equalizing access to knowledge, research participation, and learning opportunities.

Finally, it is important that we achieve a balance between portraying an optimistic future in which information technology is used to enrich and enhance the traditional activities of the university and alerting our colleagues that there may be a big, bad wolf at the door—whether it be the University of Phoenix, Unext.com, Microsoft, Time-Warner-AOL, or even the Walt Disney Company. Is it best to attempt to achieve change through hope and opportunity or through fear and a struggle for survival?

NOTES

1. John Seely Brown and Paul Duguid, "Universities in the Digital Age," *Change* (July 1996), 11–19.

2. Stan Davis and Jim Botkin, *The Monster under the Bed* (New York: Touchstone, 1994).

3. "Inside the Knowledge Factory," *The Economist* (October 4, 1997). See also Michael Gibbons, *The New Production of Knowledge* (London: Sage, 1994).

4. Ibid.

5. See the Web site: <http://www.ummu.umich.edu/>.

6. Michael G. Dolence and Donald M. Norris, *Transforming Higher Education: A Vision for Learning in the 21st Century* (Ann Arbor: Society for College and University Planning, 1995).

7. Edward A. Lee and David G. Messerschmitt, "A Highest Education in the Year 2049," *Proceedings of the IEEE* 87, no. 9 (November 1999) 1685–91.

8. Ray Kurzweil, *The Age of Spiritual Machines: When Computers Exceed Human Intelligence* (New York: Viking, 1999).

9. Lewis J. Perelman, *School's Out* (New York: Avon, 1993).

PART III

Strategies and Recommendations

The essence of strategy is the close view of distant things and the distant view of close things.

—Sun Tzu

In the next three chapters we shift from a discussion of issues and challenges facing higher education as it enters the digital age to a consideration of possible strategies and recommendations. Again we divide our discussion into three levels considered in each of the next three chapters: first, a consideration of institutional strategies; next, a broader consideration of strategies appropriate to the higher education enterprise; and finally, a discussion of strategies at the national level, including recommendations for policies and programs at the levels of both state and federal government.

Here it is important to keep in mind several characteristics of information technology. First, this is a technology that effectively eliminates the constraints of space and time. It allows the activities of the university such as teaching and research to occur anyplace at anytime and possibly involving anyone. Second, this technology tends to disaggregate activities, for example, separating the development of learning content and services from their delivery. In the digital age the instructor is less likely to be concerned with the development of educational content and increasingly will become one who guides and facilitates active learning on the part of students. Third, this technology transforms roles in the university, for example, transforming students into active learners and likely consumers of educational services, reshaping the role of faculty as teachers and scholars, and transforming the roles of university leaders and administrators.

Finally, it is important to bear in mind just how rapidly and unpredictably information technology is evolving, doubling in power roughly every year and capable of discontinuous, even disruptive change in surprising, new directions. Not only are computer networks evolving rapidly toward effectively infinite processing power and bandwidth, but they are doing so in a highly ubiquitous way that affects every aspect of the lives of citizens in the digital age. We are evolving from e-commerce, to e-learning, to e-everything. Information technology requires the reinvention of every aspect of our social institutions, not just in the near term but in a continual fashion as the technology continues to evolve. The challenge to leadership becomes one both of seeing over the horizon and of adapting leadership styles to an environment of constant change.

CHAPTER 7

Institutional Strategies

We now turn our attention to a series of recommendations for universities and their leaders faced not only with complex and costly decisions concerning the acquisition and use of information technology but, more broadly, with the task of developing institutional strategies to cope with the digital age. Perhaps our first goal should be simply capturing their attention, since many leaders of our colleges and universities have either ignored or delegated the responsibility for developing such strategies to others in the administration or on faculty committees. There is an old saying that to lead a mule, you first need to whack it over the head with a 2x4 to get its attention. The material in the first sections of this book have been intended, in part, as the 2x4 to raise awareness of the challenges and opportunities presented by digital technology.

Of course, college and university leaders will react differently to these issues, depending on the nature of their institution. For example, while the capacity of information technology to transform learning may be compelling to some institutions, it is less likely to excite or alarm leaders of research universities, since, in truth, many faculty members in these institutions regard scholarship as their highest priority and tend to pay only lip service to education, particularly at the undergraduate level. Research universities will be somewhat more concerned about the impact of for-profit competitors on the marketplace for their high-profit margin education programs since these tend to subsidize graduate education and research. Perhaps most compelling to research university leaders will be the threat of a changing marketplace for the best faculty and students. Not only will faculty tend to be attracted to those institutions with the most supportive digital environments for research and education, but as the intellectual products of the university become increasingly valued by the commercial marketplace, the mobility of faculty enabled by information technology will pose serious challenges to the ability of universities to protect and control the valuable intellectual content developed on their campuses.

The most compelling arguments will be somewhat different for liberal arts colleges. Since the finances of these institutions tend to be highly dependent upon tuition revenue, they are likely to be seriously concerned about any potential shifts in student demand. Of particular interest will be the impact of digital technology on their traditional sources of students, particularly to the degree that information and communications technology creates an open learning marketplace in which the student increasingly becomes an active consumer of educational services.

So, too, enrollment-sensitive regional colleges and universities will be threatened by the changing student marketplace and, in particular, by emerging commercial competitors offering educational services to adult learners. The rapid growth of on-line distributed learning could erode their regional monopolies. More nimble, for-profit competitors may be able to move quickly to capture new markets in workplace training and professional education.

While the threats posed to traditional roles and practices may serve usefully as the 2x4 to get the attention of colleges and universities—particularly their faculties—university leadership should not be simply reacting to threats but instead acting positively and strategically to exploit the opportunities presented by information technology. As we have suggested, this technology will provide great opportunities to improve the quality of education and scholarship. It will allow colleges and universities to serve society in new ways, perhaps more closely aligned with their fundamental academic mission and values. It will also provide strong incentives for building new alliances among diverse educational institutions, thereby providing systemic opportunities for improving the quality of higher education in America.

Hence, we believe that while college and university leaders should recognize and understand the threats posed by rapidly evolving information technology to their institutions, they should seek to transform these threats into opportunities for leadership. Information technology should be viewed as a tool of immense power to use in enhancing the fundamental roles and missions of their institutions.

PREPARING FOR CHANGE
The Current Situation

As information technology continues to evolve at its relentless, ever-accelerating pace, affecting every aspect of our society and our social institutions, organizations in every sector are grappling with the need to transform their basic processes of how they collect, synthesize, manage, and control information. Corporations and governments are reorganizing in an effort to utilize technology to enhance productivity, improve quality, and control costs (so-called e-business transformation).[1] Entire industries have been restructured to better align with the realities of the digital age.

Yet, from a structural perspective, the university stands apart, moored to its past traditions and practices, particularly in areas such as education. In spite of the information explosion and the profound impact of digital communications technology in areas such as scholarship, the nature of learning remains fundamentally unchanged in higher education. The traditional classroom remains the overwhelming focal point for learning, with the faculty still functioning largely as "talking heads" and students as passive learners.

To some degree, this is surprising, since colleges and universities are the most wired communities in our society. Surveys suggest that over 90 percent of college students access the Internet on a daily basis to communicate through E-mail, extract information from the Web, conduct a growing array of electronic transactions, and pursue academic studies (whether assigned by the faculty or not). Faculty members make extensive use of digital technology in research and scholarship, frequently driving the evolution of hardware and software to meet their particular needs. Universities have been the spawning ground for many of the digital technology and killer applications that have so transformed our society, such as electronic mail, the Web browser, and Napster-like peer-to-peer sharing.

Most colleges and universities, however, continue to ignore the technology cost learning curves so important in other sectors of society. Although both scholarship and administration have become heavily dependent on digital technology, many universities believe that it remains simply too costly to implement technology on a massive scale in instructional activities—which, of course, it certainly does as long as they insist on maintaining their traditional classroom-based character rather than reengineering educational activities to enhance productivity and quality. Their limited use of technology thus far has been at the margins, to provide modest additional resources to classroom pedagogy or to attempt to extend the physical reach of our current classroom-centered, seat time-based teaching paradigm. It is ironic that the very institutions that have played such a profound role in developing the digital technology now reshaping our world are among the most resistant to reshaping their activities to enable its effective use in their core activity, education.

Barriers to Change

What explains the reluctance of higher education to implement digital technology in the ways that other sectors such as business and government have adopted these tools? In part it has to do with leadership. Many university leaders appear to be either in a state of denial about the impact of information technology on their institutions or so confused by the complexity of IT issues that they simply hesitate making decisions or commitments. Surveys suggest that despite the profound nature of these issues, information technology usually does not rank high among the list of priorities for university planning and decision making.[2] Perhaps this is due to the limited experience that most college and university leaders have with this emerging technology. It could also be a sign of indecisiveness and procrastination. Yet, as the pace of technological change continues to accelerate, indecision and inaction can be the most dangerous course of all.

In part, too, it has to do with the culture of the university, long committed to preserving values, traditions, and practices of the past as an important role. Tenured faculty members tend to cling to stability, even as the knowledge that they create through research and scholarship reshapes our world. Governing boards, particularly those of public institutions, tend to protect the status quo in an effort to avoid agitating important constituencies. Furthermore, universities are characterized by very large and slowly changing fixed costs such as those associated with tenured faculty, physical plant, and administrative staff. Although most revenue streams are far more variable and unpredictable, dependent upon market forces and economic conditions, academic institutions tend to react very slowly to revenue shifts, even if perceived to be long-term in nature.

This tendency to protect the status quo may also arise in part from the complacency accompanying good times. As we begin a new century, many of our colleges and universities have become very prosperous. The bull market of the 1990s, coupled with successful fund-raising campaigns, has given many universities endowments that make them look and act more like banks than educational institutions.[3] Furthermore, many states have restored the priority of higher education for public tax support, although it continues to cycle up and down with the economy. Both public and private colleges and universities continue to have strong political support. During prosperous times, leaders relax, forget about discipline and sacrifice, and prefer to play golf (or read fiction).

So, too, the existing organizational and financial structures protect the status quo. Our management systems and financial processes are still geared to the organizational unit—departments, schools, libraries, telecommunications and network organizations—as the center of the institution, and this undermines the inherent power of the technology to decentralize access and control. The scholar, the student, and the administrator become the central foci of the transformed university, not the organizational unit in its traditional form as the academic department or the library.

Moreover, while corporations may view IT-based activities such as e-commerce and e-business as critical to operations and survival, many campus officials do not view either these or their academic counterparts such as e-learning as priorities for their institutions and thus may be unwilling to make the required investment of people, time, and money. Most academic administrators do not fully understand the significance of network-based activities and how digital technology supports the mission of the organization and facilitates many enterprise-to-enterprise operations. Most campus Web sites are primarily devoted to passive information (library catalogs, courses, etc.) with little capacity for financial transactions or knowledge management. Furthermore, less than 5 percent of colleges and universities have a strategic plan for e-business.[4] Ironically, as one moves up the learning curve, from community colleges, to regional universities, to research universities, there appears to be less and less activity, particularly at the level of research universities. While there are experiments such as Fathom.com and Unext.com, these are largely "hands-off," without strong participation by the faculties of the research university. As a result, the research universities are not learning how to implement this technology as have others in the enterprise.

The irony facing many college and university presidents is that despite the complexity of issues raised by digital technology, the need for making rapid decisions becomes ever more urgent. Digital technology offers numerous opportunities for both growth and decline. A temptation is to sit tight and hope that "it will go away." After all, television was supposed to drastically change education. It did not. Some suggest that the Internet, the computer, multimedia, digital appliances, e-learning, and private sector competition are all passing fads, too. There is ample evidence from other sectors, however, that ignoring technological change can lead to disaster.

Threats and Opportunities

The limited nature of the university's efforts to transform its activities to align better with the digital age cannot long continue, as other sectors of our society have learned. If the leadership in higher education does not chart a course for moving the university into the digital age, then others will attempt to chart that course for us, or they will navigate around higher education, finding other learning agents and intermediaries that can address the opportunities created by digital technology for learning.

Of course, technology will provide great opportunities. Not only will the advance of digital technology in the years ahead (to petaflop supercomputers, ubiquitous computing, forget-nothing storage, retinal displays, new software platforms, tools, and applications) provide significant opportunities to improve teaching and research, but technology will also present wonderfully fertile new areas of study, not only in science and technology but perhaps even more in the social sciences, the arts, and the humanities. Information technology will offer new pedagogical opportunities such as distributed learning, broad access to digital archives, immersive virtual reality environments, and the ability to simulate both natural and social phenomena. Most significantly, technology will allow us to link together students and faculty into new learning communities, no longer dictated by the constraints of space and time.

The emergence of electronic and network-based services will cut new channels through our myriad systems of education. Campus systems, services, and approaches will change, because it will be increasingly difficult, costly, and isolationist to provide services in the traditional way. Colleges must join the movement in other sectors to focus more on the needs of clients. Faculty will establish the standards for the demonstration of mastery of topics, but learners will demand substantial control over the conditions and timing for the acquisition of skills and demonstration of mastery. The dominant questions facing the leaders of today's colleges and universities will become what aspects to change and how fast they can be changed.

Information technology provides the university with both the opportunity and the necessity to renegotiate its linkages with every other institution in society—with secondary education, with industry, with government, with the media, and with the political system. However, without different institutional arrangements, we fear not only that these technologies will be underexploited but they may well reinforce the current limitations of the higher educational system. Some institutions may learn too late the lessons from the commercial sector: information represents the table stakes for survival in the digital age. If you are not going to invest in this technology, you may as well get out of the game.

THE DEVELOPMENT OF INSTITUTIONAL STRATEGIES

The Strategic Context for Decisions

Information technology presents us with a temporal dilemma. Because of the exponential evolution of this technology, event horizons for dramatic change are much closer than we think they are. For example, getting people to think about implications of accelerating technology learning curves as well as technology cost-performance curves is very important. There are staggering increases in efficiency for an organization if one can reorganize its fundamental activities to take advantage of technology, but many colleges and universities continue to look at IT as a cost rather than seeking to understand its cost-benefit characteristics.

Surveys of campus leaders suggest that most attention is being focused on near-term issues, for example, determining what information technology infrastructure for campus-based activities is necessary and how to finance it. Although academic leaders are most concerned with the implications of electronic learning environments and distance learning, many campus administrators and IT professionals are immersed in the challenge of upgrading antiquated administrative computer systems and replacing them with enterprise resource planning, knowledge management, or e-business systems, at rather considerable expense.

So what do presidents, trustees, and other leaders of our academic institutions need to know? What new technologies are likely to roll out next? Where are they likely to see the first impact on their institutions? Where are various possible decisions likely to take them? These may be the questions of most interest to some, but we rather think that most leaders are more concerned with how they create the academic environment that students and faculty need for high-quality teaching, learning, and scholarship. They recognize that this will require a trade-off of investments between bricks (conventional physical infrastructure) and clicks (information technology). Increasingly, most realize that they can no longer approach these issues in isolation. They must seek partners, both within the higher education enterprise and beyond to include the commercial and government sectors and possibly even international collaborators.

Certainly, it is important that both planning and decisions address the issues and realities of the present. Technology really does not tell us what will happen or what to do next year. The more distant the future, the more exciting and distracting it can become. Universities should always keep in front of them the need to make decisions about issues of today, even as they consider and influence possibilities for the future.

Time is of the essence. To capture the opportunities that will be available to universities in the knowledge-driven era—or for some, even to survive—profound and far-reaching commitments must be made quickly. These commitments must be made explicitly and publicly and must be accompanied by the investments of talent and funds that can make them real. This will be a challenge in environments long acculturated to deliberation and skepticism of fads and trends originating in industry.

University leaders need a long-term strategic context to enable near-term decisions. It is important to make informed investments and launch creative initiatives today, but within a framework for the longer term. Among all of our social institutions, universities are particularly obliged to look to the long term, seeking not just the quick fix but rather the longer-term strategy and necessary commitments.

Some Assumptions for the Near Term

In considering these issues, we make several assumptions about the evolution and availability of information technology for the near term (10 years or less):

- Information and communications technology will continue to evolve exponentially, following Moore's law for at least the foreseeable future.
- Ubiquitous, high-speed, and economically accessible network capacity will exist nationally and to a great extent globally.
- Affordable, multimedia-capable computers (including network appliances) will be commonplace, and most colleges and universities will expect student ownership of such devices.
- Most colleges will deliver some portion of their instructional missions both on campus and beyond via the Internet.
- As the ability to use technology in the support of instruction improves, the differentiators of technology-enriched course offerings will continue to be price, quality, and access.
- Nontraditional sources of university-caliber instruction, such as software developers and publishers, are likely to become increasingly important suppliers of course content and materials.
- The employment relationships between academic institutions and their faculty will become even more complex.

- Within this time frame the laws that govern intellectual property will change significantly. In particular, the application of publisher-protections to the digital distribution of copyrighted materials is likely to have enormous revenue and expense implications for higher education in general and for technology-enriched instruction in particular. The legal and economic management of university intellectual property will become a complex area of activity.

Key Recommendations

Let us now turn our attention to several specific recommendations for university leaders faced with the challenge of leading their institutions in the face of rapidly evolving digital technology. We have grouped these into seven specific recommendations or steps intended to help leaders shape a strategy unique to the circumstances, challenges, and opportunities facing their institution.[5]

Recommendation 1: University leaders should recognize that the rapid evolution of information and communications technologies will stimulate—indeed, demand—a process of strategic transformation in their institutions.

We stress throughout this book the degree to which digital technology is reshaping both our society and our social institutions. Its exponential pace of evolution drives rapid, profound, unpredictable, and discontinuous change. It is a "disruptive" technology,[6] eroding conventional constraints such as space, time, and monopoly and reshaping both the structure and boundaries of institutions. The terms used to describe IT-driven change such as "e-business" and "e-learning" are simply metaphors for the pervasive, ubiquitous connectivity between and among people, knowledge, activities, and markets enabled by digital technology. In this sense, then, "e-business transformation" or "e-learning transformation" is in reality a very fundamental transformation process, driven by technology but involving people, organizations, and cultures. It must be addressed both systemically and ecologically.

More specifically, decisions involving digital technology raise very key strategic issues for colleges and universities requiring both attention and understanding at the very highest levels of institutional leadership. Technology is comparable in importance to other key strategic issues such as finance, government relations, and private fund-raising where final responsibility must rest with the president. The pace of change is too great and the consequences of decisions too significant to simply delegate to others such as faculty committees or chief information officers. The road ahead is littered with land mines and tipping points that require informed attention by the executive leadership and governing boards of academic institutions. Leadership on technology issues must come from the president and the provost, with the encouragement and support of the governing board.

Here colleges and universities face significant challenges, since not only is their leadership frequently inexperienced or uncomfortable with digital technology, but many institutions have only limited in-house expertise in these areas. Furthermore, few academic institutions have experience in the type of broad strategic planning and transformation process required by information technology. As a consequence they all too frequently rely on outsourcing not only technology but also technology strategies, wasting both valuable time and significant financial resources on ill-conceived initiatives. While it is certainly true that the hardware, software, and applications systems are usually best procured from commercial vendors, colleges and universities must develop sufficient expertise and experience at the leadership level to launch and guide the necessary process of institutional transformation at the strategic level.

Recommendation 2: It is our belief that universities should begin the development of their strategies for technology-driven change with a firm understanding of those key values, missions, and roles that should be protected and preserved during a time of transformation.

Colleges and universities need to begin the development of a technology strategy by addressing the most fundamental questions:

- How should the university set priorities among its various roles such as education of the young, the preservation of culture, basic research and scholarship, serving as a social critic, and applying knowledge to serve society?

- Which of its values and principles should be preserved, and which should be reconsidered. Academic freedom? Openness? A rational spirit of inquiry? Sustaining a community of scholars? A commitment to excellence? Almost certainly. But what about shared governance? Tenure? Are these values to be preserved?

- How will colleges and universities define their students? As the young? As adults? As established professionals and perhaps even academics? The best and brightest? Members of broader society? The workforce? Local, regional, global populations?

- How will we define our faculty members? As the products of our graduate schools and research laboratories? As practicing professionals (à la University of Phoenix)?

- What is the role of the residential campus in a future in which knowledge-based activities such as learning become increasingly independent of space and time (and perhaps reality)?

- How should the university address the rapidly evolving commercial marketplace for educational services and content, including, in particular, the for-profit and dot-com providers?

- What policies does the university need to reconsider in light of evolving information technology (e.g., intellectual property, copyright, instructional content ownership, faculty contracts)?

- Will new financial models be required? Beyond the need to implement a sustainable model of investment in information technology infrastructure, the intensely competitive marketplace for higher education services stimulated by digital technology will put at risk the current system of cross-subsidies in funding university activities.

- Just-in-time lifelong learning and the growing desire to be educated anyplace, anytime are driving the demand for distance education. How should the university approach the challenges and opportunities of online distributed learning?

- What is the role of universities with respect to the "digital divide," the stratification of our society—our world—with respect to access to technology?

- Will more (or perhaps most) universities find themselves collaborating and competing in a global marketplace, and how will that square with regionally supported universities?

Again drawing from the experience of the business world, most companies have found that the key to e-business transformation is to first return to the fundamentals, to begin with their core mission and how they provide value to their customers.

Recommendation 3: It is essential to develop an integrated, coordinated technology strategy for the institution in a systemic and ecological fashion.

Digital technology is pervasive, affecting every aspect and function of the university, from teaching and scholarship, to organization, financing, and management, yet a major challenge on many campuses is that there are too many people doing their own thing, independently of one another. Although many faculty, staff, and students are knowledgeable about the applications of technology in their narrow field of interest, broader awareness of institutionwide issues is a challenge. Furthermore, many faculty members simply do not understand the imperative nature of the need for a technology strategy. They are unaware of both the applications and implications of technology to their own activities, much less the broader university. There is a digital divide at many levels throughout the contemporary university.

It is difficult to coordinate the various silos of activities into a coherent structure. A technology strategy must be systemic, drawing together diverse applications such as instruction, research, libraries, museums, archives, academic computing, and university presses. However, it must also recognize and accommodate the very great diversity among university activities. Like a biological ecology, a technology strategy should be open, complex, and adaptive, with sufficient robustness and diversity to respond and adapt to the diverse and ever-changing needs of academic programs.

Information and communications technologies are tools for creating and enhancing connectivity, of strengthening the sense of community across distance and time. More abstractly, this technology supports the knowledge environment to enable knowledge creation, dissemination, and preservation of knowledge communities.

Recommendation 4: Universities need to understand the unique features of digital technology and how these affect people and their activities.

We have stressed many of the unique features of digital technology, for example, its exponential rate of evolution, its pervasive and ubiquitous nature, its ability to reproduce knowledge objects with perfect accuracy at zero cost, while transcending the constraints of space and time. The ever-accelerating tempo of digital technology poses great challenges to institutions. For example, today the software testing cycle is not much longer than the software usage cycle for many applications. When the power for a given price doubles every 18 months or less, rapid obsolescence disrupts conventional infrastructure planning processes. However, the most dramatic changes are driven not by the technology itself but rather by its applications.

The expectations of today's students (not to mention faculty and staff) are rising rapidly. They are accustomed to the convenience of electronic banking, mobile communications, and Web-based retailing (à la Amazon.com or Travelocity.com) and do not tolerate well the archaic, paper-based, queue-dependent cultures of universities. They also are accustomed to independent choice, not simply in technology but in sources of information. Compounding this is the changing nature of the "e-economy" in which business processes become more dynamic and activities become more transparent. Product reviews and price comparisons are now easily accessible on the Web. Web-based auctions (e-Bay) and AI-based purchasing agents are revolutionizing the nature of commercial transactions. Barriers to the entry of new competitors are falling, leading to the vertical disintegration and restructuring of entire industries.

Several examples illustrate the profound nature of the transformations in higher education driven by these characteristics of digital technology. Thus far we have focused most of our attention on the use of digital technology in the classroom experience, enriching it through access to original materials, augmenting it with on-line student-to-faculty and student-to-student dialogue, and distributing it through networks. The pervasive nature of this technology suggests far broader application across the campus learning environment to augment and enrich all learning experiences. We have long promoted the value of the residential campus experience as an environment for the intellectual and emotional maturation of young students. From this holistic viewpoint, we need to examine the full range of learning experiences—formal, informal, experiential, collaborative—to better understand the potential applications of information and communications technologies. For example, what in the interaction between a faculty member and the student provides a richer learning experience than classroom lectures and textbooks? How could digital technology impact community service activities or the diversity objectives of the university? We need to keep in mind that information technology is not a broadcasting technology but bidirectional (actually, multidirectional) medium. It allows institutions not only to connect with alumni and others off the campus but also to enable meaningful interaction of off-campus experts with on-campus academic programs and students. One can imagine a future in which digital technology will allow students to learn all the time, taking several majors at once, interacting with others, with knowledge resources and with instruments around the world in a seamless, time- and distant-independent way.

A second and, to many, more disturbing example: we have noted that information technology makes more transparent and dynamic the various activities and transactions of institutions. In particular, it demands a more rational—or at least competitive—configuration of activities, requiring organizations to focus on those activities where they are really strong (e.g., their core competencies) and outsource those where others are more capable. When one recognizes that the current portfolio of the contemporary college or university is determined more by history and happenstance than rational decisions, much less the marketplace, it is logical to expect that academic institutions will need to think about unbundling some of the activities that they have accumulated over the years because of the digital revolution. For example, which among the typical activities of the university are truly core competencies? Undergraduate education (including socialization)? Researcher training? Knowledge creation? Knowledge archiving (libraries)? Publication? Professional training? Most would probably agree with these, but what about entertainment (intercollegiate athletics, theater, concerts)? Hotel services? Alumni travel? Health care? Lest we forget, universities do from time to time spin off activities—usually reluctantly and awkwardly but nevertheless sufficiently to demonstrate an "existence theorem" for the process.

E-learning will bring about many changes in higher education. Students, who historically have come to learning sites, will increasingly participate at locations remote from the campus and the instructor. Rather than being affiliated with a single institution, they may be associated concurrently with multiple providers and modes of instruction. Educational services will become unbundled, with different providers carrying out various functions: curricular development, delivery of instructional modules, provision of student services, student evaluation, and awarding of credentials. Students will assume greater control over their educational experiences by designing programs that fit their specific needs with regard to program content, length, delivery mode, and location. Program completion will be defined increasingly by the knowledge gained and skills mastered rather than credit hours earned.

Faculty roles and work patterns will also change. Less emphasis will be placed on lecturing and greater emphasis on facilitating the educational process, for example, by providing learning assistance in time patterns and modes tailored to the needs of individual students.

In summary, it is likely that almost every function—especially every valuable function—will be affected by and possibly displaced by digital applications. Competitors will appear and will in many cases provide more effective and less costly alternatives. Universities can embrace the new techniques themselves, outsourcing some of their functions while maintaining their vertically integrated missions, or they may find themselves on a downward economic spiral. It will likely take some time for the full impact of this unbundling to be felt, but even small shifts in the high-value activities could degrade the university's character and structure.

Recommendation 5: Universities should aim to build layered organizational and management structures, based upon broadly accepted values, strategies, heuristics, and protocols at the highest levels but encouraging diversity, flexibility, and innovation at the level of execution.

Identifying and implementing the organizational and management structure appropriate for digital technology are major issues—and barriers—at most institutions. Even the most technology-sophisticated universities have struggled to find an effective structure, oscillating between centralized and decentralized approaches, frequently seeking the counsel of information services consultants experienced with e-business transformation, and spending tens of millions of dollars. Most universities are still struggling with organizing the "IT commons" in a way that is compatible with the distributed nature of the contemporary university. Furthermore, identifying the boundary of the university becomes more difficult as the interface with society becomes ever more porous.

Such challenges are likely to continue. After all, the Net and related digital technologies are dropping the costs of transactions and data access by many orders of magnitude. Distance has become almost irrelevant, with national and global connectivity becoming both inexpensive and pervasive. The ubiquitous nature of digital technology and the distributed nature of the university seem incompatible with the traditional hierarchy of management.

All organizations, whether in higher education, commerce, or government, face a quandary: should they centralize, through growth or mergers, becoming conglomerates to take advantage of economies of scale, standardization, and globalization, or should they decentralize, seeking autonomy, empowerment, and flexibility at the level of unit execution, while encouraging diversity, localization, and customization? Which path should they choose?

Actually, both and neither. There is no unique way to organize technology-based activities, although it is likely that most colleges and universities are currently far from an effective or optimal configuration. Furthermore, flexibility and adaptability are the watchwords for any such organization during a time of extraordinarily rapid technological change. The challenge is to orchestrate and coordinate the multiple activities and diverse talent on campus that explore and transform the application of digital technology in education. In effect, technology-driven transformations can be viewed as a collective R&D project for the institution.

The key to achieving this is to build layered organization and management structures. At the highest, centralized level one should seek a clear institutional vision, driven by broadly accepted values, guided by common heuristics, and coordinated through standard protocols. Below this at the level of execution one should encourage diversity, flexibility, and innovation. In a sense, institutions should seek to centralize the guiding vision and strategy, that is, determine "where" the institution should head, while decentralizing the decision process and activities that determine "how" to achieve these institutional goals. Put another way, universities should seek to synchronize, rather than homogenize, their activities. Rather than obliterating silos of activity, one should use standard protocols and infrastructure to link them together, creating porous walls between them.

All of this may accelerate the diversification of the academic community already well under way with the expansion of institutions, the specialization of academic subjects, and the focus on outside sources of funding and support from both government and the private sector. The atomization of the academic community increases the power of institutional administration. The transformations implicit in the introduction of IT to the curriculum are beyond the powers of academic senates or committees of amateurs to govern or steer. As our society moves from elite, to mass, to universal education, the role of the central administration becomes stronger and that of academics weaker.

Public universities will face particularly serious challenges, since they are accountable to public authority and therefore averse to risk, and IT is an area where risk and success are closely linked. A large public university is too big and its authority too widely dispersed to make rapid decisions. Individuals and units need to be able to make many small, rapid, risky, and relatively inexpensive decisions from below and have the opportunities and resources to experiment.

Recommendation 6: One should recognize that the investment in technology infrastructure necessary for higher education in the digital age not only will be comparable in expense to physical and human capital but will be pervasive and continually evolving throughout the institution.

We noted earlier that the IT infrastructure necessary to sustain university activities and administration is quite extensive, including not simply hardware (computers, networks) and software (operating systems, middleware, learningware, administration applications) but as well extensive human resources and skills (support and administration of IT systems). Just as with the organization and management of the university, we need to seek a layered or tiered architecture for digital technology that is characterized by a unified "back-end" or centralized infrastructure and diverse and flexible "front-end" applications. Modularity and tiering are the keys to effective technology acquisition and implementation strategies. Connectedness and interoperability are key criteria in IT infrastructure design.

Technology synergies must be achieved when the different technologies are combined. For example, we will need ubiquitous networking of voice, data, and video. We will need many layers of systems and facilitating applications, including fully integrated academic/administrative systems, client/server-based applications, object-oriented customer service systems, enhanced input/output capabilities, such as info kiosks, workstations, personal digital assistants, notebook computers, and knowledge navigators.

Part of the challenge is the accelerating pace of evolution of this technology and the difficulty in predicting its twists and turns and the next "killer app." For example, many universities were making major investments in minicomputers (PDPs, VAXs) in the early 1980s just as the personal computer appeared. The introduction of the network browser with the appearance of Mosaic in 1994 (and then Netscape and Internet Explorer) turned traditional enterprise systems on their head, demanding new Web-based services and e-commerce. If Bell Laboratories and others are successful in stimulating the transition from electronics to photonics and wireless technology, the massive investments that colleges and universities have made in networking infrastructure (their "wire plant") may rapidly become obsolete.

The same can be said for software evolution and administrative systems. Many universities have made massive investments in reengineering legacy administrative systems, in part to prepare for Y2K and in part to drive change in administrative processes. However, the promises of reengineering remain unrealized for many institutions. In many instances, large, expensive systems designed to institute change have been only partially implemented, often with less than expected results. Many institutions have moved on to enterprise systems implementations to integrate student, financial, and human resources systems that are an order of magnitude more expensive. All too often these centralized systems make the organization conform to technology rather than vice versa. They essentially force academic activities such as teaching and research to conform to business IT systems. While administrative systems such as enterprise resource planning (ERP), customer relationship management (CRM), and knowledge management systems (KMS) can be useful to the administrative side of the university, they can sometimes work at odds with the academic activities.

So, too, the changing nature of the core academic activities will demand changes in infrastructure. A new educational model is evolving to serve the needs of the digital age. Barriers to learning must be replaced with mechanisms to facilitate the new styles of learning for the digital age: open learning (open access), just-in-time learning, and just-for-you learning (unbundled, customized learning). In a world in which both the student body and the professorate become more and more mobile, telecommuting and telelearning, physical infrastructure, although still necessary, may decline in relative importance to robust network connectivity. Expensive research facilities will become increasingly shared resources rather than the responsibility of a single campus, but then requiring high-speed data links. Digital technology will not only facilitate but drive collaboration and hence alliances.

Recommendation 7: Getting from here to there requires a well-defined set of operational strategies and tactics aimed at institutional transformation.

We are in the very early stages of technology-driven tectonic shifts that will reshape our institutions and our enterprise. Although the university as a social institution has survived largely intact for over a millennium, it has done so in part because of its extraordinary ability to change and adapt to serve society. Beyond vision, organization, and investment, universities need a well-defined set of operational strategies and tactics. Technology-driven transformation should be viewed as steps up a ladder rather than down a road, since at each level a new set of challenges will arise. Timing and the pace of change are everything, since if these are incompatible with the capacity of the institution, strong resistance and possibly even chaos can be the consequences.

Change became the watchword in many sectors of our society during the late 20th century as globalization and rapidly changing market conditions required many companies—indeed, entire industries—to restructure themselves in order to survive. Costs were cut, quality was improved, and new management philosophies such as just-in-time production and customer relationship management became popular. We must take care, however, in simply assuming that the transformation strategies of the business world can be transferred directly to the university. As history has demonstrated, change in the university is rarely driven from within. After all, one of the missions of the university is to preserve time-honored values and traditions. So, too, tenured faculty appointments tend to protect the status quo, and the process of shared governance provides the faculty with a mechanism to block change. Most campus administrators tend to be cautious, rarely rocking the boat in the stormy seas driven by politics either on campus or beyond. Governing boards are all too frequently distracted from strategic issues in favor of personal interests or political agendas.

Earlier examples of change in American higher education, such as the evolution of the land-grant university, the growth of higher education following World War II, and the evolution of the research university, all represented reactions to major forces and policies at the national level. The examples of major institutional transformation driven by internal strategic decisions and plans from within are relatively rare. Change is a particular challenge to the public university, surrounded as it is by powerful political forces and public pressures that tend to be conservative and reactionary.

Of course, transforming an institution as complex as the university is neither linear nor predictable. Transformation is an iterative process, since as an institution proceeds, experience leads to learning that can modify the transformation process. Furthermore, a university must generally launch a broad array of initiatives in a variety of areas such as institutional culture, mission, finance, organization and governance, academic programs, and external relations, all of which interact with one another.

It is important to challenge an institution with high demands and expectations. However, leaders should also recognize that for most institutions the limiting factors will be the availability of human resources. Few among the faculty or administrative staff understand adequately the nature and implications of digital technology. There are even fewer capable of leading a process of change. While universities typically look to their IT organizations or libraries for such leadership, it is more likely to exist among the faculty, with those who have actually utilized state-of-the-art digital technology in the fundamental academic activities of the university, teaching and research.

There is another important constituency capable of driving change in the university: students. This should not be surprising to those familiar with the history of higher education, since students have frequently driven change in the university, ranging from the stimulation of new academic programs to its responsiveness to rapid social change. Furthermore, many students, particularly at the graduate level, drive much of the intellectual momentum of the university through their research activities. As we noted earlier, the plug-and-play generation is far more comfortable with digital technology than most of the current generation of university faculty and leaders. They not only are more adept in applying the technology to their own activities but frequently play key roles in its development (as the numerous IT start-ups led by undergraduate and graduate students make apparent). With technology, just as with other issues, students are likely to be a powerful force driving change in higher education.

Each of our colleges and universities will face different challenges and pursue different strategies during this period of change, and appropriately so. Small, private colleges and universities are likely to focus more on niche markets, determined by geography or academic interests or socioeconomic status. Elite research universities will first attempt to use their wealth—and fund-raising capacity—to build breakwaters against the crashing waves of market changes, buying time for more leisurely, although still inevitable, change. The large public universities will likely be the last to change, constrained by political and social pressures, and could well become like the dinosaurs, unable to adapt.

SOME RECOMMENDATIONS CONCERNING TACTICS

Campus Networking

The transformative power of information technology arises from both its pervasive nature and its ability to link together people, activities, and knowledge resources. Hence, the network becomes both the metaphor for the technology architecture of the contemporary university and the focus of most of its infrastructure investment. Both Internet access to off-campus resources and "intranet" capability to link students, faculty, and staff together are the highest priority. The key theme will be connectivity, essential to the formation and support of digitally mediated communities.

As with so many other aspects of digital technology, networking is best envisioned as a layered architecture. At the highest organizational level (and of primary concern to the central administration) is network connection to the Internet backbone through commercial telecommunications vendors and to higher education networks such as the Abilene network of the Internet2 project.[7] The wide area networks characterizing the campus environment require major attention and considerable investment. The variability in the technology needs of various academic and administrative units will generally require considerable diversity in local area networks, but great care should be taken to establish clear standards and protocols so that interoperability and robust connectivity are achieved. The final layer of networking is to the individual, or various applications, and this will increasingly be wireless, utilizing commercial technologies such as Wi-fi, G-3, and Bluetooth.

Although colleges and universities have traditionally focused on campus-based infrastructure, whether bricks or clicks, the availability of ubiquitous connectivity beyond the campus has become increasingly important since students, faculty, and staff will expect robust access to their colleagues, work, and play wherever they are, whether on campus, at home, or on the road. Universities are already straining to keep up with the connectivity demands of students. Today's undergraduates are already spending hours every day interacting with faculty, students, and home while accessing knowledge distributed about the world. Simply keeping pace with an adequate number of modem ports to meet the demands of off-campus students for access to campus-based resources and the Internet is overloading many universities. Many institutions have already given up on providing such access and instead depend upon local telecommunications providers such as DSL or cable networks to link the surrounding community with the campus. Since the quality of connectivity available both on campus and in the community will be an increasingly important factor in attracting high-quality students and faculty, universities need to play an active role in influencing the quality of networking in their surrounding environments.

Creative students will always find new ways to overload even the most carefully designed network. The experiences with Napster and streaming video make this all too apparent. Similar surprises can occur with faculty projects, such as the SETI (Search for Extraterrestrial Intelligence) Web site, which utilizes millions of personal computers to assist in the analysis of radio astronomy data to search for extraterrestrial intelligence and now consumes more than 25 percent of UC-Berkeley's bandwidth. At some point the capacity to invest in further bandwidth reaches its limits, and policies concerning network use become key.

Hardware

As digital technology becomes increasingly ubiquitous, universities will have to make intelligent decisions as to just what components they will provide and which should be the personal responsibility of students, faculty, and staff. While networks and specialized computing resources will remain the responsibility of the university, the purchase of other digital devices such as personal digital appliances will almost certainly be left to the individual.

There continues to be a debate about whether students should be required to purchase their own computers. Student experience with information technology is evolving rapidly. For example, in recent surveys the University of Michigan found that over 90 percent of its first-year students arrived on campus with at least three years of computer experience, and essentially all graduating seniors indicated that they made extensive use of computers during their education. Over 60 percent owned computers when they first arrived on campus, and a far higher percentage owned personal computers by the time of graduation. Our students currently spend about 12 to 14 hours a week on a computer, with roughly half of this on the Net. By way of comparison, faculty indicated that they spend about 20 hours a week working on computers; a significant fraction of this work was done at home. Over 90 percent of faculty own computers.[8]

The penetration of technology into the academic community will continue to change as the ever-evolving microchip and miniaturization shrink today's desktop or laptop computer to a personal digital appliance (e.g., a Palm or Net-enabled cellular phone) always on and always linked into the Net through wireless connectivity ("always-on" technology). These are likely to be the primary devices used by students in both their academic and personal activities. In the near term they may be supported by "docks" in their rooms or at university sites providing larger displays, mass storage, and other specialized functions. Within the decade, however, these links to the Net are likely to become ubiquitous, with human–machine interfaces provided by heads-up displays in glasses or direct retinal scans, coupled with voice and gesture recognition (thereby eliminating the keyboard and pointing devices such as the mouse). In a sense, today's personal computers and PDAs will merge with telephones, televisions, and radios into powerful digital appliances.

The principal university investment will be in the network and server infrastructure and wireless connectivity to support these Web-client digital devices, much in the way that most colleges and universities now install and support the wire plant and switches to support telephone connectivity. The availability of digital appliances will not eliminate entirely the need for physical sites where special-purpose computers are provided, for example, for scientific computation or software development or virtual reality simulations, but these will tend to be more discipline-specific rather than the general computer clusters dotting today's university campuses.

Universities will need to strive for synergies in the integration of various technologies. Beyond the merging of voice, data, and video networks, there will be possibilities as well to merge applications across areas such as instruction, administration, and research. The issue of financing will become significant as institutions seek a balance between institution-supported central services and point-of-access payments through technologies such as smart cards.

Universities should avoid hitching their wagons to a small set of vendors. As information technology becomes more of a commodity marketplace, new companies and equipment will continue to appear. The great diversity in needs of various parts of the university community also will demand a highly diverse technology infrastructure. Humanists will seek robust network access to digital libraries and graphics processing. Scientists and engineers will seek massively parallel processing. Social scientists will likely seek the capacity to manage massive databases, for example, data warehouses and data mining technology. Artists, architects, and musicians will require multimedia technology. Business and financial operations will seek fast data processing, robust communications, and exceptionally high security. And the list goes on.

Linking these complex, multivendor environments together will be a challenge, since they use different equipment for varying purposes and diverse software and operating systems. For this reason, it is important to insist on open-systems technology rather than relying on proprietary systems. Fortunately, most information technology has long since moved away from proprietary mainframe systems ("big iron"), to client-server systems and peer-to-peer networks based on standard operating systems such as Unix, Linux, or Windows.

Software, Systems, Applications, and Solutions

So, too, the days of universities' designing and developing most of their software applications for administrative or academic purposes have long since past. At the desktop level, most applications rely upon commercial products such as Microsoft Office or Adobe Photoshop, while the local networks rely on standard solutions such as Ethernet or Wi-fi. In a similar fashion, most academic functions increasingly rely on commercial software vendors to supply applications or, in some cases, entire solutions.

There is still a significant amount of customization in the development of enterprise-level administrative systems, generally outsourced from information services companies such as PeopleSoft, SAP, or Oracle. Even here, however, there are signs of change as an increasing number of institutions are choosing to outsource entirely administrative functions to a growing array of application services providers (ASPs), who actually run the necessary applications on their hardware and software systems.

An example of the new tools for management provided by information technology is knowledge management, the process of transforming information and intellectual assets into enduring value.[9] Although first developed in the business environment, knowledge management tools can also be used in universities not only for administrative services but also for knowledge about teaching and learning. It can lead to better decision-making capabilities, reduced producing development cycle time, and improved academic and administrative services and cost. For example, it could tap the knowledge possessed by individual faculty and staff, like the faculty member who has led a successful curriculum effort, a department secretary who knows how to navigate the complex proposal submission process, or the special assistant to the president who knows where all the useful reports are. The challenge is to convert the information that currently resides with those individuals and make it widely and easily available to any faculty member, staff person, or other constituent.

Financial Issues (Cost vs. Investment)

Most colleges and universities view the greatest challenge of information technology as its cost. However, as industry has learned, if one is able to reengineer activities to better take advantage of information technology, then not only significant increases in efficiency and quality but also economic benefits that can cover, at least in part, the costs of the technology are possible. Put another way, organizations have found that by reengineering work itself, they are able to recast expenditures on information technology as investments with high payoff in quality, efficiency, and avoided expense.

Distance learning provides an example. Information technology is the instrument that should enable higher education to push its boundaries to serve learners everywhere. Learners will access not only faculty who reside on their campus but faculty anywhere on the knowledge network. The greatest impact of the knowledge network approach will be the ability to reach learners in literally any location off-campus and at any time. This will increase the capacity of higher education to serve more learners—by an order of magnitude. This vision provides the promise of expanded opportunities for educators who are willing to develop new approaches to match the learning metaphors of the information age.

In tomorrow's learning and knowledge navigation network, institutions will serve not only traditional residential learners but also a heterogeneous assemblage of off-campus learners, researchers, and community problem solvers. The number of off-campus learners will begin to vastly outnumber on-campus learners. In the digital age, educators must discover ways to increase access to legions of perpetual learners, unbundling services so that learners pay only for what they use. They can also distribute campus-based learning services to expanded, parallel communities of learners (e.g., other colleges, K–12, businesses). Taken together, these approaches could dramatically increase higher education revenues, which can form the basis for the investment in technology necessary to achieve transformation.

E-learning will prompt new categories of costs, including infrastructure (bandwidth, facilities), equipment (computers, routers), software (operating systems, applications), student–faculty support (training help desks), and content (courseware development or acquisition). The search to do more with less will continue unfettered, so that colleges can aggressively pursue strategic opportunities in the midst of increasing competition. To accomplish these objectives, institutions increasingly will look to e-business applications to reduce administrative costs.

The business case for adopting an e-business strategy is compelling, and the urgency to do so will grow. Multiple vendors with a broad array of products will cause increased confusion as institutions determine whether to build or buy and compete or collaborate. The Internet will affect process, organization, and policies. It will raise a host of other new issues—tax, legal, security, and skills. Integrating information management will be a crucial challenge to enable institutions to leverage fully the benefits of doing business electronically.

It seems clear that technology will shift higher education's expenditure mix and change faculty roles and responsibilities, but will it actually reduce cost? Conventional wisdom inside the academy says no, but a good many outsiders are increasingly prone to say yes. The answer depends less on the nature of a particular technology than on the willingness of higher education to reengineer the fundamental processes characterizing teaching, scholarship, and administration. Historically, technology has been seen as a capital expenditure for universities or as an experimental tool to be made available to only a few. In the future, higher education should conceive of information technology both as an investment and as a strategic asset that will be used by the entire faculty, staff, and study body to sustain and enhance the mission of the university.

It is essential to integrate investments in information technology into the ongoing process, since otherwise it will just appear as a cost and not as an investment. One approach is to treat information technology as we do physical infrastructure, depreciating it as we would a building but on a much shorter timescale. Similar to physical infrastructure, some degree of central management is desirable rather than a totally decentralized approach requiring units to be responsible for their own IT infrastructure.

Of particular importance here are the IT professionals necessary to build and maintain sophisticated digital infrastructure. Top technical talent will require competitive compensation programs that set them apart from many other university staff. Universities may be required to set up new job classification schemes to recognize the competitive marketplace for IT professionals.

We can learn from the commercial sector in this regard. Most companies devote considerable attention and resources to training and personnel development. In contrast, most universities do not even take advantage of what they offer on campus, much less utilizing commercially available courses in areas such as networks and operating systems. Corporations have learned that poor IT implementation can lead to extinction in the private sector, where there is no safety net. It is not enough just to commit resources. You have to succeed.

Cultural Issues

Although information technology today is used primarily to augment and enrich traditional instructional offerings, over the longer term it will likely change the paradigms for learning and scholarship, and it will certainly change the relationship between faculty and staff and the university. For example, as the university is viewed increasingly as a "content provider," with the evolution of the commodity classroom, learningware, and the like, we will need to rethink issues such as ownership of faculty course materials.

As one example of this phenomenon, many students are already moving rapidly to embrace Net-based learning and take increasing control over their own education. They are still enrolling in traditional academic programs and participating in time-tested pedagogy such as lecture courses, homework assignments, and laboratory experiments, but many students approach learning in very different ways when they work on their own. They use the Net to become "open learners," accessing worldwide resources and Net-based communities of utility to their own learning objectives.

Today's students are technologically savvy and proficient. They have grown up accustomed to automated teller machines, MP3 players, next-day delivery, and the Internet. They are able to procure books, CDs, and even term papers over the Web and increasingly expect the same type of instant fulfillment of needs and wants. Queues on campus for course registration, feedback from advisers, financial aid decisions, degree audits, and other services will be met with disdain and vocal dissatisfaction. Similarly, just like the services that they are able to receive from other Web-based companies, students and faculty increasingly will expect services to be available on a 24/7 basis and to be personalized to their needs and interests. As in other industries, only the Web and associated e-business applications can provide this functionality for colleges.

The culture and character of the faculty pose a particular challenge. One measure of the fluidity of an institution is the average time it takes to get a 50 percent turnover in personnel. For a high-tech firm, this duration may be only six months, but for a university with its tenure system, it is closer to 20 years! Part of the challenge is the transient nature of digital technology. In part this is simply due to the short half-life characterizing its exponential evolution. When a given piece of hardware or software is likely to remain viable for only a few years or less, faculty are reluctant to invest the time necessary to learn how to use and exploit it in their academic activities. Similarly, the interest of academic leaders in information technology tends to fluctuate with each appointment of a chair, dean, provost, or president. When faculty see the pendulum swinging, little wonder that many decide to wait—this, too, shall pass. Developing, sustaining, and institutionalizing a university technology strategy that aligns with the decentralized nature of the academic culture are major challenges.

Policies and Practices

Universities will face a considerable challenge in retaining instructional mind-share among their best-known faculty. We have long since adapted to the reality of those faculty members negotiating very substantial freedom and perhaps even release time from teaching as a consequence of their success in generating research grants, yet few institutions have developed policies and practices to address the growing commercial value of instructional content, particularly in digital form. Universities are responding to the new opportunities available to celebrity faculty by enacting and/or enforcing various policies directed at restricting the faculty's ability to contract with outside organizations in the instructional arena, yet such policies may be self-defeating, since they could well drive professors to other institutions with more flexible policies.

One of the most hazardous policy minefields, both for institutions and for individuals, involves the ownership of course materials or perhaps even courses themselves. There has been a long-standing tradition in higher education that in contrast to research, where university ownership of intellectual property is well established, the intellectual property associated with teaching is owned by the professor. Faculty members have long been able to publish textbooks or other materials based on their teaching activities. In fact, some faculty members with popular textbooks in high-enrollment courses such as introductory economics or mathematics have become millionaires from publishing royalties. Some professors would even maintain that they have control amounting to effective ownership of their course itself (particularly when they have taught the same course for many years in a row).

Today, however, information technology threatens to disrupt this long-standing practice. Some fear the image of celebrity professors selling their courses to the highest bidder, even if this is a for-profit, on-line dot-com competing directly with their host institution. Others are concerned about entrepreneurial faculty launching their own for-profit venture based on their instructional activities within the university. Still others seek ways that the universities can capture and profit from the intellectual property produced by their faculties in instructional activities just as they have through commercializing the products of research.

Surveys of those academic leaders, however, suggest more pragmatism.[10] Few believe that on-line courses and course materials will become a gold mine (although institutions with established brand names such as the Harvard Business School may be an exception). They are also skeptical that universities are sophisticated or flexible enough in business ventures to compete with commercial vendors such as publishers or dot-coms in the development, marketing, or distribution of learningware. In fact the real dispute may be less over control of valuable resources than a growing concern about the evolution of the teaching mission and objectives of universities in the digital age.

There are several approaches that universities can take to policy in this area. They can assert ownership over the copyrightable works of the faculty, citing the agency principles of works made for hire. They can allow faculty members to continue to assert ownership over their copyrightable works. They can attempt to allocate ownership via contract. They can simply place all instructional content in the public domain, much in the spirit of open source software development (à la Linux or MIT's Open Courseware project).

If we recognize the importance of encouraging faculty participation in the development and delivery of technology-based instruction, then it becomes clear that institutions should proceed cautiously in asserting ownership, especially when previous policy or practice has been to the contrary. Probably one of the most demoralizing things that an institution could do would be to change the intellectual property ownership by saying, "We used to let you own your course materials, but that was before there was money to be made off them. Now *we* will own everything!" Of course, if the institution has made a substantial contribution to the creation of course materials, it may want to hold on to those rights that it needs in order to preserve the integrity of their instructional programs.

All institutions need to have a framework for thinking through these issues and the implications of the electronic revolution for their institutions and faculty. Having a framework for discussion and decision making is quite different from writing elaborate policies. Our experience suggests that the default position for all institutions should be that the faculty member owns the course materials that he or she has created. Rather than trying to anticipate all the possible exceptions and include them in a policy, one might include trigger mechanisms; for example, if course materials are commercialized by someone other than the university and actually make money, the university should get a small cut (5 percent). Who commercializes the products—who markets and distributes them—is a critical issue.

LONGER-TERM STRATEGIC ISSUES

Although we recognize the hazards in speculating about the longer-term future, say a decade and beyond, even a highly speculative exercise can be useful in providing the framework for near-term strategies.

Assumptions for the Longer Term

To this end, we base our further discussion on the following assumptions:

- Information and communication will continue to evolve exponentially over the next several decades (perhaps even superexponentially), evolving from giga, to tera, to peta, to exo, to yetta, and beyond.
- Digital technology will provide the primary interface for human interaction with one another, with our environment, and with our various activities such as learning, work, and play.
- The human–machine interface will evolve rapidly, with immersive telepresence, artificial intelligence, and neural implants.
- Knowledge media will change the relationship between people and knowledge. (Here knowledge media are the convergence of computing, telecommunications, and the cognitive sciences.)
- Education will become the key strategic issue for a knowledge-based society.

Strategic Planning for the Longer Term

Although difficult and speculative, we simply must consider longer-term institutional strategies that at least are influenced by the potential developments in information technology. Traditional planning simply does not work in times of great change. One of the false assumptions plaguing traditional strategic planning is that the future can be forecast based on current climatic conditions in the environment. Part of the problem is that "discontinuities" like technological innovations make forecasting practically impossible, and discontinuity is the primary characteristic of the digital technology-driven environment. The current batch of new technologies, including the global computing network, inexpensive, high-speed data transmission and storage, wireless mobility, and a revolution of new software interfaces, is sending shock waves into the information component of every endeavor. The effects cannot be easily predicted or systematically addressed—not, in any case, by the traditional methods of planning. Executives in industries as varied as manufacturing, retailing, and services tell us that their basic assumptions about products, channels, and customers will be completely changed by digital technology in the next several years, perhaps more than once—even if they don't know exactly how.

The new planning horizon is now closer to 12 to 18 months, and as Moore's law continues its superexponential journey, it is a vanishing horizon at that. This acceleration means less time to respond and therefore less time for analysis or detailed planning. Managers, executives, and entrepreneurs are increasingly embracing the prospect of implementing strategy well before it is entirely thought through or before a detailed business case can be developed, in part because of the shrinking window of opportunity.

How might we approach planning for such an uncertain future? First, we have to understand that the real impact of digital technology is on basic human processes such as work, play, learning, collaboration, and decision making. Hence, as the technology evolves from giga, to tera, to peta, to exo, and beyond, we need to keep an eye out for applications that could really unravel our existing structures for human activities. For example, if microcommerce and auctioning for transactions in the fractions of a cent really evolve, then pay-for-bit knowledge resources might replace the current fair-use practices. As the plug-and-play generation continues to embrace and push the technology, do we run the risk that their elders will be forced to become plug-and-pray users? What Amazon.com commercial entities might evolve in a world in which information and communications technology is a million or a billion times more powerful, with intelligent microsensors "on every cockroach," real artificial intelligence, and ubiquitous nanotechnology?

The Long-Term Objective: Institutional Survival

The opportunities and threats presented by information technology preclude the option of waiting for the technologies to mature and the implications to become discernible. The rising popularity of the Internet, increasingly demanding customers and unrelenting expectations for expedited services, continuing cost constraints, and emerging opportunities for new revenues will compel universities to adopt an e-business strategy. Failure to provide e-business functionality will result in competitive disadvantages for institutions.

With only slight exaggeration, it might be possible to assert that the only parts of the traditional educational programs of the university (apart from doctoral training of the next generation of faculty and other advanced degrees) that would be untouched by private sector competition would be the residential 18–22-year-old market because of its capital-intensive nature and its focus on both the intellectual development and socialization of young adults. This seems large now, but how big will that market be when students can choose among a full range of alternatives covering a spectrum of prices? Indeed, such an education may become a luxury good for the richest class of society.

This implies that universities should attach a great urgency to debates about their future. Rather than sitting back and observing how the market develops, university presidents and administrators should be proactively determining the future of the institutions. Otherwise, they will be condemned to be the bystanders that get swept away in the tides of change. The future of the university may well depend upon an early commitment to enter many of the new market opportunities that are today opening the floodgates of private sector attention and capital. The biggest sin that universities can commit today is of omission, not of commission.

A WORD ABOUT LEADERSHIP

Looking across the landscape of higher education, one finds that leadership in the application of digital technology in colleges and universities tends to vary considerably, both among institutions and with respect to time. The leadership provided by a particular institution may last only a few brief years before being overtaken by others. It is surprising how little stability there is in an institution's standing in the use of technology. Unlike other measures such as academic reputation, things can change very fast in a very short time.

To some degree, the rapid evolution and obsolescence of the technology drive some of this fluctuation, but institutional leadership in information technology also appears to depend significantly on executive leadership. Of course, other key academic leaders such as deans or provosts can create pockets of innovation within a given institution. Generally, however, the unusual interest or commitment of the campus chief executive officer drives institutional leadership in this area. In contrast to most academic activities that are bottom-up in nature, surf riding the information technology wave appears to require institutional strategies emanating directly from the office of the president.

Here it is important to stress that leadership comes in many guises and is not necessarily the preserve of the elite research universities. For example, several community colleges and regional universities have provided leadership in the use of on-line distance learning to reach new student populations commensurate with their outreach mission. Some liberal arts colleges have demonstrated considerable leadership in the application of information technology to undergraduate education. These successes illustrate yet again the importance of aligning technology strategies with other institutional goals.

Some institutions are wealthy enough that they can pursue a "close follower" strategy, watching carefully and following closely on the footsteps of those attempting to blaze new trails with digital technology. Others have yet to see the imperatives for technology investments and are unlikely to climb the learning curve necessary to take advantage of the opportunities offered by information technology. They could well be left behind as higher education evolves into a component of a global knowledge and learning industry.

Why should a college or university want to be perceived as a leader in the exploitation of such an expensive and rapidly changing technology? After all, leadership does engender certain risks. However, leadership attracts outstanding students, faculty, and staff seeking technology-intensive environments for learning and research. Leadership can also attract significant resources from both public and private sources, necessary to sustain such environments.

NOTES

1. Mohan Sawney, *Seven Steps to Nirvana: E-Business Transformation* (Cambridge: Harvard Business School Press, 2000).

2. "Convocation on Stresses on Research and Education at Colleges and Universities" (Government-University-Industry Research Roundtable and National Science Board. Washington, DC: National Academy of Sciences, 1997), <http://www2.nas.edu/guirrcon/>.

3. The endowments of elite institutions such as Harvard, Yale, and Stanford have soared to $10 billion to $20 billion, invested in a range of activities from off-shore oil wells to Las Vegas casinos.

4. James Roche, "Checking the Radar: Survey Identifies Key IT Issues," *Educom Quarterly*, no. 2 (2000), 4–16.

5. Why seven? Beyond the fact that our culture is filled with numerous examples of seven steps to one objective or another (e.g., weight loss, profit, or even nirvana), it is also the case that psychologists tell us that seven is the maximum number of points that most people can remember.

6. Clayton M. Christensen, *The Innovator's Dilemma* (Cambridge: Harvard Business School Press, 1997).

7. For information concerning the Internet2 project, see the Web site for the University Corporation for the Advancement of Internet Development at <http://www.internet2.edu>.

8. Student-Faculty Computer Survey, Information Technology Division, University of Michigan, Ann Arbor, 1997.

9. Gerald Bernbom, ed., *Information Alchemy: The Art and Science of Knowledge Management*, Educom Leadership Strategy Series 3 (San Francisco: Jossey-Bass, 2000).

10. Carol Twigg, "Who Owns Online Courses and Course Materials?" Pew Learning and Technology Program <http://www.center.rpi.edu/PewSym/mono2.html>.

CHAPTER

Responding to Market Forces

We now turn our attention from institutional strategies to a series of recommendations concerning the evolution of the higher education enterprise. We noted earlier the array of economic, social, and technological forces driving change in our world, in many cases manifested in the appearance of powerful market forces. As each wave of transformation sweeps through our economy and our society, with an ever more rapid tempo, the existing infrastructure of educational institutions, programs, and policies becomes more outdated and perhaps even obsolete. While the pervasive need for advanced education dictated by the high-performance workforce has expanded significantly the student population, it has also transformed it significantly in character and need. While young adults continue to seek the experience of intellectual maturation and socialization associated with undergraduate education, their numbers are now exceeded by working adults seeking knowledge and skills of direct relevance to careers and expecting professional, businesslike relationships with learning institutions. For these learners, convenience and cost-effectiveness have become comparable to academic quality and institutional reputation in importance. They demand that institutions focus on providing educational services that meet their needs, rather than stressing the scholarly achievement of faculty, providing public services such as health care or entertainment (intercollegiate athletics), or building institutional prestige (brand name).

Even within the traditional higher education enterprise, there is a sense that the arms race is escalating, as institutions compete ever more aggressively for better students, better faculty, government grants, private gifts, prestige, and winning athletic programs. Beyond this is growing competition from beyond the campuses from for-profit universities, publishers, information services companies, and other emerging educational services providers. These market forces are fueled not only by the growing and changing educational needs of a knowledge-based society but as well by emerging digital technologies that are rapidly restructuring the competitive landscape.

Beyond the traditional institutions, the postsecondary enterprise of tomorrow will also contain computer hardware and software companies, telecommunications carriers, information services companies, entertainment companies, information resource organizations, and corporate and governmental educational organizations. Furthermore, new competitors are appearing that attempt to capitalize on emerging technologies to exploit the profit potential of some elements of higher education such as executive business education. Nontraditional consumers of educational services such as working adults, corporations, and government agencies are increasingly price-sensitive and place more value on the acquisition of demonstrated skills than brand-name association. Faculty members, as the key sources of intellectual content in both instruction and research, increasingly view themselves as independent contractors and entrepreneurs, seeking ownership and personal financial gain. Furthermore, faculty loyalty will increasingly be to scholarly communities distributed through cyberspace rather than campus communities and institutions.

Regardless of who or what drives change, the higher education enterprise is likely to be dramatically transformed over the next decade.[1] It could happen from within, in an effort to respond to growing societal needs and limited resources, but it is more likely to be transformed by new markets, new technologies, and new competition. In this rapidly evolving knowledge business, the institutions most at risk will not be of any particular type or size but rather those most constrained by tradition, culture, or governance.

With the emergence of new competitive forces and the weakening influence of traditional regulations, education is evolving like other "deregulated" industries, for example, health care, communications, and energy. In contrast to these other industries, which have been restructured as government regulation has disappeared, the global knowledge industry will be unleashed by emerging information technology as it releases education from the constraints of space, time, and the credentialing monopoly. As our society becomes ever more dependent upon new knowledge and educated people, upon knowledge workers, this global knowledge business will represent one of the most active growth industries of our times.[2]

Today it is estimated that higher education represents roughly $237 billion of the $740 billion education market in the United States,[3] but even these markets are dwarfed by the size of the "knowledge and learning" marketplace, estimated in excess of $2.2 trillion. Furthermore, with the current population of 84 million students enrolled in higher education worldwide estimated to double over the next two decades, the size of the global marketplace is considerably larger.

Little wonder that many believe that the market forces created by the workforce skills needs of a knowledge economy and driven by new competitors and technologies will present a formidable challenge to existing colleges and universities. Although the expanding educational needs of a growing population, the high-performance workplace, and developing nations will sustain the size of the market served by the traditional higher education, this market share is almost certain to decline as new, technology-based competitors appear to serve new educational markets.

How should traditional colleges and universities approach the challenges and opportunities presented by an evolving postsecondary education market? Should they remain focused on their traditional roles and clients, allowing new competitors to serve the growing marketplace of nontraditional students and educational/knowledge needs without challenge? Should they develop the capacity to serve these new and growing needs of a knowledge-intensive society? Where would the resources come from to support such an expansion of educational missions? Students? Taxpayers? Corporate clients? Perhaps of even more immediate concern, how can colleges and universities cope with the potential erosion of revenue from high profit-margin activities such as general education and professional education that appear to be the early targets of for-profit competitors?

More generally, how can conventional academic institutions accommodate the likely evolution and integration of education into a global knowledge and learning industry? Should universities seek to establish their traditional academic activities as sufficiently world-class to be competitive in this global marketplace, or should they outsource world-class services provided by other institutions to their regional market and instead focus on homegrown educational products designed for local markets? How important will reputational characteristics such as prestige or brand name be in such a global marketplace? Clearly, there will not be a single best educational approach that works for all institutions. The diverse nature of learning and learners will provide many opportunities for differentiation.

In fact, one of the advantages of information and communications technology is that it facilitates a greater diversity of learning opportunities.

This chapter focuses on a series of recommendations concerning market issues for colleges and universities—as individual institutions, as associations, and possibly as new forms of alliances. In effect, we discuss business strategies for higher education in the digital age.

A GLOBAL KNOWLEDGE
AND LEARNING INDUSTRY, REVISITED

Our colleges and universities are in the very early stages of technology-driven transformations that will reshape both our institutions and the broader higher education enterprise. Although the university as a social institution has survived largely intact for over a millennium, it has done so in part because of an extraordinary ability to change and adapt to serve a changing world. Change in higher education is frequently difficult to perceive and certainly occurs at a different pace than in industry or government, yet the remarkable diversity that we see today among institutions—from small liberal arts colleges, to gigantic university systems and from proprietary colleges, to global "cyberspace" universities—demonstrates both the survival and evolution of the species as well as how profound change in higher education can become.

From a broader perspective, we can see the rapid evolution of a global knowledge and learning industry as a continuation of an ever-expanding role and presence of the university during the past century. From the commitment to universal access to higher education after World War II, to the concern about cost and efficiency in the 1980s, to the economic role of the university in a knowledge-driven society, there have been both a growth in the number and complexity of the missions of the university and the entry into postsecondary education of new players and competitors. Today we think of the postsecondary education industry as consisting of a core of research, doctoral, and comprehensive institutions; four-year colleges; two-year colleges; proprietary institutions; and professional and specialized institutions. This core is supported, sustained, and augmented by an array of external players, including state and federal government, business and industry, and foundations. The traditional postsecondary institutions will be joined at the core of the emerging knowledge and learning industry by new players: telecommunications companies, entertainment companies, information technology companies, information service providers, and corporate and governmental education providers.[4]

At the top of the food chain are the elite research universities, the Harvards and the Stanfords, the UC–Berkeleys and the Michigans, that provide an intellectually rich—and economically very expensive—educational experience to a relatively small number of students. For example, even a large university such as UC–Berkeley enrolls fewer than 30,000 students compared to the 260,000 enrolled in the California State University System. Harvard and Stanford enroll even fewer, about 10,000 each. The elite liberal arts colleges such as Amherst and Oberlin are even more focused, with only about 2,000 students participating in their faculty-intensive residential campus experience.

At the other extreme are adult education institutions such as the University of Phoenix and the British Open University that use a combination of standardized regional centers and on-line technology to reach hundreds of thousands of students. Addressing the educational needs of even larger numbers are the systems of regional state universities and community colleges. Although these institutions do not provide the rich educational experience of a residential campus with low student-to-faculty ratios—indeed, most of their students are commuters, and many are part-time with full-time jobs—they do educate the bulk of the roughly 14 million students enrolled in higher education programs in the United States.

In understanding how these diverse institutions relate to the higher education marketplace, it is important to keep several points in mind. First, most younger students tend to pay for the credential of a college degree rather than for an educational experience, since they perceive this to be the ticket to satisfying and well-compensated careers. Furthermore, for those who can afford it, the prestige of a college or university is usually viewed as more important than the quality of the educational experience that they will receive in its academic programs. Of course, university brand names have long been important because of the social networks based upon college and alumni experiences. Branding has become even more important in recent years as federal funding and private giving have become increasingly correlated with faculty reputation, and as the college ratings provided by publications such as *U.S. News and World Report* have established the rankings of various institutions firmly in the minds of the marketplace.

One of our colleagues refers to the past several decades as the "Harvardization" of higher education in America, in which our colleges and universities, whether large research universities or small community colleges, aspired to emulate elite universities such as Harvard. This elitist model was reinforced by national priorities such as the space race of the 1960s, which focused attention on educating "the best and the brightest" to be leaders in our society. Today, as we enter an age of knowledge in which the learning and skills of the broader workforce have become key to our national prosperity, security, and social well-being, such an elitist model that aims at spending more and more on fewer and fewer, whether students or faculty, seems increasingly incongruent with our national needs. Competing for the gold standard of elite education will become a less attractive course for market-driven institutions.

Rather, the premium will be on the development of unique missions for each of our institutions, missions that reflect not only their tradition and their unique roles in serving society but as well their core competence. As industry has learned, in an increasingly competitive global marketplace, you have to focus on what you can do best, where you are truly world-class, and outsource other products and services.

This will require not only that each of our colleges and universities develop a unique vision but, beyond that, that they be prepared to focus resources to achieve it. They must be prepared to shift resources when necessary, possibly reducing or even eliminating some programs and activities in order to improve or initiate others. In such decisions, they must keep in mind the important criteria of quality, centrality, and cost-effectiveness.

Which institutions are most vulnerable to intensifying market forces and emerging competition? Some suspect that small, underfunded private colleges face the most risk. So, too, regional public colleges and universities that ignore their original mission and instead attempt to add expensive new research, graduate, or professional programs could find themselves overextended and vulnerable to the marketplace. There is a general assumption that least vulnerable will be the best-known and best-endowed universities, inoculated against emerging competition by prestige and wealth.

However, there will be winners and losers in all ranks. There is ample evidence that strong leadership, vision, and a willingness to change can produce winning strategies for any type of institution, whether it be a local community college, a small, private, liberal arts college, a regional university, or a major research university. It is also the case that sooner or later, even the wealthiest brand-name institutions will be at significant risk from market competition if they are without a strategy and an ability to change.

For the most expensive institutions, the early impact could well be price pressures. For all but the most elite institutions (the most prominent brand names), the cost pressure imposed by comparisons of student tuition rates could be enormous. How can a family justify spending $20,000 to $30,000 per year on tuition when a new entrant may be able to provide academic offerings of comparative quality at $5,000 to $10,000, based on actual measurement and comparison of student learning achievements? Similarly, public officials and politicians will also become conscious of such comparisons during a time when state and federal budgets are under increasing pressure from limited revenues and competing public priorities such as health care, corrections, and K–12 education. Already we see some states beginning to question the need to invest in more campus-based facilities when distance learning may provide lower-cost alternatives.

Perhaps even more immediate will be significant price competition from new competitors in low-cost, high profit-margin academic programs such as business education and general education. Technology-intensive, for-profit competitors such as Jones International University and Unext.com initially target business education for adults in the workplace because these are frequently subsidized by employers, and on-line education can offer significant cost savings by eliminating travel and time-off-job expenses. As experience is gained in these on-line programs, it is logical to expect them to compete more directly with established business schools both for degree programs and for executive education. Moving further up the learning curve, several for-profit competitors have already announced their intention to enter the general education market, which is also characterized by relatively low instructional costs and large student populations.

The most significant impact of the Net, of computer-mediated learning, will be to break apart this monolithic nature of the university, much as other industries have been broken apart through deregulation. As universities are forced to evolve from "faculty-centered" to "student-centered," they may well find it necessary to unbundle their many functions, ranging from admissions and counseling, to instruction, and to certification.

Over the longer term, there may be erosion in universities' monopolistic claim on the teaching franchise, currently sustained by regional accrediting associations and empowered by state and federal government. As Dolence and Norris suggest, computer networks are likely to enable a transition to a learning franchise characterized by access to powerful learning systems, information and knowledge bases, scholarly exchange networks, or other mechanisms for the delivery of learning.[5] Learning modules and systems are open to anyone who wishes to access them and has the resources to compensate the provider. Measurement and certification of mastery will remain important for many learners, but they will be separable from the learning franchise. An array of organizations is positioned to vie for the learning franchise—institutions of higher education, corporations, technology companies, for-profit educational enterprises, and research laboratories. New strategic alliances and commercial ventures will be formed to tap these potentials.

Electronic classrooms, information networks, on-line learning, continuing education, and contract learning are examples of higher education's increasing commitment to distributed education. The sort of learning that goes on the Net outside classrooms with no one in charge but the learner is closer to what has been called "open learning."[6] Open learning advocates seek to bring down barriers that prevent learners from taking charge of their own learning as much as possible. Unlike on-line learning, the promotion of open learning cannot be taken as primarily a technological issue. Institutions will have to cede significant amounts of control if learners are to actively take charge of their own learning.

MARKET STRATEGIES

What are the options available to traditional colleges and universities to respond to the changing marketplace for educational services?

Stay the Course: Some of the most elite institutions may adopt a strategy of relying on their prestige and their prosperity to isolate themselves from change, to continue to do just what they have done in the past, and to be comfortable with their roles as niche players in the higher education enterprise, but for most of the larger and comprehensive institutions, the activities of elite education and basic research are simply too expensive to sustain without some attention to sustaining the cross-subsidies determined by the marketplace.

Dabbling: Some institutions may choose to track the evolution of technology-intensive education by mounting limited experiments in on-line learning, without major investment or commitment. Although such efforts are unlikely to create significant risks—or identify significant opportunities, for that matter—they do provide some direct experience in distributed learning. Indeed, one might make the case that all colleges and universities should experiment sufficiently with technology-based education to learn its potentials and limitations.

Alliances: Extending this role somewhat, colleges and universities might enter into alliances with other types of educational institutions or even newly emerging competitors such as for-profit or cyberspace universities. For example, a university might retain most of its traditional activities while selectively including its on-line courses and other on-line educational offerings under the umbrella of a virtual university, such as an open university operated by a state's university system or some other profit or nonprofit broker. One could also imagine forming alliances with organizations outside higher education, for example, information technology, telecommunications, or entertainment companies, information services providers, or even government agencies. We return later in this chapter to discuss alliance strategies.

Pathfinders: Although some universities may conclude that it would be inappropriate to launch major technology-based distributed learning efforts, they may encourage their faculty to become involved in developing the templates, or paradigms that others could use. It is clear that there are significant research opportunities in the areas of technology-assisted learning and distributed learning systems. To play this role, the universities should be prepared to participate in experiments in creating possible futures for higher education.

Whole Hog: Some universities will conclude that a major effort in technology-based distributed learning is consistent with their missions. Building on existing academic programs and strengths, they will build national and perhaps global distributed learning programs, aggressively targeting new markets while perhaps modifying significantly both the nature and extent of their traditional on-campus activities.

Clearly, colleges and universities should play to their strengths as they approach the challenges and opportunities of technology-based distributed learning. The capabilities of the faculty and student body; the vast physical, financial, and intellectual resources; and the reputation of major research universities represent very considerable assets in competing for the new educational markets opened by communications and information technology. Many public universities already have both a mission and a culture supportive of off-campus activities, particularly land-grant institutions with decades of experience in sophisticated extension activities in agriculture, industrial development, and adult education.

Ironically, even as digital technology enables a rapid expansion of educational opportunities through distributed learning, the value of a traditional, campus-based liberal arts degree may become more apparent in comparison with cyberlearning, particularly for young college students. By stressing the value of this form of education, perhaps even augmented with faculty-intensive activities such as tutorial systems or student living-learning environments, some colleges and universities may be able to solidify and sustain their efforts in traditional, campus-based education. This is a likely strategy not only for many liberal arts colleges but perhaps also for those research universities characterized by strong undergraduate colleges.

However, other institutions without strong traditions in residential, campus-based education will have little choice but to develop the capacity for technology-based distributed learning in an effort to retain market share.

This is likely to be the case for most regional universities and community colleges, already heavily engaged in adult education, since these compete most directly with emerging for-profit providers such as the University of Phoenix.

Characteristics

As they develop strategies for technology-intensive distributed learning, institutions should bear in mind that designing, developing, and deploying effective on-line learning systems are both difficult and expensive. Most efforts to date have simply repackaged the traditional lecture/course notes format of the classroom for distribution over computer networks (a "talking heads" format), yet effective distributed learning will require reconceptualizing the learning experience, taking advantage of the unique features of digital communications.

Properly implemented, on-line learning has the potential for very significant advantages beyond that of distance-independence. It allows 24/7 access to students, although if poorly designed, it can also place unrealistic time burdens on faculty. It facilitates the repackaging of learning experiences to better align with the learning needs of the students ("just-in-time" and "just-for-me"), particularly when combined with interactive Web portal or database technology that adapts both content and the learning environment to the characteristics of each particular student. On-line learning allows sophisticated knowledge management systems capable of tracking student progress and supporting administrative functions such as student records and tuition payments. If designed appropriately, on-line learning systems should be capable of scaling to large student populations, thereby holding the promise of significant cost savings, at least for certain academic programs.

Diversification and Specialization

Although eventually all colleges and universities will undergo a profound transformation primarily as a consequence of the quickly evolving information and communication technologies, this does not necessarily imply the disappearance of site-specific educational venues. Although significant components of the curriculum will be reaggregated to form a centralized content-producing and widely based distribution network, there will continue to be considerable diversity in how these resources are utilized and augmented at the campus level.

One result of this intense competition associated with a restructured postsecondary marketplace could be not only harder times for institutions of higher education but also the potential unraveling of the traditional, vertically integrated, full product-range university. In its place one could imagine the university as a smaller, more specialized provider of a limited set of educational programs, probably based around a three-year residential liberal arts degree that socializes students and teaches them how to learn but does not dispense a particular body of knowledge that is expected to satisfy their need for life.

We are already beginning to see signs of market segmentation that will reverse the past several decades of homogeneity in higher education as colleges and universities recognize the importance of focusing on particular markets. Some will continue to emphasize campus-based undergraduate education for recent high school graduates. Research universities may find their competitive strengths in graduate and professional education, particularly in a global marketplace. Some institutions, particularly in the commercial sector, will focus on the rapidly growing population of adult learners attempting to adapt to the high-performance workplace. Some will become more regional in focus, while others may attempt to develop national or global markets.

The Tolerance for Risk

As we noted earlier, the rapid and disruptive evolution of digital technology tends to make prediction a hazardous exercise. Speculation about the evolution of this technology and its impact on our society is notorious for its inaccuracy. We tend to overestimate the near term and seriously underestimate the long term. Hence, it seems useful to conclude this chapter with several caveats.[7]

As the financial collapse of the dot-coms in 2000 illustrated, the potential market for Internet-based commodities is frequently exaggerated. Such is almost certainly the case for the various estimates of the market for distributed learning, at least for the near term. Furthermore, to paraphrase Mark Twain rather than Peter Drucker, the demise of the residential campus is also exaggerated. Campus-based education within the traditional college curriculum and lecture format has proven to be a highly effective mechanism for transforming young adults into valuable citizens. To be sure, should the cost of this form of education continue its upward spiral, other less costly alternatives such as commuter education and online learning will become more attractive alternatives, but the expanding population of young adults makes it highly likely that the market for campus-based education will continue to be robust.

Although many colleges and universities are experimenting with technology-based learning, it is highly unlikely that most will find it cost-effective to develop their own distributed learning environments. The cost and complexity of such systems, coupled with the intense competition from the commercial sector, will demand alliances. Many universities will simply turn to application service providers (ASPs) to outsource complete distributed learning solutions, including network operations, software, E-mail services, database services, and administrative and instructional services. Moreover, the learner-centered, commodity nature of effective distributed learning solutions will likely conflict with traditional faculty culture (faculty control of classroom content and curriculum, faculty governance, tenure) and may require the creation of new learning organizations external to the university. These will also require quite different forms of faculty incentives and compensation, more akin to the medical practice plans of university medical centers.

MANAGEMENT OF INTELLECTUAL CONTENT

Knowledge is increasingly being not only distributed and archived in digital form but actually created in this form. Although we tend to think first of scientific data such as the capture of astronomical data on photon detectors or the genomics of the human DNA, in reality, most creative work in the arts and humanities rapidly acquires a digital form (e.g., through word processors, digital photography, or video). Furthermore, this digital knowledge has increasing value in the commercial marketplace, as the dot-com spin-offs of Silicon Valley or the patents on genetically engineered biological materials make apparent. Digital technology has played an important role in coupling the university to the commercial marketplace as a source of valuable digital knowledge. How should the university view this role? As a public good and public responsibility? Or as commercial business of great value?

Universities and academic scholars in many fields have come increasingly to think of products of all of their activities as "intellectual property," to be developed and protected rather than shared. This shift has resulted in part from changes in patent and copyright laws.[1] These changes have been accompanied by industry's growing reliance on academic research and rapidly expanding federal research investments in areas that have strong interest for the private sector (such as biomedical research and computer science). University technology transfer offices work actively to encourage faculty to patent significant results, so that the institutions and researchers may share the stream of royalties that result from licensing the patents to companies. Academic research is growing more competitive generally.

The latter approach has been endorsed and stimulated by federal policies such as the Bayh-Dole Act of 1980, which allows universities to retain the ownership of commercially valuable intellectual property produced in government-sponsored research. Many universities have sophisticated technology transfer offices to identify, protect, patent, license, and perhaps even spin off commercially valuable products and companies, yet digital technology has challenged this conventional approach through "killer applications" such as Napster through which enterprising students are forcing the commercial recording industry to restructure itself by creating a "virtual commons" in cyberspace for the swapping of digital recordings, without compensation. Although this particular activity has been slowed by federal court decisions, it represents only an early example of the "open source movement" in which digital products such as the Linux operating system are created and distributed entirely in the public domain. Clearly, there is a contradiction between the open source peer-to-peer approach of Napster and Linux and the "pay-for-bit" approach of most university intellectual policies.

There is considerable uncertainty concerning just how universities should approach the commercialization of the intellectual property associated with higher education. What is most problematic for the research university is how to develop and exploit commercial courseware in ways that are consistent with faculty ownership of the curriculum and how to venture outside the boundaries of the institution, either to make money, expand access, or control cost. How can universities get into the mass market for courseware within the constraints of their own values and structures? The answer may lie in three directions: the creation of new structures—schools, institutes, and the like—whose mission is to project the university's resources beyond its boundaries for a price; the use of the university's own extension service to perform the same functions; and the development of partnerships with other institutions.

Although many faculty members will be uncomfortable with university efforts to respond to (or resist) the market pressures of technology-based distributed learning, others will seek to participate, either through their institution's efforts or with external organizations. We noted earlier that this will demand a serious review not only of intellectual properties policies but as well the nature of faculty contracts. Rather than the university seeking total possession of the intellectual activities of faculty, perhaps it should rather be content with purchasing only a piece of their effort, while providing a platform for activities outside the university (much as in the world of classical music, a famous maestro can serve as the conductor or music director of several orchestras simultaneously).

Transferring university-developed knowledge to the private sector provides clear benefits to society. Stimulated by federal policies such as the Bayh-Dole Act and state investment and encouragement, universities have mounted aggressive efforts to capture, develop, market, and defend the intellectual property resulting from their scholarly and instructional activities. However, this commercialization of the academy also poses threats to the fundamental academic values such as open scholarly exchange and academic freedom. It also encumbers the university with additional layers of regulations and bureaucracy as it attempts to contain and manage intellectual property development and transfer.

A sharply contrasting model is provided by the "open source movement" in software development. In this model, a user community develops and shares publicly available intellectual property (e.g., software source code), cooperating in its development and improvement and benefiting jointly from its use. Perhaps the leading example is the development of the Linux operating system, now evolving to pose a major competitive threat to proprietary systems such as Microsoft Windows and Unix. This "gift economy" represents an emergent phenomenon from a community working together with no immediate form of recompense except social capital intertwined with intellectual capital.

The Massachusetts Institute of Technology (MIT) has recently taken a major leadership step in exploring this alternative approach with its Open-CourseWare project, which aims at putting MIT course materials on the Web for public use. As noted by MIT president Charles Vest,

> The glory of American higher education is its democratizing reach. At MIT we plan to speed this process to Internet time, by making the primary materials for nearly all of our 2,000 courses available on the WWW [World Wide Web] for use by anyone anywhere in the world. We see this project as opening a new door to the powerful, democratizing, and transforming power of education. Almost all of our faculty see this as a way to enhance our service to society and to improve education worldwide, goals they consider to be more important than revenue possibilities.[8]

Note that Vest believes that the real key to learning at MIT is "the magic that occurs when bright, creative young people live and learn together in the company of a highly dedicated faculty." In this sense, they view the OpenCourseWare project as more a form of academic publishing than of teaching, since it puts materials in the hands of others to use as they see fit. From this perspective they agree with many other members of the scholarly community that the spirit of open systems should prevail.

Although MIT has moved forward with this vision (with the help of $10 million from private foundations), their course materials will be at the very high end of the science and engineering curriculum spectrum and aimed at only the most advanced students. Suppose, however, that a major public research university (or, better yet, a small consortium of leading public universities) were to extend this vision by providing in the public domain (via the Internet) not only the digital resources supporting their curriculum but also the open source middleware to actually use these resources. In fact, this might well be the digital version of the land-grant extension role of the public university in the twenty-first century. It responds well not only to recent efforts such as the Kellogg Commission on the Future of the Land-Grant University but also, more broadly, to the ongoing debate concerning just how public universities will serve our rapidly changing world.

Let us suggest an even bolder approach. Suppose that in return for strong public support, the nation's public universities could be persuaded to regard *all* intellectual property developed on campus through research and intellectual activity as in the public domain. They could encourage their faculty to work closely with commercial interests to enable these knowledge resources to serve society, without direct control or financial benefit to the university, perhaps by setting up a "commons" environment adjacent to the campus (either geographically or virtually) where technology transfer was the primary mission. This might be just as effective a system for transferring technology as the current Bayh-Doyle environment for many areas of research and instruction. Furthermore, such an unconstrained distribution of the knowledge produced on campuses into the public domain seems more closely aligned with the century-old spirit of the land grant university movement.

There is a compelling need to develop a cohesive and consistent set of policies to guide the academic community in a number of areas, but this will not occur in a vacuum. As higher education develops such policies, it will encounter many obstacles, arising from the nature of our litigious society and its overwhelming burden of regulations. It is already clear that the legislation of electronic media promoted by the entertainment industry and its lobbyists could deliver a crippling blow to scholarly publication and education. Concepts such as fair use for instructional purposes are at great risk, not to mention the evolution of digital libraries and data repositories, if a meaningful set of policies governing research, scholarship, and education is not developed at the federal level.

ALLIANCES

Again, drawing on the experience of restructured industries in the private sector, technology-driven change provides strong incentives for colleges and universities to explore alliances, both within higher education and with other sectors. The financial pressures of the early 1980s and 1990s taught most universities the wisdom of focusing resources to achieve quality in selected areas of strength rather than attempting to be all things to all people. An increasingly competitive and rapidly changing marketplace will demand even more focus and differentiation. There are strong incentives to meet the broad expectations of various stakeholders through alliances of institutions with particular focused strengths rather than continuing to broaden institutional mission with the consequent dilution of resources, since the breadth and extent of the diverse demands of society tend to exceed the resources and capacities of a single institution.

Examples are useful here. During the 1990s, the Big Ten universities (actually there are 12, including the University of Chicago and Penn State University) merged many of their activities, such as their libraries and their federal relations activities. They explored ways to allow students at one institution to take courses or even degree programs from another institution in the alliance in a transparent and convenient way.

Another example is instructive. Many students and families believe that the teaching-intensive residential campuses of small liberal arts colleges provide a far more effective learning environment that the megacampuses of large research universities. In contrast, research universities provide extraordinary resources such as libraries, laboratories, and performance centers, not to mention faculty members who are leading scholars in a broad array of disciplines and professional fields. One might imagine combining the strengths of both types of institutions by forming alliances among liberal arts colleges and research universities, essentially using information technology to create a virtual analog to the Oxbridge style of learning and scholarship. This might allow the students enrolling at large research universities to enjoy the intense, highly personal experience of a liberal arts education at a small college while allowing the faculty members at these colleges to participate in the type of research activities occurring only on a large research campus.

There are also strong incentives to form alliances involving traditional universities and for-profit education companies. Universities can benefit from the experience gained from commercial competitors as well as their ability to access private capital markets to invest in product development and assessment. The corporate partners, in turn, can benefit from the "brand name" of established universities. In fact, since past experience suggests that digital technology rewards those who enter early, adapt rapidly, and are ready to seize opportunities when they arise, it is important for established colleges and universities to enter alliances or joint ventures with leading competitors before they have made commitments to other institutions. The case studies of companies such as Microsoft and AOL that have achieved effective monopoly or industry dominance because of their role in determining technology architectures such as desktop operating systems or Internet access suggest some urgency. While it is not obvious that higher education would ever again be able to re-create their earlier monopoly on higher education, the value of brand name and the huge fixed-cost, low variable-cost nature of the new business suggest that early movers will have sustainable advantages.

HIGHER EDUCATION ASSOCIATIONS

Colleges and universities have long joined together in national associations to pursue common agendas such as influencing federal legislation or enhancing public visibility. Notable among these is the One Dupont Circle group, named after the location in Washington where many of the associations are (or were) located, which include the American Council on Education (ACE), the Association of American Universities (AAU), the National Association of State Universities and Land-Grant Colleges (NASULGC), the American Association of State Colleges and Universities (AASCU), and so on. Such associations have been instrumental in assisting colleges and universities to cope with major forces of change such as information technology, as evidenced by the formation and evolution of organizations such as EDUCOM and CAUSE in the 1980s (now a merged organization known as Educause). Such organizations can play important roles by hosting meetings or workshops, by identifying and distributing key issues and viewpoints through publications, by creating learning opportunities through demonstrations and case studies, or by attempting to influence legislation. They also provide neutral turf where university leaders can come together to address complex issues such as intellectual property ownership.

However, it is also the case that rapidly evolving strategic issues such as those driven by information technology can pose a challenge to these national associations. For the most part, their attention and efforts are focused on very near-term issues such as federal funding and regulation. The great diversity among the membership of many associations—particularly the American Council on Education, whose membership spans the range from small liberal arts colleges to gigantic university systems—can make it difficult to develop a cohesive strategic agenda.

The national higher education associations can be remarkably effective, for example, when reacting to a threat such as a proposed cut in federal research funding or financial aid, since these are generally seen as priorities by most of their membership. However, longer-term strategic issues and actions are more problematic, since first a consensus must be developed among the member institutions concerning the importance of an issue. Nevertheless, there are examples of important steps taken at this level, such as the Millennium Commission, formed by NASULGC to explore opportunities to use on-line education to stimulate a twenty-first century analog to the land-grant acts of the nineteenth century.

To this end, let us suggest several possible actions for the national higher education associations:

- There needs to be an ongoing body of university leaders (perhaps supported by a staff of campus chief information officers) that continually monitors the evolution of digital technology, identifying trends that could impact higher education and bringing these to the attention of university leaders.

- Organizations such as EDUCAUSE merit strong and sustained support by the higher education community.

- Beyond that, there probably should be a more formal knowledge management system to serve as a resource for colleges and universities in their efforts to develop strategic technology road maps.

- National associations should continue to serve as the launching pad for broad collaborative experiments such as the University Consortium for Advanced Internet Development.

THE BRAVE NEW WORLD
OF MARKET-DRIVEN EDUCATION

The experience with market-driven restructuring in other industries has not been altogether encouraging, particularly with technology or media-based enterprises. The broadcasting and publication industries suggest that commercial concerns can lead to mediocrity, an intellectual wasteland in which the lowest common denominator of quality dominates. While the dissolution of the AT&T monopolies stimulated competition in telecommunications, it also resulted in the weakening of one of this nation's greatest intellectual assets, the Bell Laboratories. Furthermore, anyone who has suffered through the cattle-car experience of hub-spoke air travel can question whether the deregulation of commercial aviation has been worth it. Although the rate of increase in the cost of health care was slowed by the competition unleashed in a restructured marketplace, there are increasing concerns about the quality and convenience of health care delivery in our intensely competitive—and many would maintain chaotic—deregulated health care marketplace.

Driven by market pressures, many colleges and universities might choose to focus on more lucrative professional or training degree programs, rather than the broader intellectual and socialization experience generally associated with a liberal arts education. Institutions might also shy away from controversial issues either in their educational or research programs that might rile donors, corporate sponsors, and political constituencies—a not infrequent characteristic of for-profit competition in the marketplace. Institutions might tend to focus their energy and resources on those students who are easier to educate and better able to pay, abandoning those whose financial and intellectual needs are more challenging to the marketplace.

Some institutions may be able to shield themselves from these cost pressures by relying on their established reputations and relative prosperity to continue to attract and retain the best students and faculty and to attract the massive resources necessary to sustain quality programs. While this may allow them to protect their traditional missions, quality, and character, it could also isolate them from the critical restructuring efforts that will likely occur in the broader higher education enterprise, as new learning paradigms evolve to serve a radically different future. One might well ask whether it is in the best long-term interests of the leading universities— or of the higher education enterprise more generally—for a few institutions to skim the cream off the top of the resources pool simply to maintain their traditional roles. Such a strategy could lead to the decoupling and increasing irrelevance of such universities to the rest of higher education in America and throughout the world, thereby calling into question their leadership roles.

For example, a small group of elite institutions could capture the high end and give instant credibility to new entrants by making their courses available for use; the University of Phoenix, the Open University, and other convenience and/or distance learning entrants could capture mature students. On-line publishers could pick off the low end of the market re-selling courses developed by faculty for their own institutions. Information services companies such as Accenture and similar corporate universities could take over executive education and specific skills training. When the list is extended from these specific names to all the companies of each generic type, the result is the disappearance of huge chunks of the traditional market for universities.

With only a slight exaggeration, it might be possible to assert that the only parts of the traditional educational programs of the university, apart from doctoral training of the next generation of faculty and other advanced degrees, that would be untouched by private sector competition would be the residential 18-year-old market. This seems large now, but how big will that market be when students can choose among a full range of alternatives covering a spectrum of prices? Although the campus will not disappear, the escalating costs of residential education could price this form of education beyond the range of all but the affluent, relegating much, if not most, of the population to low-cost (and perhaps low-quality) education via shopping mall learning centers or computer-mediated distance learning.

There is a broader issue here, as emphasized in the 1997 report by the Commission on National Investment in Higher Education.[9] While some individual institutions may be able to cope with the current environment of limited resources, the implications for the higher education enterprise and for our nation are far more serious. At a time when the level of education needed by our society is increasing, the opportunity to attend college could be denied to millions of Americans unless a coordinated effort can be made to control costs while increasing public support. Given current funding projections, it will be difficult even to maintain the present enrollment levels, much less respond to the growing educational needs of the future. It is estimated that the level of underfunding of the higher education enterprise will grow to almost $40 billion by the year 2015 without concerted action. There is no way that tuition income alone can compensate for this funding gap—to rely entirely on this revenue source would drive the cost of higher education beyond the capacity of millions who need it. A unified effort to enhance productivity and restore public support will be needed—and even this may not be adequate if higher education insists on retaining its current paradigms for teaching and service.

There is an important lesson here. Without a broader recognition of the growing learning needs of our society, an exploration of more radical learning paradigms, and an overarching national strategy that acknowledges the public purpose of higher education and the important values of the academy, higher education will be driven down roads that would indeed lead to a nation at risk. Many of the pressures on our public universities are similar to those that have contributed so heavily to the current plight of K–12 education, where education has been viewed increasingly as an industry, demanding higher productivity according to poorly designed performance measures. The political forces associated with mass education have intruded on school management in general and governing boards in particular.

BALANCING MARKET FORCES WITH PUBLIC PURPOSE

Today we are evolving rapidly into a knowledge-based society in which the key strategic resource to our future has become knowledge itself—ideas and educated citizens. The educational needs of the nation have evolved from focusing on the leaders of our society to providing broad, quality educational opportunities for our entire population, in a sense, universal and pervasive educational opportunities. Furthermore, it has become increasingly evident that the level of one's education—and the access to continuing educational opportunities—has become a primary factor in determining the quality of life.

Societies everywhere expect from their schools and universities the provision of an education that can permit them to compete in the changing global economic landscape. Institutions that can continually change to keep up with the needs of the transforming economy that they serve will survive. Those that cannot or will not change will become irrelevant and perhaps ultimately expire.

Of course, technology will play a critical role in this, since digital technology is emerging as a primary delivery mechanism for educational services and intellectual content. The burgeoning use of the Internet and the national and international networks it enables is creating environments where intellectual capacity, information and knowledge bases, methodologies, and other valuables are made available to learners anywhere, anytime. Because the network is ubiquitous and open, higher education will no longer own the franchise as provider. Instead, it will compete for learners with commercial firms and other intermediaries. Almost every function of the contemporary university will be affected by—and might even be displaced by—digital technology. New competitors will appear, threatening the status quo with more effective and less costly alternatives. With over 100 million new learners at stake globally, the competition will be intense. As individuals, businesses, and government turn to network alternatives, the franchise of the college degree or college credit will face significant challenges. Although it will take a long time for the full impact of technology-driven transformation of the marketplace to be fully appreciated, even small shifts in the core activities of the university could have dramatic impact.

While we generally think of the providers in the higher education enterprise as traditional organizations such as individual schools, colleges, and universities and the market as individual students, in reality both providers and consumers are becoming increasingly systemic in nature. Universities are frequently organized into statewide systems, and educational services are increasingly sought by corporations or governments for broad classes of students. Furthermore, there are signs that the knowledge industry will stimulate entirely new social structures and institutions. A good example is provided by the evolution of the public library a century ago, which became the nexus of public culture in our communities. In every town and city in America, the public library, as a central and valued community meeting space, became the civic integrator, the focal point of culture, knowledge, and learning available to all.

The market forces driven by increasing demand for higher education and unleashed by technology are very powerful. However, if commercial interests are allowed to dominate and reshape the higher education enterprise, some of the most important values and traditions of the university fall by the wayside.[10] Will higher education retain its special role and responsibilities, its privileged position in our society? Will it continue to prepare young students for roles as responsible citizens? Will it provide social mobility through access to education? Will it challenge our society in the pursuit of truth and openness? Or will it become, both in perception and reality, just another interest group driven along by market forces? As we assess these market-driven emerging learning structures, we must bear in mind the importance of preserving the ability of the university to serve a broader public purpose.

The American university has been seen as an important social institution, created by, supported by, and accountable to society at large.[11] The key social principle sustaining the university was the perception of education as a *public good*—that is, the university was established to benefit all of society. Like other institutions such as parks and police, it was felt that individual choice alone would not sustain an institution serving the broad range of society's education needs. Hence, public policy dictated that the university merited broad support by all of society, rather than just by the individuals benefiting from its particular educational programs.[12]

Today, even as the needs of our society for postsecondary education intensify, we also find an erosion in the perception of education as a public good deserving of strong societal support.[13] State and federal programs have shifted from investment in the higher education enterprise (appropriations to institutions or students), to investment in the marketplace for higher education services (tax benefits to students and parents). Whether a deliberate or involuntary response to the tightening constraints and changing priorities for public funds, the new message is that education has become a private good that should be paid for by the individuals who benefit most directly, the students. At the same time, this shifted the perspective of higher education from that of a social institution, shaped by the values and priorities of broader society, to, in effect, an industry, increasingly responsive to the marketplace of individual students and clients.

Colleges and universities and their various stakeholders should guide this process in such a way as to preserve our core missions, characteristics, and values. In particular, the nature of higher education as a public good rather than simply a market commodity needs to be reestablished by strong public policy and public action both at the federal level and at the level of our states and communities, since the future of the university in the digital age is clearly a national concern.

NOTES

1. Donald N. Langenberg, "Taking Control of Change: Reinventing the Public University for the 21st Century," in *Reinventing the Research University*, ed. Kumar Patel (Los Angeles: University of California Press, 1994).

2. Marvin W. Peterson and David D. Dill, "Understanding the Competitive Environment of the Postsecondary Knowledge Industry," in *Planning and Management for a Changing Environment*, ed. Marvin W. Peterson, David D. Dill, Lisa Mets, and associates (San Francisco: Jossey-Bass, 1997), 3–29.

3. Diane Oblinger, Carole A. Barone, and Brian Hawkins, *Distributed Education and Its Challenges: An Overview* (Washington, DC: American Council on Education, 2001).

4. Marvin W. Peterson and David Dill, "Understanding the Competitive Environment of the Postsecondary Knowledge Industry."

5. Michael G. Dolence and Donald M. Norris, *Transforming Higher Education* (Ann Arbor, MI: Society for College and University Planning, 1999).

6. John Seely Brown and Paul Duguid, *The Social Life of Information* (Boston: Harvard Business School Press, 2000), 224.

7. Brian Hawkins, "Technology, Higher Education, and a Very Foggy Crystal Ball," *Educause* (Nov/Dec 2000).

8. Charles M. Vest, *Disturbing the Educational University: Universities in the Digital Age: Dinosaurs or Prometheans?* (Cambridge: MIT Press, 2001).

9. Joseph L. Dione and Thomas Kean, *Breaking the Social Contract: The Fiscal Crisis in Higher Education,* Report of the Commission on National Investment in Higher Education (New York: Council for Aid to Education, 1997).

10. Frank Newman and James Scurry, "Online Technology Pushes Pedagogy to the Forefront," *Chronicle of Higher Education* (July 13, 2001).

11. Patricia J. Gumport, *Academic Restructuring in Public Higher Education: A Framework and Research Agenda* (Stanford, CA: National Center for Postsecondary Improvement, 1998), 111.

12. Howard R. Bowen, *The Costs of Higher Education* (San Francisco: Jossey-Bass, 1980).

13. Robert Zemsky, "Rumbling," in *Policy Perspectives,* Pew Higher Education Roundtable, sponsored by the Pew Charitable Trusts (Philadelphia: Institute for Research on Higher Education, April 1997).

CHAPTER

Addressing the Needs
of the Nation

Since the impact of rapidly changing technologies such as computers and telecommunications is seen initially as a market force, it is natural to first examine the impact of digital technology on higher education through the lens of a changing marketplace for students, faculty, and resources. The history of higher education in America would suggest, however, that public policy and public investment have been far more influential than market forces in determining the nature of our colleges and universities.

From the earliest days of the nation, the benefits of the American university were expressed in terms of its public, democratic role. Through the writings of Jefferson and early legislation such as the Federal Ordinance of 1785, education was seen as important to the nation's democratic and economic well-being. Government policies and social priorities were clearly conveyed through a series of important actions such as the Land-Grant (Morrill) Acts, the GI Bill, the various Higher Education Acts, and federal financial aid programs such as the Pell Grants. The intent was to promote equal liberty to differing individuals and groups and to enable citizens to understand their responsibility as citizens of a free society. During this period higher education expanded from its traditional role of educating the elite for leadership roles, to providing mass education, perhaps best captured by the belief of the Truman Commission in 1952 that every high school graduate should have the opportunity for a college education. Today, we have evolved still further toward universal education, where our institutions have been asked to address the educational needs of our citizens throughout their lives with affordable, high-quality learning opportunities.

As we enter the new millennium, there is an increasing sense that the social contract between the public university and American society may need to be reconsidered and perhaps even renegotiated once again.[1] The university's multiple stakeholders have expanded and diversified in both number and interest, drifting apart without adequate means to communicate and reach agreement on priorities. Higher education must compete with an increasingly complex and compelling array of other social priorities for public and private resources. Both the public and its elected leaders today view the market as a more effective determinant of social investment than government policy. Perhaps most significant of all, the educational needs of our increasingly knowledge-intensive society are both changing and intensifying rapidly, and this will require a rethinking of the appropriate character and role of higher education in the twenty-first century.

The American experience suggests that the marketplace needs to be tempered by public policies. After all, antitrust legislation ensures fair competition in commercial markets; federal regulation governs sectors such as transportation and communication with important public responsibilities; and states regulate monopolistic utilities to ensure that they act in the public interest in areas such as energy and telecommunications. Although many policymakers argue for less regulation and more use of market forces in higher education, here, too, we need policies aimed at capturing the benefits of market competition while avoiding the dangers of market forces.

In this chapter we turn our attention to the role of public policy in shaping the evolution of higher education in the digital age. We first examine the role of the university from the perspective of state and federal governments facing new imperatives for intellectual and human capital in an age of knowledge. We next suggest a framework for public policy by laying out a vision for a new social contract between higher education and the nation aimed at building a *society of learning,* a society in which pervasive learning opportunities become universal and available to all citizens. Finally, we provide a series of recommendations to state and federal government as well as to other patrons of higher education such as foundations and corporations.

THE NEW IMPERATIVES
FOR A KNOWLEDGE-DRIVEN SOCIETY

There are powerful forces driving an increasing societal demand for higher education services in the United States. In today's world, knowledge has become the coin of the realm, determining the wealth of nations. It has also become the key to one's personal standard of living, the quality of one's life. We might well make the case that today it has become the responsibility of democratic societies to provide their citizens with the education and training that they need throughout their lives, whenever, wherever, and however they desire it, at high quality and at a cost that they can afford. Many countries have already made this commitment.

The Skills Race

Ask any governor about state priorities these days, and you are likely to hear concerns expressed about education and workforce training. The National Governors Association notes, "The driving force behind the 21st Century economy is knowledge, and developing human capital is the best way to ensure prosperity."[2]

The skills race of the twenty-first-century knowledge economy has become comparable to the space race of the 1960s in capturing the attention of the nation. Seventy percent of Fortune 1000 CEOs cite the ability to attract and retain adequately skilled employees as the major issue for revenue growth and competitiveness. Corporate leaders now estimate that the high-performance workplace will require a culture of continuous learning in which as much as 20 percent of a worker's time will be spent in formal education to upgrade knowledge and skills. Tom Peters suggests that the twenty-first century will be known as the "Age of the Great War for Talent," since in the knowledge economy, talent equals wealth.[3]

Information technology is allowing knowledge to spread almost instantly, making it accessible to anyone and everyone. As Peter Drucker has stressed, the next society will be a knowledge society. Knowledge will be its key resource, and knowledge workers will be the dominant group in its workforce. It will be characterized by (1) borderlessness, because knowledge travels even more effortlessly than money, (2) upward mobility, available to everyone through easily acquired formal education, and (3) the potential for failure as well as success, since while anyone can acquire the means of production, not everyone will be successful. Together, these three characteristics will make the knowledge society a highly competitive one for organizations and individuals.[4]

People have always looked to education as the key to prosperity and social mobility, but now more than ever, people see education as their hope for leading meaningful and fulfilling lives. The level of one's education has become a primary determinant of one's economic well-being. Just as a high school diploma became the passport for participation in the industrial age, today, a century later, a college education has become a requirement for economic security in the age of knowledge. The fastest growing group in the workforce today is composed of knowledge workers, who have two main needs: formal education that enables them to enter knowledge work in the first place and continuing education throughout their working lives to keep their knowledge up-to-date. In industrial societies, schooling traditionally stopped when work began. In the knowledge society, it never stops.

The implications of the knowledge-intensive nature of our society can be seen by comparing the wages of groups with differing education levels. The single most important factor in determining the level of income has become the level of one's education. The pay gap between high school and college graduates continues to widen, doubling from a 50 percent premium in 1980 to 111 percent today. Not so well known is an even larger earnings gap for those with graduate degrees. This income gap is expected to continue to widen as we move further into the twenty-first century. This growing education divide has been driven by a mismatch between the supply of higher education and a growing demand for people with knowledge-based skills, as well as the erosion in earning power of those without advanced education.[5]

Beyond the impact on individual earnings, there are many other economic indicators of the importance of knowledge in determining the prosperity both of companies and our broader society. Relative indices such as the productivity per employee or market-capitalization per employee are substantially larger for information services companies than for those in more traditional manufacturing. In the knowledge economy, the key asset driving corporate value is no longer physical capital or unskilled labor. Instead, it is intellectual and human capital.

We might define human capital as the knowledge and skills that people acquire through education, on-the-job training, or other types of schools and other types of learning. It can take many different forms. In previous centuries, economies were based on manpower, strength, and some machinery, but not really so systematically on knowledge. In today's world, knowledge is making the difference not only in how an individual does but also in how well a company does and, for that matter, in how well a country does. At no previous time has human capital been so important, meaning that finding, developing, and retaining knowledge workers will be the mission-critical functions in the new economy. In today's knowledge-based global marketplace, human capital is replacing physical capital as the source of competitive advantage. Where the resources of the physically based economy were coal, oil, and steel, the resources of the new, knowledge-based economy are brainpower and the ability to effectively acquire, deliver, and process information. Those who are effectively educated and trained will be the ones who will be able to survive economically and thrive in our global, knowledge-based economy. Those who do not will be rendered economically obsolete.

However, it has become increasingly clear that we are simply not providing our citizens with the learning opportunities needed for a twenty-first-century knowledge economy. Recent Third International Mathematics and Science Study (TIMMS)[6] scores suggest that despite school reform efforts of the past two decades, the United States continues to lag behind other nations in the mathematics and science skills of our students. Despite the growing correlation between the level of one's education and earning capacity, only 21 percent of those in our population over the age of 25 have graduated from college.

Nowhere is the shortage of skilled people more evident than in the technology-intensive occupations. As Michael Moe of Merrill Lynch notes, scientists and engineers are the heroes of the new economy; they influence the spending for any organization, and they are in extremely short supply. In fact, there are currently 700,000 open IT jobs, or one-third of all IT jobs, with the shortage expected to double in the next five years. Compounding the complexity of the dearth of IT professionals is Moore's law, making some IT skills obsolete in the blink of an eye. Furthermore, enrollments in graduate programs have held constant or declined (particularly in technical fields such as engineering) over the past two decades.[7]

The space race galvanized public concern and concentrated national attention on educating the elite of our society in advanced disciplines such as science and engineering. The skills race of the twenty-first century will value instead the skills and knowledge of our entire workforce as a key to economic prosperity, national security, and social well-being. It is within this context that there is growing concern about whether our existing institutions have the capacity to serve these changing and growing social needs—indeed, even whether they will be able to survive in the face of the extraordinary changes occurring in our world.

As we have observed, both young, digital media-savvy students and adult learners will likely demand a major shift in educational methods, away from passive classroom courses packaged into well-defined degree programs and toward interactive, collaborative learning experiences, provided when and where the student needs the knowledge and skills. The increased blurring of the various stages of learning throughout one's lifetime—K–12, undergraduate, graduate, professional, job training, career shifting, lifelong enrichment—will require a far greater coordination and perhaps even a merger of various elements of our national educational infrastructure.

The growing and changing nature of education needs will trigger strong economic forces. Already, traditional sources of public support for higher education such as state appropriations or federal support for student financial aid have simply not kept pace with the growing demand. This imbalance between demand and available resources is aggravated by the increasing costs of education, driven as they are by the knowledge- and people-intensive nature of the enterprise as well as by the difficulty that educational institutions have in containing costs and increasing productivity.

For almost two decades, since the publication of A Nation at Risk,[8] most attention of state, federal, and business leaders has been focused on reforming K–12 education. Higher education was largely ignored, in the belief that despite its flaws, it was nevertheless world-class. However, today, as the implications of an age of knowledge become more apparent, the university has come onto the radar scope of political and business leaders because of the role that it must play in producing and sustaining the new cadre of knowledge workers critical to the twenty-first-century economy.

The age of knowledge holds an even deeper significance for higher education. In a sense, knowledge is the medium of the university. Through the activities of discovery, shaping, achieving, transmitting, and applying knowledge, the university serves society in myriad ways: educating the young, preserving our cultural heritage, providing the basic research so essential to our security and well-being, training our professionals and certifying their competence, challenging our society, and stimulating social change. In a world in which knowledge and educated people have become the key to prosperity and security, there has been an increasing tendency for society to view the university as an engine for economic growth through the generation and application of new knowledge. From a broader perspective, just as the loss of faith in government intervention has shifted political attention away from the distribution of wealth to its production, there has been a shift of emphasis within the university away from simply distributing and analyzing knowledge, for example, "teaching" and "scholarship," to creating knowledge, to activities such as "innovation" and "creativity."

The university has long played both a personal and a civic role in providing each new generation of students with the opportunity to better understand themselves, to discover and understand the important traditions and values of our past, and to develop the capacity to cope with their future. Today, 65 percent of America's high school graduates seek some level of college education, and this will likely increase as a college degree becomes the entry credential to the high-performance workplace in the years ahead.

Even those with college degrees will find themselves hard-pressed to keep up as they face a future that will in all likelihood demand frequent career changes; even a college education will serve only as a stepping-stone to a process of lifelong education. The ability to continue to learn and to adapt to—indeed, to manage—change and uncertainty will become one of the most valuable skills of all.

Our central theme is that education, broadly defined, will play a pivotal role in the coming economic transition and its impact on individuals. Previous economic transformations were closely associated with major public investment in infrastructure such as railroads, canals, electric networks, and highways. In the coming economic transition, an equivalent infrastructure will be an educated population.

Cradle-to-Grave Education

Knowledge is unlike traditional skills, which change very slowly. Rather, knowledge rapidly becomes obsolete, and knowledge workers regularly have to go back to school to refresh their educations. As knowledge continues to expand, doubling in some fields every few years, the content of many educational programs also rapidly becomes obsolete. Here we must stress that the skills and perspectives provided by a liberal education are generally lasting in value. However, the more particular knowledge and skills characteristic of professional education have an ever-shorter shelf life. As a result, the fastest growing industry in any developed country may turn out to be the continuing education of already well educated adults, which is based on values that are all but incompatible with those of the youth culture traditionally served by our colleges and universities.[9]

This knowledge explosion is accompanied by an unprecedented employment churn, which is making a potential student out of every worker. The "free agent" mind-set of today's knowledge worker is evidenced by the fact that the average person entering the workforce today will work for between 8 and 10 different employers, versus 4 to 6 a decade ago. Labor Department officials claim that an estimated 50 million workers, or about 40 percent of the workforce, change employers or jobs within any one year. To accomplish this, the nation's industry needs management and a workforce that have been educated and retrained to be cross-functional, cross-skilled, self-managed, able to communicate and work in teams, and able to change on a moment's notice. In this far more demanding workplace, managers and others who do not meet the criteria are usually the first to be dropped, but the more fortunate are retrained or reeducated.

Today's typical college graduates will change careers several times during their lives, requiring additional education at each stage. Furthermore, with the ever-expanding knowledge base of many fields, along with the longer life span and working careers of our aging population, the need for intellectual retooling will become even more significant. Even those without college degrees will soon find that their continued employability requires advanced education. Some estimate that just to keep an individual on pace with evolving workplace skills and knowledge will require a time commitment of roughly one day of education per week.[10] This translates to one-fifth of the workforce in college-level educational programs at any time, equivalent to roughly 28 million full-time students—compared to the 12.1 million full-time students currently enrolled in our colleges and universities.[11]

Knowledge workers are likely to make less and less distinction between work and learning. In fact, continuous learning will be a necessity for continued work relevance and security. Employers will seek individuals who can consistently learn and master new skills to respond to new needs. They will place less emphasis on the particular knowledge of new employees than on their capacity to continue to learn and grow intellectually throughout their careers. From the employee's perspective, there will be less emphasis placed on job security with a particular company and more on the provision of learning opportunities for acquiring the knowledge and skills that are marketable more broadly.

We need to rethink educational goals from this lifetime perspective. Undergraduate education and graduate education are just steps—important steps, to be sure—down the road toward a lifetime of learning. Importantly, they can ensure a person's ability and desire to continue to learn, to become attuned to change and diversity and adaptable to new forms of knowledge and learning of the future. From this perspective, we may be able to better match both learning content and experiences with the intellectual maturation as well as the needs of the learner. While some individuals will always be learners throughout their lives, others need both incentives and opportunities for lifetime learning.

For example, primary and secondary education should focus on the development of fundamental skills in areas such as language and quantitative reasoning. Undergraduate education would prepare the student for lifelong learning, while providing the skills and competence to succeed in the workplace. The early years of one's career might be the time for experimentation, for risk taking, since it is frequently then that the most creativity occurs. Later in life, there may be more of an interest in, and acceptance of, the need for a liberal education, to enrich one's later years.

In a world driven by knowledge, learning can no longer be regarded as a once-is-enough or on-again, off-again experience. Rather, people will need to engage in continual learning in order to keep their knowledge base and skills up-to-date. Since the need for learning will become lifelong, perhaps the relationship between a student/graduate and the university will similarly evolve into a lifetime membership in a learning community. In this system, enrollment should be viewed less as participation in a particular degree program and instead as a lifetime association with the university, in which the university agrees to provide whatever learning resources are required by its learner/members throughout their lives, whatever, whenever, and wherever their educational needs. Clearly, the rapid evolution of distance learning technology will increasingly allow this. We also see increasing interest on the part of alumni in remaining connected to their university and to learning opportunities throughout their lives.

This need for lifelong learning poses great challenges to higher education, since it is becoming increasingly clear that our old paradigms of campus-based degree programs will not serve this emerging need. Although many institutions have created separate educational divisions to serve adult learners—for example, extension, continuing education, lifelong learning—these have been viewed traditionally as lower-priority activities. To keep pace with the changing educational needs of our society, the university will have to consider lifelong learning activities as a far more strategic component of its mission.

Diversity

When Americans hear references to the demographic changes occurring in our nation, we probably first think of the aging of our population.[12] It is true that the baby boomers have moved into middle age and soon will be approaching retirement, with worrisome consequences for our current entitlement programs such as Social Security and Medicare. After a brief decline in the number of young adults during the 1980s and 1990s, we once again are seeing a growth in the number of college-age students, an echo of the baby boom generation, yet this growth in the number of young people is far exceeded by the growth in the number of senior citizens. In this country, there will soon be more people over the age of 65 than there are teenagers, and this situation is certain to continue for the remainder of our lives. Furthermore, the growth rate in both our population and our workforce is declining to the lowest level in our nation's history. Since fertility and mortality rates are below their long-term averages, it has become clear that the United States will not be a nation of youth again in our lifetimes. As our society ages, it has become more conservative, with national priorities increasingly focusing on the concerns of the elderly rather than the needs of the young.

There is a certain irony here. While America and much of Europe are aging, the rest of the world is becoming ever younger. Today, half of the world's population is under the age of 20, with over 2 billion teenagers on planet Earth, most living in Asia, Africa, and Latin America. Just as the 40 million teenagers born in America during the postwar decade determined our culture, drove our consumption patterns during the 1950s, dominated our politics during the 1960s, and contributed our president in the 1990s, so, too, will teenagers around the globe have a profound impact on world culture.

Add to this youth-dominated world the capacity for cheap, global communication, and you can imagine the scenario.[13] Within a decade, hundreds of millions of young people will be linked together by the ubiquitous information technology rapidly appearing throughout the world. A glance at early forms of popular culture arising from such "wired communities" of young people—MTV or *Wired* magazine—provides ample evidence that their future is certainly *not* our present. While these networked teenagers will not homogenize world culture, they will certainly incorporate and mix cultures from around the world to spawn new societies, and their demand for education will be staggering. Even to sustain current participation rates for higher education would require creating a major new university on-line every week to serve this growing population of young people.[14]

An equally profound demographic phenomenon is the increasing diversity of American society with respect to race, ethnicity, and nationality. Women, minorities, and immigrants now account for roughly 85 percent of the growth in the labor force, currently representing 60 percent of all of our nation's workers. Those groups we refer to today as minorities— African, Hispanic, Asian, and Native Americans—have already become the majority population in states such as California, Arizona, and Texas. By the late twenty-first century, the United States could become a nation of minorities, without a majority ethnic group. Women, who have already become the predominant gender in our nation and our educational institutions, are rapidly assuming leadership roles in both the public and private sectors.

The full participation of currently underrepresented minorities and women is crucial to our commitment to equity and social justice, as well as to the future strength and prosperity of America. Our nation cannot afford to waste the human talent, the cultural and social richness represented by those currently underrepresented in our society. If we do not create a nation that mobilizes the talents of all our citizens, we are destined for a diminished role in the global community and increased social turbulence. Most tragically, we will have failed to fulfill the promise of democracy upon which this nation was founded. The challenge of increasing diversity is complicated, however, by social and economic factors. Far from evolving toward one America, our society continues to be hindered by segregation and nonassimilation of minority cultures.

What are the implications of these demographic changes for higher education in the digital age? Throughout its history, higher education in America has always responded to the needs of a changing population. As America expanded to the frontier and then evolved into an industrial society, our universities expanded enrollments, developed professional schools, and rapidly transformed themselves to stress applied fields such as engineering, agriculture, and medicine favored by the federal land-grant acts. Higher education expanded both scope and mission again after World War II to absorb returning veterans and the baby boom generation in the 1950s and 1960s. With the help of federal programs such as the Higher Education Act of 1965, our colleges and universities have reached out to increase the participation of those racial, ethnic, and cultural groups not adequately represented among our students, faculty, and staff. We have tried to build supportive environments that accept, embrace, and sustain diversity as essential to the quality of our missions of teaching, research, and service.

Today our college-age population is growing once again, with a 30 percent growth projected in the number of traditional college students by the year 2015.[15] Some regions of the nation will face a particular challenge with growing populations and changing demographics, such as California's Tidal Wave II of almost 500,000 additional college-age students over the next decade or the Texas challenge of a college population dominated by heretofore underrepresented minorities.

The changing character and needs of the American population are driving a major redefinition of the concept of a college student and hence the character of our institutions. Only 17 percent of students enrolled in college today are in the 18–22-year-old group that we generally think of as traditional college students. No longer are the students on our campuses drawn primarily from the ranks of middle- and upper-class high school graduates. Colleges and universities are increasingly challenged to build educational programs for a student population diverse in essentially every human characteristic: age, gender, race, socioeconomic background, and so on.

However, events of the past several years suggest that the road to serving an increasingly diverse population may also become even more difficult. Even as universities come to understand the educational benefits of a diverse student population and faculty, they are increasingly constrained in the mechanisms that they may use to achieve diversity. Throughout society we see a backlash against earlier social commitments and programs. Both the courts and legislative bodies are now challenging long-accepted programs such as affirmative action and equal opportunity. The polarization of our society by race, class, and nationality has become ever more intense, ironically even as our nation and the world have become more linked together in a political, economic, and cultural sense by modern communications and transportation technologies.

The growing pluralism of our society is one of our greatest challenges as a nation. It is also among our most important opportunities, because it gives us an extraordinary vitality and energy as a people. As both a reflection and leader of society at large, the university has a unique responsibility to develop effective models of multicultural, pluralistic communities for our nation. We must strive to achieve new levels of understanding, tolerance, and mutual fulfillment for peoples of diverse racial and cultural backgrounds both on our campuses and beyond. It has also become increasingly clear that we must do so within a new political context that will require new policies and practices. It is also clear that we must utilize the power of digital technology to provide learning opportunities that not only reach beyond the campus into homes and the workplace but also can be adapted to meet unique educational needs of an increasingly diverse population.

A SOCIETY OF LEARNING

As we enter the new millennium, there is an increasing sense that the social contract between the public university and American society may need to be reconsidered and perhaps even renegotiated once again.[16] The university's multiple stakeholders have expanded and diversified in both number and interest, drifting apart without adequate means to communicate and reach agreement on priorities. Higher education must compete with an increasingly complex and compelling array of other social priorities for limited public funding. Both the public and its elected leaders today view the market as a more effective determinant of social investment than government policy. Perhaps most significant of all, the educational needs of our increasingly knowledge-intensive society are both changing and intensifying rapidly, and this fact will require a rethinking of the appropriate character and role of higher education in the twenty-first century.

The Kellogg Commission

In 2000 the Kellogg Commission on the Future of the Land-Grant University[17] proposed a vision for the future of education known as "a learning society," a term implying socially inclusive learning opportunities for all of its members, including children, young and older adults, the elderly, the employed and the unemployed, the advantaged and the disadvantaged. In such a society, all students are educated to the highest levels that they can reach, recognizing that everyone can learn but that not everyone learns in the same way.

Such a society would value and foster habits of lifelong learning, ensuring that there are responsive and flexible learning programs and learning networks to address all students' needs. Of particular importance would be the use of emerging information technologies, capable of enriching, distributing, and customizing learning opportunities. This vision would require new public policies that ensure equity of access to learning, information, and information technologies, recognizing that investments in learning contribute to overall competitiveness and the economic and social well-being of the nation.

From Asynchronous to Ubiquitous Learning

The Kellogg Commission identifies the key elements of a learning society as follows:

- It values and fosters habits of lifelong learning and ensures that there are responsive and flexible learning programs and learning networks available to address all students' needs.
- It is socially inclusive and ensures that all of its members are part of its learning communities.

- It recognizes the importance of early childhood development as part of lifelong learning and develops organized ways of enhancing the development of all children.

- It views information technologies, including new interactive, multimedia technologies, as tools for enriching learning by tailoring instruction to societal, organizational, and individual needs.

- It stimulates the creation of new knowledge through research and other means of discovery and uses that knowledge for the benefit of society.

- It values regional and global interconnections and cultural links.

- Finally, it fosters public policy that ensures equity of access to learning, information, and information technologies and recognizes that investments in learning contribute to overall competitiveness and the economic and social well-being of the nation.

From a broader perspective, we have entered an era in which educated people and the knowledge that they produce and utilize have become the keys to the economic prosperity and well-being of our society. Education, knowledge, and skills have become primary determinants of one's personal standard of living. Just as our society has historically accepted the responsibility for providing needed services such as military security, health care, and transportation infrastructure in the past, today education has become a driving social need and societal responsibility.

Of course, this has been one of the great themes of higher education in America. Each evolutionary wave of higher education has aimed at educating a broader segment of society, at creating new educational forms to do that—the public universities, the land-grant universities, the normal and technical colleges, the community colleges. So what would be the nature of a university of the twenty-first century capable of creating and sustaining a society of learning? It would be impractical and foolhardy to suggest one particular model. The great and ever-increasing diversity characterizing higher education in America makes it clear that there will be many forms, many types of institutions serving our society, but a number of themes will almost certainly factor into at least some part of the higher education enterprise.

With increasing differentiation, there will be many "new" universities as institutions attempt to define themselves in the marketplace both by core competencies and by differences. Some colleges and universities may continue to focus on the traditional educational paradigms discussed in earlier chapters, but many will undergo or exploit significant transformations to explore an array of themes:

Learner-centered: Just like other social institutions, our universities must become more focused on those whom we serve. We must transform ourselves from faculty-centered to learner-centered institutions, becoming more responsive to what our students need to learn rather than simply what our faculties wish to teach.

Affordable: Society will demand that we become far more affordable, providing educational opportunities within the resources of all citizens. Whether this occurs through greater public subsidy or dramatic restructuring of the costs of higher education, it seems increasingly clear that our society—not to mention the world—will no longer tolerate the high-cost, low-productivity paradigm that characterizes much of higher education in America today.

Lifelong learning: In an age of knowledge, the need for advanced education and skills will require both a personal willingness to continue to learn throughout life and a commitment on the part of our institutions to provide opportunities for lifelong learning. The concepts of student and alumnus will merge. Our highly partitioned system of education will blend increasingly into a seamless web, in which primary and secondary education; undergraduate, graduate, and professional education; on-the-job training and continuing education; and lifelong enrichment become a continuum.

Interactive and collaborative: Already we see new forms of pedagogy: asynchronous (anytime, anyplace) learning that utilizes emerging information technology to break the constraints of time and space, making learning opportunities more compatible with lifestyles and career needs; and interactive and collaborative learning appropriate for the digital age, the plug-and-play generation.

Diverse: The great diversity characterizing higher education in America will continue, as it must to serve an increasingly diverse population with diverse needs and goals.

Intelligent and adaptive: Knowledge and distributed intelligence technology will increasingly allow us to build learning environments that are not only highly customized but adaptive to the needs of the learner.

Many colleges and universities have already launched major strategic efforts to understand these themes and to transform themselves into institutions better capable of serving a knowledge-driven society. Yet such efforts to explore new learning paradigms extend far beyond the traditional higher education enterprise to include an array of new participants, ranging from publishing houses (e.g., Harcourt-Brace), to entertainment companies (e.g., Disney), to information services providers (e.g., Accenture), to information technology corporations (e.g., IBM). It is clear that the access to advanced learning opportunities not only is becoming a more pervasive need but could well become a defining domestic policy issue for a knowledge-driven society.

Perhaps access to advanced educational opportunities will be the defining domestic policy issue for a knowledge-driven society. If so, however, we will need to develop new paradigms for delivering education to even broader segments of our society, perhaps to all of our society, in convenient, high-quality forms, at a cost that all can afford. Fortunately, today's technology is rapidly breaking the constraints of space and time. It has become clear that most people, in most areas can learn and learn well using asynchronous learning, that is, "anytime, anyplace, anyone" education. Lifetime education is rapidly becoming a reality, making learning available for anyone who wants to learn, at the time and place of his or her choice, without great personal effort or cost. With advances in modern information technology, the barriers in the educational system are no longer cost or technological capacity but rather perception and habit.

Even this may not be enough. Perhaps we should instead consider a future of "ubiquitous learning"—learning for everyone, every place, all the time. Indeed, in a world driven by an ever-expanding knowledge base, continuous learning, like continuous improvement, has become a necessity of life.

In a society of learning, people would be continually surrounded by, immersed in, and absorbed in learning experiences. Information technology has now provided us with a means to create learning environments throughout one's life. These environments not only are able to transcend the constraints of space and time but, like us, are capable as well of learning and evolving to serve our changing educational needs.

THE FEDERAL POLICY ENVIRONMENT

Although policymakers at the state and federal level have increasingly relied on market forces to address many of the priorities of contemporary society, there is nevertheless a strong role for government in shaping and guiding higher education in the digital age so that it serves the needs of a changing society.

Federal Policies, Programs, and Investments

Here it is important to note the different roles played by the federal government in the two primary missions of the university, education and research. In the case of research, there is a long-standing partnership between the federal government and the university involving the support of basic and applied research in the national interest. The federal government has long been involved in developing and funding programs aimed at not only supporting but shaping the university research enterprise. In contrast, the federal government's role in the support of higher education is actually quite limited. It does provide financial aid programs for students and also regulates much of the instructional enterprise, yet its capacity to stimulate and shape educational innovation is quite limited since the states and the students pay most of the bills. Yet here, too, we maintain that there is an important federal role, particularly during a period of change.

We begin our discussion of possible federal roles with three premises:

Premise 1: We have entered an age of knowledge, in which educated people and their ideas have become the keys to social prosperity, security, and well-being. Furthermore, in such an age, education has become the key determinant of one's personal prosperity and quality of life.

Premise 2: It has become the responsibility of democratic societies to provide their citizens with the education and training that they need, throughout their lives, whenever, wherever, and however they desire it, at high quality and at an affordable cost, that is, to create a society of learning in which lifelong educational opportunities become not only available to, but pervasive in, the lives of all of our citizens.

Premise 3: Although the major investments in the learning infrastructure necessary to create and sustain a society of learning will come from the private sector and local government at the state and community levels, leadership, vision, and a policy framework must come from the federal government.

As the United States enters a new century, we face social and economic challenges triggered by globalization, technological change, and demographic change that have established the development of our nation's human and intellectual capital as our highest domestic priority. There are strong precedents for federal policies, programs, and investments that work through our colleges and universities to address such national priorities. Although recent tax cut legislation combined with new national priorities such as defense against terrorism may restrict federal tax revenues and expenditures for the next several years, federal funding patterns are cyclic, and sooner or later higher education is certain to become a priority for new initiatives. However, there is a more serious issue here: the absence of a vision for the nation concerning the use of information and communications technology in education. If we were given a few billion dollars of federal funds, what would we use it for?

Hence, our first challenge is to stimulate a process at the national level aimed at developing a vision for the future of higher education—indeed, more generally, all of education—in the digital age. Without the vision, it will be difficult to develop a strategy for the rest of the agenda. The "society of learning" theme articulated earlier in this chapter might provide the seeds for just such a vision, but without broad participation and buy-in to its articulation and development, such a very general concept remains only an abstraction.

Knowledge Creation

For the past half century, the American research enterprise has been a triad, consisting of research universities as a primary source of basic research and graduate education, corporate R&D laboratories as the backbone of the applied research necessary for product development and commercial application, and federal research laboratories to perform the basic and applied research aimed at particular national priorities such as nuclear defense and space exploration. There is a wide consensus that U.S. scientific preeminence and economic growth depend on maintaining the share of GDP devoted to R&D, with a target goal of 3 percent. Indeed, total R&D spending increased over the past decade, rising to $247 billion or 2.8 percent in fiscal year (FY) 2001. Yet since 1987, industry R&D has increased by 196 percent while the federal share of total R&D, $92 billion in FY 2001, has dropped from 46 percent to 27 percent.[18]

In part, this remarkable growth in private sector R&D has been stimulated by the importance of applied research and development in a technology-driven economy. It also depends on the flow of basic research findings and the associated training of scientists and engineers, principally the concern of the federal government. Hence, the growth of industry spending on R&D should not lull observers into minimizing the importance of the federal R&D budget. In fact, one might well question whether the current federal investment is adequate to sustain the necessary private sector investment in these activities, so critical to our economic prosperity.

Furthermore, there are many sources of creative inspiration and innovation, just as there are many competing ways to create knowledge, including think tanks, industrial research, venture-funded spin-offs, and faculty-owned companies. In many cases these are more focused, efficient, interdisciplinary, and able to take advantage of information technology to gain speed and competitive advantage than more traditional research programs. Furthermore, we already see the early signs of new forms of research organizations such as collaboratories and knowledge networks stimulated directly by evolving information and communications technology. It seems likely that the current structure of the national research enterprise will change significantly.

We also believe it unlikely, however, that the research university will be replaced as the primary source of basic research in our nation, at least for the near term. There is no evidence of rapid growth of not-for-profit institutes or academies (such as those in Europe) focused on basic research, although several have been created for applied research in fields such as biotechnology (e.g., Celera). Furthermore, the large corporate laboratories such as Bell Labs, IBM Research Labs, and Xerox PARC seem constrained by the quarterly profit-and-loss statements of their parent companies to focus increasingly on product-related research. Microsoft is one of the few companies rapidly increasing investments in basic research, but this should not be surprising, since recent history has shown that only monopoly industries can support large research laboratories.

In fact, industry is depending increasingly upon universities for both basic and applied research. To the degree that computers and networks allow faculty members to leverage their activities more effectively, the information technology may solidify even further the university's unique role in basic research. The university will continue to be the primary source of new knowledge and creativity in our nation. Hence, federal support of the university research enterprise will continue to be of great importance in responding to national needs and priorities.

Cyberinfrastructure

Some changes in the nation's research enterprise will be necessary. Research support should move beyond bricks (facilities) and even clicks (digital technology) to support the development of systems and organizations appropriate for knowledge work in the digital age. In the past the federal government has played an essential role in the development of information technology, through the defense needs for computers and networks and its support of campus-based research in areas such as computer science and engineering, electrical engineering, physics, and mathematics. So, too, have major corporate R&D laboratories such as Bell Laboratories and IBM Research Laboratories played very key roles in performing the basic and applied research necessary for technological breakthroughs. One might well argue that this triad character of the national research enterprise consisting of research universities, federal research laboratories, and corporate research laboratories was and remains key to the continued evolution of digital technology. No single sector or purpose is sufficient to sustain the remarkable evolution of information and communications technology.

Despite this interlinked character of our national research enterprise, one occasionally encounters skepticism about the degree of federal involvement. After all, the massive resources available to companies such as Microsoft, IBM, and Cisco dwarf the R&D investments of the federal government in information technology. Why are major federal research programs even necessary?

Looking back over the past several decades, the answer seems obvious. Most of the key technological advances, from supercomputers, to networks, to "killer applications" such as Internet browsers, were stimulated not by commercial markets but by the needs of scientific investigators. In fact, the rapid evolution of so-called e-science, those areas of fundamental research such as higher-energy physics, proteomics, and global systems simulation that depend particularly heavily on "cyberinfrastructure," is likely to drive the evolution of information technology far more rapidly than the commercial marketplace.

There are challenges here unique to the character of digital technology itself. Perhaps most significant is the challenge of anticipating and accommodating the wildly different and changing rates of exponential evolution of various elements such as processing speed, bandwidth, storage, and software. The technology is driven by whichever exponential is rising the most rapidly. "Riding the exponential wave" means, in effect, continually jumping from one technology to another, an ability far more characteristic of research projects than commercial product development.

Beyond the diversity in the rates of evolution of various aspects of information technology, the diversity in needs and applications of the technology leads to a cacophony that makes coordination difficult. Not only is it very difficult to achieve coordination and cooperation among various federal agencies such as the Department of Energy, the National Aeronautics and Space Administration (NASA), and the National Institutes of Health, but the situation is sometimes just as bad even within a single agency. The United States has vast assets in these areas, but they are not well coordinated. There is a lack of converged standards and middleware. Few research projects are funded for the archiving and distribution of digital data.

An example illustrates the point. Even within a basic research agency such as the National Science Foundation, there is difficulty in developing and implementing a policy that clearly defines a role in not only building but sustaining the digital infrastructure necessary for scientific research. The NSF has played a critical role in stimulating the evolution of major resources such as supercomputers and high-bandwidth networks. However, the voices of those researchers who have become heavily dependent on these technologies for their e-science projects are sometimes drowned out by those of computer scientists and engineers more concerned with research on digital systems than sustaining the infrastructure necessary for their application to scientific research.

The problem is that we are not treating e-science infrastructure as a system that requires both coordination and support at the level of the federal government. Furthermore, efforts to develop policy at a more systemic level frequently run into the tired argument that industry should do the infrastructure while government and higher education should focus on basic research. Many other nations have recognized the need for coordinated efforts and are making investments that could well move them ahead of the United States, while we continue to tolerate both competition and confusion among and within federal agencies, not to mention between publicly funded research and development and commercial application.

Federal R&D in the "Science of Education"

We have argued that the development of human capital is becoming a dominant national priority in the age of knowledge, comparable in importance to military security and health care, yet our federal investment in the knowledge base necessary to address this need in minuscule. In FY 2001, the nation invested over $247 billion in R&D. Of the federal government's share of $92 billion, $20.4 billion was invested in the National Institutes of Health (NIH), $8 billion in space, $4.4 billion in NSF, and $2 billion in high-energy physics. How much will the federal government invest in research directed toward learning, education, and schools? Less than $300 million—less than 0.2 percent of our investment in the biosciences or 1 percent of that in high-energy physics.

To view this paltry investment from a somewhat different perspective, most industries spend between 3 percent and 10 percent per year of revenues for R&D activities. By this measure, the education sector of our economy (including K–12, higher education, and workforce training), which amounts to $700 billion, should be investing $20 billion or greater each year in R&D, roughly the same order of magnitude as the health care sector. However, currently only about 0.3 percent of public spending on children and education is devoted to R&D. Evidence from other domestic areas in crisis that are primarily public sector responsibilities, such as air traffic control systems, suggests that inadequate investment in R&D is a key factor resulting in inadequate innovation and adoption of new technology. If the public sector is unwilling to invest in R&D where it bears prime responsibility, perhaps it is not surprising that progress in education and improving learning outcomes for our children has been slow and uncertain.

Of course, one might raise the question of how we define R&D in education. It is not our intent to wade into the swamp of discussing whether the bulk of the activity supported by the Department of Education, such as the Office of Educational Research and Improvement, is actually "research," at least in the sense that most other scientists would understand it.[19] Nor will we address the growing investments of for-profit competitors such as Unext.com and the University of Phoenix in the development of educational products or assessment tools.

Rather, we would like to focus our discussion on what many term the "science of education," meaning research that would be classified by scientists as guided by the scientific method and subject to rigorous review by the scientific community. Included in this would be research in areas such as neuroscience, cognitive psychology, organizational theory, the quantitative social and behavioral sciences, and, of course, the application of digital technology to learning. There are currently very real constraints imposed by those in the administration and Congress who have difficulty accepting a more revolutionary educational role for the federal government. Although education is clearly felt to be a priority in our society, it is generally viewed and supported within the constraints of existing perspectives, policies, and programs. It may well be true that the current problems plaguing education in America are political, organizational, and economic, but without a firm scientific understanding of how learning actually occurs and how learning environments should be developed, progress will be limited. The radical rethinking of the learning ecology necessitated by a knowledge-driven society is very threatening to most public leaders.

New opportunities for breakthroughs in understanding children's cognitive development are emerging in brain research. A strong scientific infrastructure could be developed to link basic brain research with more applied areas of cognitive, emotional, physical, and social development, similar to that which occurred in the understanding of solid-state physics necessary for microelectronics or the science of genomics and cellular biology important for modern medicine.

There are similar opportunities in systemic issues such as the design of learning systems. For example, how would one explore different architectures of learning environments, institutions, and enterprises for the digital age? Here the goal would be to set aside the constraints of existing educational structures (e.g., schools, colleges, workplace training) and practices and begin with a clean slate to consider how one might meet the lifelong educational needs of citizens in a global, knowledge-driven society. How would one design learning experiences, resources, and institutions that exhibit the various characteristics suggested for learning institutions in the twenty-first century: learner-centered, interactive and collaborative, asynchronous and ubiquitous, intelligent and adaptive, lifelong and evolutionary, diverse, and affordable?

Of particular interest here is the redesign of the national learning infrastructure that provides technical knowledge and skills (science, math, technology) and the learning skills necessary for a knowledge-driven society. There also needs to be consideration given to how to design a learning architecture that narrows the digital divide, with particular concern given to providing educational opportunities to those who have been traditionally disadvantaged by our current educational systems.

Although the U.S. Department of Education has traditionally been assigned the responsibility for federal leadership and policy development in education, particularly at the K–12 level, it could be that the most appropriate federal agency for providing national leadership in creating a new learning infrastructure might well be the National Science Foundation. This is suggested by several considerations: (1) much of the knowledge most critical to our future will be based upon science, mathematics, and technology; (2) the NSF is unique among federal agencies in having both a charter and experience in the conduct of fundamental research concerning education at all levels; and (3) the NSF is also unique in its ability to engage the entire research community in high-quality, merit-driven research directed at national priorities such as education. In fact, much of the innovation in lifelong learning will be based upon research and development sponsored by the NSF in fields such as information technology, cognitive science, and the social and behavioral sciences.

The current Interagency Education Research Initiative, involving NSF, NIH, and DOEd, provides one interesting approach to rapidly scaling up federal investment in educational research. All federal agencies have human capital needs and therefore some responsibility for investment in education and skills development (much as they have been assigned roles in economic development through the Small Business Research Initiative program). Each could be a player in a broader interagency program, similar to the strategic Information Technology Research or Nanotechnology Research programs of the past several years.

There are serious limitations in using such conventional approaches to stimulate creative and innovative research during a period of rapid change and uncertainty. Particularly in the area of digital technology and its application to learning, we need far more out-of-the-box projects that frequently push the envelope far beyond what conventional programs (and peer review) are willing to tolerate.

An even more interesting model for the conduct of research on education and learning is provided by the DOD's Defense Advanced Research Programs Agency (DARPA). Through a process using visionary program managers to channel significant, flexible, and long-term funding to the very best researchers for both basic and applied research undergirding key defense technologies, DARPA has been able to capture contributions of the very best of the nation's scientists and engineers in highly innovative projects. Many of today's technologies such as microelectronics, computer science, materials science, and nanotechnology can be traced to earlier DARPA programs. Perhaps we need an Education Advanced Research Programs Agency (EARPA) to focus the capabilities of the American research enterprise on what many believe to be our nation's most compelling priority, the quality of education for a knowledge-driven society. Since the Department of Education has so little experience in merit-driven basic research activities and limited credibility with the broader scientific community, other federal agencies such as the NSF and NIH might serve as partners to provide guidance and oversight during the start-up phase of an EARPA. This might also provide a source of intellectual energy and vitality in the Department of Education, similar to that provided by basic research activities in other mission agencies (DOD, DOE, NASA, etc.). To convince the research community that this is a serious effort and not simply channeling more money into the education establishment, it might even be useful to get the National Academies' participation in such activities.

Another approach would be to adopt the model used in health research, which is undergirded by solid basic and applied research based on the use of clinical trials and of ongoing longitudinal studies tracking health behavior and status focusing on virtually every health problem. Health research also has an institutional infrastructure based on teaching hospitals, schools of public health, and academic research centers that closely link research to training, practice, and public education. Another component is extensive cross-training among disciplines and between researchers and practitioners. All of this is aided by a central funding agency—the National Institutes of Health—that is guided by scientific peer review and is able to set priorities and achieve more investment in infrastructure. In contrast, research on children outside of physical health often lacks a vibrant basic research component, has almost no scientifically structured clinical trials, and has relatively few major longitudinal surveys tracking children and no equivalents of teaching hospitals or schools of public health that combine research with practice. The R&D community is fragmented across disciplines and federal departments that invest in infrastructure, making investment inefficient. Research centers tend to be university-based and far removed from schools or communities where children's learning and development occur.

Beyond new mechanisms to stimulate and support research in the science of education, we also need to develop more effective mechanisms to transfer what we have learned into schools, colleges, and universities. For example, the progress made in cognitive psychology and neuroscience during the past decade in the understanding of learning is considerable,[20] yet almost none of this research has had an impact our schools.

A Learn-Grant Act for the Twenty-first Century

Recall that a century and a half ago, America was facing a period of similar change, evolving from an agrarian, frontier society into an industrial nation. At that time, a social contract was developed between the federal government, the states, and public colleges and universities designed to assist our young nation in making this transition. The land-grant acts were based upon several commitments. First, the federal government provided federal lands for the support of higher education. Next, the states agreed to create public universities designed to serve both regional and national interests. As the final element, these public or land-grant universities accepted new responsibilities to broaden educational opportunities for the working class while launching new programs in applied areas such as agriculture, engineering, and medicine aimed at serving an industrial society, while committing themselves to public service, engagement, and extension.

As we noted earlier, today our society is undergoing a similarly profound transition, this time from an industrial to a knowledge-based society. Hence, it may be time for a new social contract aimed at providing the knowledge and the educated citizens necessary for prosperity, security, and social well-being in this new age. Perhaps it is time for a new federal act, similar to the land-grant acts of the nineteenth century, that will help the higher education enterprise address the needs of the twenty-first century. A twenty-first century land-grant act is not a new concept.[21] Some have recommended an industrial analog to the agricultural experiment stations of the land-grant universities. Others have suggested that in our information-driven economy, perhaps telecommunications bandwidth is the asset that could be assigned to universities much as federal lands were a century ago. Unfortunately, an industrial extension service may be of marginal utility in a knowledge-driven society. Furthermore, Congress has already given away much of the available bandwidth to traditional broadcasting and telecommunications companies.

There is a more important difference. The land-grant paradigm of the nineteenth and twentieth centuries was focused on developing the vast natural resources of our nation.[22] Today, however, we have come to realize that our most important national resource for the future will be our people. At the dawn of the age of knowledge, one could well make the argument that education itself will replace natural resources or national defense as the priority for the twenty-first century. We might even conjecture that a social contract based on developing and maintaining the abilities and talents of our people to their fullest extent could well transform our schools, colleges, and universities into new forms that would rival the research university in importance. In a sense, the twenty-first-century analog to the land-grant university might be termed a learn-grant university.

A learn-grant university for the twenty-first century might be designed to develop our most important asset, our human resources, as its top priority, along with the infrastructure necessary to sustain a knowledge-driven society. The field stations and cooperative extension programs—perhaps now as much in cyberspace as in a physical location—could be directed to the needs and the development of the people in the region. Furthermore, perhaps we should discard the current obsession of research universities to control and profit from intellectual property developed on the campus through research and instruction by wrapping discoveries in layer after layer of bureaucratic regulations defended by armies of lawyers and instead move to something more akin to the "open source" philosophy used in some areas of software development. That is, in return for strong public support, perhaps public universities could be persuaded to regard all intellectual property developed on the campus through research as in the public domain and encourage their faculty to work closely with commercial interests to enable these knowledge resources to serve society, without direct control or financial benefit to the university.

In an era of relative prosperity in which education plays such a pivotal role, it may be possible to build the case for new federal commitments based on just such a vision of a society of learning. But certain features seem increasingly apparent. New investments are unlikely to be made within the old paradigms. For example, while the federal government–research university partnership based on merit-based, peer-reviewed grants has been remarkably successful, this remains a system in which only a small number of elite institutions participate and benefit. The theme of a twenty-first-century learn-grant act would be to broaden the base, to build and distribute widely the capacity to contribute both new knowledge and educated knowledge workers to our society, not simply to channel more resources into established institutions.

An interesting variation on this theme is the Millennium Education Trust Fund, proposed by Lawrence Grossman and Newton Minow.[23] This fund would be established by investing the revenues from the sale or lease of the digital spectrum and would serve the diverse educational, informational, and cultural needs of American society by enhancing learning opportunities, broadening our knowledge base, supporting the arts and culture, and developing the skills that are necessary for the information age. Grossman and Minow estimate that the auctions of unused spectrum over the next several years could yield at least $18 billion. These revenues, placed in a Millennium Education Trust Fund, would work just as the Northwest Ordinance and Morrill Act did in past centuries, investing proceeds from the sale of public property in our nation's most valuable asset, our people.

Whatever the mechanism, the point seems clear. It may be time to consider a new social contract, linking together federal and state investment with higher education and business to serve national and regional needs, much in the spirit of the land-grant acts of the nineteenth century.

STATE POLICIES, PROGRAMS, AND INVESTMENTS

Although the federal government does exert some influence on higher education through its sponsorship of key programs and federal regulations, the primary responsibility for most colleges and universities resides at the state or local level. In an abstract sense, one can think of the primary responsibility of state government as creating and maintaining institutions of higher education as societal assets by providing relatively unrestricted operating support. This is to be contrasted with the federal role, where public policies and targeted funding are used to influence higher education to address national priorities (e.g., the land-grant act, the GI Bill, the government-research partnership).

It is at the state level where the conflicting forces of market pressures and public purpose must be reconciled. Of course, we should acknowledge that despite the rapid evolution of digital technology and the emergence of new competitors over the past decade, market competition, particularly for public universities, has been relatively benign, mitigated by both traditional monopolies and government regulation. State governments continue to operate higher education systems that are essentially cartels, with the mission, funding, and management of institutions largely dictated by state policies and governing boards.

This relatively stable, if not stagnant, situation is likely to change in the years ahead as market forces driven by economic, social, and technological change overwhelm traditional roles, policies, and regulations. Now is the time for the states to give serious consideration to the policies and actions that will be necessary both to protect their higher education resources and to meet the rapidly growing and evolving educational needs of their citizens.

The relationship between higher education and state government is a complex one and varies significantly from state to state. Increasingly, state governments have moved to regulate public higher education, thereby lessening the institutional autonomy of universities. In many states, public universities are caught in a tight web of state government rules, regulations, and bureaucracy. Statewide systems and coordinating bodies exercise greater power than ever over public institutions. An example here is the rise of performance funding, in which state appropriations are based on institutional performance as measured by a set of quantitative outcome indicators, often developed by the state legislature and rarely related to program quality.

The contemporary disconnect between what traditional higher education providers, especially research institutions and four-year colleges, want and what society wants can be gleaned in part through a 1998 poll of the 50 state governors. The aptly titled study, "Transforming Postsecondary Education for the 21st Century," reveals that the governors' four priorities were

- to encourage lifelong learning (97 percent),
- to allow students to obtain education at any time and in any place via technology (83 percent),
- to require postsecondary institutions to collaborate with business and industry in curriculum and program development (77 percent), and

- to integrate applied or on-the-job experience into academic programs (66 percent).

In contrast, the bottom four items in priority were (1) maintaining faculty authority for curriculum content, quality, and degree requirements (35 percent); (2) maintaining the present balance of faculty research, teaching load, and community service (32 percent); (3) ensuring a campus-based experience for the majority of students (21 percent); and (4) in last place—enjoying the support of only one of the governors responding—maintaining traditional faculty roles and tenure (3 percent).

More states than ever (at least two dozen, at last count, including California, Florida, Pennsylvania, Texas, New York, and Wisconsin) are using strategic or "master" plans to chart a course for their public colleges, mainly out of a belief that the institutions must be better positioned to deal with rapid technological and economic change. The key priorities in these plans are:

- Offering access to college to large populations that are not currently being served and that run the risk of being left behind by continuing shifts in the economy.
- Getting public colleges much more involved in efforts to improve public schools, as a result of the belief that inadequate teacher-training programs have contributed to the problems of public education.
- Managing and exploiting new technology to provide more access to college, link all sectors of education, and help public institutions hold their own in an increasingly competitive market.

The views and needs of business are at the heart of nearly all of the long-range higher education plans that states have adopted or are considering. Both California and Florida are coupling their master higher education plans to K–12. In fact, Florida has eliminated the state's separate college systems and combined them with K–12.

Here it is also important to recognize the very great differences among states in needs, scale, and traditions. California and Texas, facing the challenge of soaring enrollments of students from minority populations, are far different from Rust Belt states such as Michigan and Ohio, which are likely to face relatively static enrollments of traditional 18–22-year-olds but rapidly accelerating needs of adult learners as their economies evolve from manufacturing to knowledge services. Furthermore, many states such as New York and Ohio have long-standing experiences with statewide higher education systems, while others such as Michigan have long believed that the anarchy of constitutional autonomy for each university provided more flexibility and resilience.

The real learning infrastructure is funded at the state or local level, not at the federal level (although the federal government can sometimes fund experiments). In the digital age, networking infrastructure, on the campus, in the surrounding community, and statewide, becomes all-important. All too often, however, states allow the powerful telecommunications industry to control the quality of this infrastructure, blocking the attempts to open up intrastate connectivity to competition. Furthermore, most states do not have adequate independent advisory bodies concerned with digital technology. All too frequently, state strategies are outsourced to commercial consultants or lobbyists. Every once in a while a particularly creative governor gets a brainstorm, and something happens, only to disappear once again into the swamp when a new administration is elected. Progress at the state level is episodic, at best ... two steps forward and one step back.

Many actions are obvious. If universities are to have the flexibility to respond to market forces, they must be provided with relief from the red tape and regulations of state government bureaucracy. Decentralization of decision making and budget authority is essential at the state, university, and academic program level. States should consider structural changes in legislative charters or perhaps even state constitutions to allow more university autonomy, perhaps even creating the opportunity for charter universities or public authorities that operate largely independently of state government. Public institutions should be provided with the capacity to launch independent, for-profit subsidiaries. More broadly, to stimulate market competition, states should encourage the entry of new providers, including for-profit and cyberspace institutions, perhaps from other states or even nations.[24]

Given the current policy framework, it is little wonder that many colleges and universities face the dilemma of operating their traditional campus-based programs within the conventional, heavily regulated environment of state government, while launching their on-line or adult education programs in an intensively competitive commercial marketplace. Despite the strong interest in market forces on the part of policymakers, there is always a tendency to revert to regulation (particularly at election time). Efforts to provide the incentives for quality and efficiency such as performance funding have frequently led to only more layers of regulation and bureaucracy. Little wonder that universities are concerned that promises of increased autonomy could lead to a loss of state subsidy while facing the difficult demands of competition.

However, it is also clear that during a time of accelerating change, universities need to become more flexible and entrepreneurial. The key challenge to state government is to provide policies that help to overcome the naturally slow and cautious mode of the present forms of university government and the constraints of state government and university system bureaucracy. Policies need to encourage universities to become more innovative and risk-tolerant.

CONCLUSIONS

We have entered a period of significant change in higher education as our universities attempt to respond to the challenges, opportunities, and responsibilities before them.[25]

Clearly, higher education will flourish in the decades ahead. In a knowledge-intensive society, the need for advanced education will become ever more pressing, both for individuals and for society more broadly. It is also likely that the university as we know it today—rather, the current constellation of diverse institutions constituting the higher education enterprise—will change in profound ways to serve a changing world. The real question is not whether higher education will be transformed, but rather *how* and by *whom*. Much of this change will be driven by market forces—by a limited resource base, changing societal needs, new technologies, and new competitors. We also must remember that higher education has a public purpose and a public obligation.[26] It is possible to shape and form the markets that will, in turn, reshape our institutions with appropriate civic purpose, but only with enlightened public policy and sustained public investment.

NOTES

1. Vernon Ehlers, "Unlocking Our Future: Toward a New National Science Policy," a report to Congress by the House Committee on Science (September 24, 1998).

2. National Governors Association, *Postsecondary Education Policy*, National Governors Policy Statement HR-44 (Washington, DC: National Governors Association, 2001); see also <http:www.nga.org/nga/legislativeupdate>.

3. Michael Moe, *The Knowledge Web: People Power—Fuel for the New Economy* (New York: Merrill-Lynch, 2000).

4. Peter Drucker, "The Next Society," *The Economist*, (November 3, 2001), 3–20.

5. Joseph L. Dionne and Thomas Kean, *Breaking the Social Contract: The Fiscal Crisis in Higher Education*, Report of the Commission on National Investment in Higher Education (New York: Council for Aid to Education, 1997).

6. *The Third International Mathematics and Science Study—Repeat* (Washington, DC: National Science Foundation and Department of Education, 2001).

7. Douglas S. Massey, *Higher Education and Social Mobility in the United States 1940–1998* (Washington, DC: Association of American Universities, 2000).

8. David Gardner, chair, National Commission on Excellence in Education, *A Nation at Risk* (Washington, DC: U.S. Department of Education, 1983).

9. Drucker, "The Next Society."

10. Michael G. Dolence and Donald M. Norris, *Transforming Higher Education: A Vision for Learning in the 21st Century* (Ann Arbor: Society for College and University Planning, 1995).

11. Ibid.

12. Harold L. Hodgkinson, *All One System: Demographics of Education—Kindergarten through Graduate School* (Washington, DC: Institute for Educational Leadership, 1985).

13. Peter Schwartz, *The Art of the Long View* (New York: Doubleday Currency, 1991), 124–140.

14. John S. Daniel, *Mega-Universities and Knowledge Media* (London: Kogan Page, 1996).

15. Diane J. Macunovich, "Will There Be a Boom in the Demand for U.S. Higher Education among 18- to 24-Year-Olds?" *Change* 29 (May–June 1997), 34–44.

16. Ehlers, "Unlocking Our Future."

17. Kellogg Commission on the Future of the State and Land-Grant Universities, *Renewing the Covenant: Learning, Discovery and Engagement in a New Age and Different World* (Washington, DC: National Association of State Universities and Land-Grant Colleges, 2000).

18. Federal R&D as a percentage of total R&D in the United States reached a high point in 1964 at 66.8 percent, equaled 46.4 percent in 1987, and in 1999 was 26.7 percent. See NSF, *National Patterns of Research and Development Resources 1999 Data Update* (NSF 00–306); see also National Science Board, *Science and Engineering Indicators* (Washington, DC: National Science Foundation, 2000), 2-9–2-21.

19. Committee on Scientific Principles for Education Research, National Research Council, *Scientific Research in Education*, ed. R. J. Shavelson and L. Towne (Washington, DC: National Academy Press, 2002).

20. Committee on Developments in the Science of Learning, National Research Council, *How People Learn: Brain, Mind, Experience, and School* (Washington, DC: National Academy Press, 2000).

21. *Renewing the Covenant*; Walter E. Massey, "The Public University for the Twenty-First Century: Beyond the Land Grant," 16th David Dodds Henry Lecture, University of Illinois at Chicago (1994); J. W. Peltason, "Reactionary Thoughts of a Revolutionary," 17th David Dodds Henry Lecture, University of Illinois at Urbana-Champaign (October 18, 1995).

22. Frank Rhodes, "The New American University," in *Looking to the Twenty-First Century: Higher Education in Transition* (Champaign-Urbana: University of Illinois Press, 1995).

23. Lawrence K. Grossman and Newton N. Minow, *A Digital Gift to the Nation: Fulfilling the Promise of the Digital and Internet Age* (New York: Carnegie Corporation of New York, 2000).

24. Frank Newman, "State Policy Development for the Digital Age," Forum on the Future of Higher Education, Brown University (2001).

25. "The Glion Declaration: The University at the Millennium," *The Presidency* (Fall 1998), 27–31.

26. Robert Zemsky and Gregory Wegner, "A Very Public Agenda," *Policy Perspectives* 8, no. 2 (1998), 1–12.

The Future of the University in the Digital Age

Higher education has entered a period of significant change as our universities attempt to respond to the challenges, opportunities, and responsibilities facing them in the new century. The forces driving change are many and varied: the globalization of commerce and culture, the advanced educational needs of citizens in a knowledge-driven global economy, the exponential growth of new knowledge and new disciplines, and the compressed timescales and nonlinear nature of the transfer of knowledge from campus laboratories into commercial products. We have entered a period of social transformation where intellectual capital is replacing financial and physical capital as the key to prosperity and social well-being. Our rapid evolution into a knowledge-based, global society has been driven in part by the emergence of powerful new information technologies such as digital computers and communications networks.

In this book we attempt to identify and examine the key themes of such technology-driven change:

1. The exponential pace of the evolution of information technology.
2. The ubiquitous/pervasive character of the Internet.
3. The relaxation (or obliteration) of the conventional constraints of space, time, and monopoly.
4. The democratizing character of information technology (universal access to information, education, and research).
5. The changing ways that we handle digital data, information, and knowledge.

6. The growing importance of intellectual capital relative to physical or financial capital in the "new economy."

As knowledge-intensive social institutions, colleges and universities will be particularly affected by the rapid evolution of digital technology. Further, if past experience is any guide, the impact of this technology on the university and the consequent changes in its activities, structure, and environment are likely to be rapid, profound, and discontinuous. The future of the university will be characterized by ever-greater uncertainty. From some perspectives, the university has changed remarkably little in values, roles, structure, and function over the past several decades—indeed, over the past several centuries, at least compared to most other social institutions. However, we should not delude ourselves into thinking that higher education will be unperturbed by the transforming character of digital technology. After all, even the most pronounced exponential change starts off with a very modest slope.

As we conclude our consideration of the future of the university in the digital age, it is important once again to distinguish between two different time periods. For the near term, meaning a decade or less, it is likely that most colleges and universities will retain their current form, albeit with some evolution in pedagogical and scholarly activities and in organization and financing. This is the period that we have addressed in this book. While change will occur, and while it is likely to be both profound and unpredictable, it will at least be understandable.

What about the longer term, perhaps a generation from now? After all, if the pace dictated by Moore's law continues to characterize the evolution of information technology, over the next several decades we would see the power of this technology (and related technologies such as biotechnology and nanotechnology) increase by factors of 1,000, 1 million, 1 billion, and so on, likely reshaping our society and most social institutions into unrecognizable forms. We must leave speculation concerning these longer-term possibilities to futurists (and perhaps science fiction writers).

THE KEY CONCLUSIONS

It is useful to summarize in this final chapter our conclusions concerning the evolution of digital technology and its impact on the university. First, we believe that the extraordinary evolutionary pace of information technology is likely to continue for the next several decades and even could accelerate on a superexponential slope. Photonic technology is evolving at twice the rate of silicon chip technology (e.g., Moore's law), with minia-turization and wireless technology advancing even faster, implying that the rate of growth of network appliances will be incredible. For planning pur-poses, we can assume that within the decade we will have computer power, bandwidth, and connectivity a hundred times—perhaps a thousand times—beyond current capabilities.

The event horizons for disruptive change are moving ever closer. It is important to challenge people to think about the implications of acceler-ating technology learning curves as well as technology cost-performance curves. There are likely to be major technology surprises, comparable in significance to the appearance of the personal computer in the 1970s and the Internet browser in 1994, but at more frequent intervals. The future is becoming less certain.

The impact of information technology on the university will likely be profound, rapid, and discontinuous—just as it has been and will continue to be for the economy, our society, and our social institutions (e.g., corpo-rations, governments, and learning institutions). It will affect our activi-ties (teaching, research, outreach), our organization (academic structure, faculty culture, financing and management), and the broader higher edu-cation enterprise as it evolves into a global knowledge and learning in-dustry.

For at least the near term, meaning a decade or less, the university will continue to exist in much its present form, although meeting the challenge of emerging competitors in the marketplace will demand significant changes in how we teach, how we conduct scholarship, and how our in-stitutions are financed. Universities must anticipate these forces, develop appropriate strategies, and make adequate investments if they are to pros-per during this period.

Over the longer term, the basic character and structure of the univer-sity may be challenged by the IT-driven forces of aggregation (e.g., new al-liances, restructuring of the academic marketplace into a global learning and knowledge industry) and disaggregation (e.g., restructuring of the ac-ademic disciplines, detachment of faculty and students from particular uni-versities, decoupling of research and education).

Although information technology will present many complex challenges and opportunities to university leaders, we suggest that procrastination and inaction are the most dangerous courses during a time of rapid technolog-ical change. After all, attempting to cling to the status quo is a decision in itself, perhaps of momentous consequence. To be sure, certain ancient val-ues and traditions of the university should be maintained and protected, such as academic freedom, a rational spirit of inquiry, and liberal learning. However, just as in earlier times, the university will have to transform itself once again to serve a radically changing world if it is to sustain these important values and roles.

Although we feel confident that information technology will continue its rapid evolution for the foreseeable future, it is far more difficult to predict the impact of this technology on human behavior and upon social institutions such as the university. It is important that higher education develop mechanisms to sense the changes that are being driven by information technology and to understand where these forces may drive the university. Because of the profound, yet unpredictable, impact of this technology, it is important that institutional strategies include (1) the opportunity for experimentation, (2) the formation of alliances both with other academic institutions as well as with for-profit and government organizations, and (3) the development of sufficient in-house expertise among the faculty and staff to track technological trends and assess various courses of action.

In summary, for the near term (meaning a decade or less), we anticipate that information technology will drive comprehensible, if rapid, profound, and discontinuous, change in the university. For the longer term (two decades and beyond), all bets are off. As we have noted, implications of a millionfold increase in the power of information technology are difficult to even imagine, much less predict for our world and even more so for our institutions.

A POLICY FRAMEWORK

Many questions concerning the future of the university in the digital age remain unanswered. Who will be the learners served by these institutions? Who will teach them? Who will administer and govern these institutions? Who will pay for them? What will be the character of our universities? How will they function? Will the campus be a physical place or a Web site portal in cyberspace?

Perhaps the most profound question of all concerns the survival of the university in the face of the changes brought on by the emergence of new competitors. That is the question raised by Peter Drucker and other futurists.[1] Could an institution such as the university, which has existed for a millennium, disappear in the face of such changes? Most of us, of course, believe quite strongly that the university as a social institution is simply too valuable to disappear. On the other hand, there may well be future forms of the university that we would have great difficulty in recognizing from our present perspective.

Rather than debating the survival of the university, it seems more constructive to suggest first a somewhat different set of questions in an effort to frame the key policy issues facing higher education and its various stakeholders:

1. How do we respond to the diverse educational needs of a knowledge-driven society? Here we must realize that while the educational needs of the young will continue to be a priority, we will be challenged also to address the sophisticated learning needs of adults in the workplace while providing broader lifetime learning opportunities for all of our society, for example, serving a "society of learning."

2. How do we take advantages of the opportunities offered by emerging information technology (e.g., freeing our activities from the constraints of space and time, allowing significant improvements in both quality and efficiency, expanding the population of those we serve) while facing its challenges (e.g., the intense competition of an open learning marketplace, the radical changes that will likely be required in both pedagogy and scholarship)?

3. The powerful market forces stimulated by digital technologies raise particularly important policy issues for higher education. How can we provide our colleges and universities with the flexibility to respond to market forces while protecting their core missions of education and scholarship? More broadly, how do we balance the roles of market forces and public purpose in determining the future of higher education in America? Can we control the powerful market forces driven by changing societal needs and evolving digital technology through public policy and public investment so that the most valuable roles and values of the university are preserved? Or will the competitive and commercial pressures of a technology-driven marketplace sweep over our institutions, leaving behind a higher education enterprise characterized by mediocrity or perhaps even irrelevance?

These are some of the issues that should frame the debate about the future of higher education in the digital age. As social institutions, universities reflect the values, needs, and character of the society that they serve. These issues of access and opportunity, equality and justice, private economic benefits and public purpose, freedom and accountability are all part of a broader public debate about the future of our nation. They provide the context for any consideration of the future of the university.

There is an important caveat in such a national dialogue concerning the future of higher education in the digital age. Information technology is evolving so rapidly that any fixed set of policies and programs is likely to be overtaken. Instead, what the higher education community really needs is an ongoing process capable of tracking technology changes and their implications, identifying key issues, challenges, and opportunities, and making recommendations for actions or further studies.

Furthermore, there needs to be a concerted effort to raise the awareness of these issues on the campuses and guide the development of a strategic framework for making decisions. Such a process should bring together leaders from diverse institutional types such as research universities, liberal arts colleges, and regional colleges and universities: deans from various academic and professional disciplines, leaders of faculty governance, and university trustees. Efforts should also be made to link together and coordinate a number of related projects concerning the impact of technology on the broader postsecondary education enterprise.

BRIDGING THE DIGITAL DIVIDE

Here it seems appropriate to make one further comment concerning "the digital divide," the concern that many have about a widening gap between those who can afford access to information technology and those who cannot. Such stratification in our society among the haves and have-nots would be of great concern if information technology were not evolving so rapidly. However, this technology is migrating rapidly toward "thin client" systems, in which the personal computer becomes an inexpensive and ubiquitous commodity available to anyone and everyone like today's calculator or telephone, while the real investment occurs in the supporting network infrastructure.

The most significant advantage of computer-mediated distance learning is access. The powerful new tools provided by information technology have the capacity to enrich all of education, stimulating us to rethink education from the perspective of the learner.

In reality, the concern should not be with the digital divide but rather with the growing gap in prosperity, power, and social well-being between those who have access to quality education and those who do not, because of economic circumstances, jobs, families, or location. From this perspective, the development of technology-based methods for delivering educational services such as asynchronous learning networks and virtual universities may actually narrow the educational gap by providing universal access to quality educational opportunities. In a sense, computer networks might even be regarded as a force that will tend to equalize access to learning, since it will extend educational opportunities to those currently underserved by traditional colleges and universities.

AN ACTION AGENDA FOR COLLEGES AND UNIVERSITIES

Let us now turn our attention to the issues and decisions facing leaders of our colleges and universities. How do they grapple with the many challenges and opportunities posed by digital technology?

They should begin with the basics by launching a conversation on their campuses that identifies those key roles and values that should be protected and preserved during a time of transformation. For example, how would the university set priorities among its various roles such as education of the young, preservation of our culture, basic research and scholarship, serving as a social critic, and applying knowledge to serve society? Which of its values and principles should be preserved, and which should be reconsidered (e.g., academic freedom, a rational spirit of inquiry, a community of scholars, a commitment to excellence, shared governance, and tenure)?

Next, while learning and scholarship require some independence from society, it is nevertheless important to listen carefully to the many stakeholders of the university to learn their changing needs, expectations, and perceptions of higher education and to understand the various forces driving change in our world. This conversation also provides a context for decision making during a time of rapid, technology-driven change.

To this end, it is important to prepare the academy for change. While launching the conversation is important, so, too, will be a reconsideration of the academic culture that sometimes allows the demand of consensus to thwart action, that rarely links accountability with privilege, and that defines tenure as lifetime employment security rather than a device to protect academic freedom. University governance may also need to be restructured—particularly lay boards and shared governance models—so that it responds to the changing needs of society rather than defending and perpetuating an obsolete past. Colleges and universities will need to develop a tolerance for strong leadership.

It seems increasingly clear that colleges and universities will need to develop new financial models if they are to thrive in the digital age. Beyond the need to implement a sustainable model of investment in information technology infrastructure, the intensely competitive marketplace for higher education services stimulated by digital technology will put at risk the current system of cross-subsidies in funding university activities.

Since the future will become increasingly uncertain, universities should encourage experimentation with new paradigms of learning, research, and service by harvesting the best ideas from within the academy (or elsewhere), implementing them on a sufficient scale to assess their impact, and disseminating their results. Examples might include increasing the opportunities for interactive and collaborative learning, developing tutorial and studio teaching enhanced by digital tools, producing and utilizing advanced simulation and visualization technology, and developing platforms for sharing Web-based materials and for managing the educational enterprise. More broadly, we should recognize that digital technology will force us to rethink the very nature of education in the university, redefining the roles of students, teachers, and learners.

Furthermore, universities should place far greater emphasis on building alliances among institutions that will allow individual institutions to focus on core competencies while relying on alliances to address the broader and diverse needs of society. Such alliances should be encouraged not only among institutions of higher education (e.g., partnering research universities with liberal arts colleges and community colleges) but also between higher education and the private sector (e.g., information technology and entertainment companies). Differentiation among institutions should be encouraged, while relying upon market forces rather than regulations to discourage duplication.

Finally, university leaders should approach issues and decisions concerning information technology not as threats but rather as opportunities. To be sure, there will be many challenges such as those posed by emerging competitors in the for-profit sector or the potential loss of outstanding students and faculty members to institutions with superior technology infrastructures for teaching and research. So, too, will the status quo be threatened by a technology driving rapid, profound, and discontinuous change, but creative, visionary leaders will tap the energy created by such threats to lead their institutions in new directions that will reinforce and enhance their most important roles and values. They will use digital technology to help their students learn more effectively, to help their faculty members become better teachers and scholars, and to enable their institutions to better serve a rapidly changing society.

THE DAWN OF THE DIGITAL AGE

Clearly, the digital age poses many challenges and opportunities for the contemporary university. For most of the history of higher education in

America, we have expected students to travel to a physical place, a campus, to participate in a pedagogical process involving tightly integrated studies based mostly on lectures and seminars by recognized experts. As the constraints of time and space—and perhaps even reality itself—are relieved by information technology, will the university as a physical place continue to hold its relevance?

Many view the computer as a symbol of the depersonalizing nature of modern science and technology, yet, if ever there was a tool for empowering the individual, it is information technology. This has become truly a liberating force in our society, not only freeing us from the mental drudgery of routine tasks but linking us together in ways that we never dreamed possible, overcoming the constraints of space and time. William F. Buckley put it well when he proclaimed: "Let our teachers encourage the use of the tools of learning and foreswear nonsense about how Shakespeare would have written flatly if he had a word processor. It is likelier that he'd have written even more masterpieces, one of them at the expense of the Luddites."[2]

In the near term it seems likely that the university as a physical place, a community of scholars, and a center of culture will remain. Information technology will be used to augment and enrich the traditional activities of the university, in much their traditional forms. To be sure, the current arrangements of higher education may shift. For example, students may choose to distribute their college education among residential campuses, commuter colleges, and on-line or virtual universities. They may also assume more responsibility for, and control over, their education. In this sense, information technology is rapidly becoming a liberating force in our society, not only freeing us from the mental drudgery of routine tasks but also linking us together in ways that we never dreamed possible, overcoming the constraints of space and time. Furthermore, the new knowledge media enable us to build and sustain new types of learning communities, free from the constraints of space and time.

It also poses certain risks to the university. It will create strong incentives to standardize higher education, perhaps reducing it to its lowest common denominator of quality. It could dilute our intellectual resources and distribute them through unregulated agreements between faculty and electronic publishers. It will almost certainly open up the university to competition, both from other educational institutions as well as from the commercial sector.

There is an increasing sense that the digital age will not permit business as usual for most universities. Rather, it will demand radical changes in the institutional arrangements among students, faculty, and educational institutions. The current concept of distance learning, even if implemented via the Internet through virtual universities, is still bound to traditional ideas and approaches, but as true learning communities are constructed in cyberspace, traditional educational institutions will feel increasing competition and pressure to change.

It is ironic that the cyberspace paradigm of learning communities, in reality, represents a mechanism to return higher learning to the historic ways of the university, with the scholar surrounded by disciples in an intense interrelationship. In a sense, it recognizes that the true advantages of universities are in the educational process, in the array of social interactions, counseling, tutorials, and hands-on mentoring activities that require human interaction.

Those universities that understand their strengths in building learning communities, providing students with the capacity to interact and learn within these communities, and then certifying the learning process may well find the coming digital revolution an extraordinary opportunity. Universities that understand both their unique role and the profound nature of the new technology could well evolve into truly global institutions, using information technology to provide educational services to an increasingly knowledge-dependent world.

The digital age poses many challenges and opportunities for the contemporary university. Evolving information technology is freeing the activities of the research university—its teaching, scholarship, and service to society—from the constraints of space, time, monopoly, and perhaps even reality itself. While the university campus as a physical place serving a community of learners is likely to remain at least for the near term, the nature of its activities, organization, management, and funding is likely to change quite rapidly and dramatically. While the challenges will be significant, so, too, will be the opportunities to enhance the important role of these institutions in our society.

It is our collective challenge to develop a strategic framework capable of understanding and shaping the impact that this extraordinary technology will have on our institutions. We are on the threshold of a revolution that is making the world's accumulated information and knowledge accessible to individuals everywhere, a technology that will link us together into new learning communities never before possible or even imaginable. This has breathtaking implications for education, research, and learning and, of course, for the university in the digital age. It is a profoundly democratic revolution that should involve us all.

NOTES

1. Peter Drucker, "The Next Society: A Survey of the Near Future," *The Atlantic Monthly* 356 (November 2001), 3–20; William A. Wulf, "Warning: Information Technology Will Transform the University," *Issues in Science and Technology* 11, no 4 (Summer 1995), 46–52.

2. William F. Buckley, *Buckley: The Right Word*, ed. Samuel S. Vaughan (New York: Random House, 1996), 205.

Bibliography

THE EVOLUTION OF INFORMATION TECHNOLOGY

Berners-Lee, Tim, James Hendler, and Ora Lassila. "The Semantic Web." *Scientific American* (May 2001); see also <http://www.sciam.com/2001/0501issue/0501berners-lee.html>.

Brown, John Seely, and Paul Duguid. *The Social Life of Information*. Cambridge: Harvard Business School Press, 2000.

Deming, Peter J., and Robert M. Metcalfe. *Beyond Calculation: The Next Fifty Years of Computing*. New York: Springer-Verlag, 1997.

Feldman, Stuart. Presentation on "Technology Futures" at the Workshop on the Impact of Information Technology on the Future of the Research University. January 22, 2001. <www.researchchannel.com/programs/na/itfru.html>.

Kurzweil, Ray. *The Age of Spiritual Machines: When Computers Exceed Human Intelligence*. New York: Viking, 1999.

Mitchell, William J. *City of Bits: Space, Place, and the Infobahn*. Cambridge: MIT Press, 1995. <http://www-mitpress.mit.edu/City_of_Bits>.

"2001: A Disappointment?" A Survey on Artificial Intelligence. *The Economist* (December 22, 2001), 96–98.

SOCIAL, ECONOMIC, AND TECHNOLOGICAL CHANGE IN AN AGE OF KNOWLEDGE

Attali, Jacques. *Millennium: Winners and Losers in the Coming World Order*. New York: Times Books, 1992.

Barlow, John Perry. "The Economy of Ideas: A Framework for Rethinking Patents and Copyrights in the Digital Age," *Wired* 2, no. 3 (March 1994), 84–90, 126–129.

Cristensen, Clayton M. *The Innovator's Dilemma*. Cambridge: Harvard Business School Press, 1997, Supplement/Special Section 1–22.

David, Peter. "Universities: Inside the Knowledge Factory." *The Economist* (October 4, 1997), Supplement-Special Section.

Drucker, Peter. "Beyond the Information Revolution.", *Atlantic Monthly* 284, no. 4 October 1999. <www.theatlantic.com/issues/99oct/9910drucker.htm>.

———. "The Next Society: A Survey of the Near Future." *The Economist* 356, no. 32, (November 2001), 3–20.

Gibbons, Michael. *The New Production of Knowledge*. London: Sage, 1994.

Schwartz, Peter. *The Art of the Long View*. New York: Doubleday/Currency, 1991.

SCHOLARSHIP IN THE DIGITAL AGE

Buildings, Books, and Bytes: Libraries and Communities in the Digital Age. Washington, DC: Benton Foundation, 1996.

Fuchs, Ira H., James J. Duderstadt, and Deanna B. Marcom, "The Diffusion of Knowledge in the Digital Age." *Proceedings of the American Philosophical Society* 145, no. 1 (March 2001), 45–82.

Lanham, Richard. *The Electronic Word: Democracy, Technology, and the Arts*. Chicago: University of Chicago Press, 1993.

National Research Council. *Issues for Science and Engineering Researchers in the Digital Age*. Washington, DC: National Academy Press, 2001.

THE PLUG-AND-PLAY GENERATION

Brown, John Seely. "Growing Up Digital." *Change* 32, no. 2 (March 2000), 11–20.

National Research Council. *How People Learn: Brain, Mind, Experience, and School*. Washington, DC: National Academy Press, 2000.

Tapscott, Don. *Growing Up Digital: The Rise of the Net Generation*. New York: McGraw-Hill, 1999.

THE FUTURE OF THE UNIVERSITY

Brown, John Seely, and Paul Duguid. "Universities in the Digital Age." *Change* 28, no. 4 (July 1996), 11–19.

Duderstadt, James J. *A University for the 21st Century*. Ann Arbor: University of Michigan Press, 2000.

Rhodes, Frank H. T. *The Creation of the Future: The Role of the American University*. Ithaca, NY: Cornell University Press, 2001.

THE IMPACT OF DIGITAL TECHNOLOGY
ON THE UNIVERSITY: ITFRU PROJECT

Daniel, John S. *Mega-Universities and Knowledge Media*. London: Kogan Page, 1996.

de Alva, Jorge Klor. "Remaking the Academy in the Age of Information." *Issues in Science and Technology*. Washington, DC: National Academy Press, 1999.

Dolence, Michael G., and Donald M. Norris. *Transforming Higher Education: A Vision for Learning in the 21st Century*. Ann Arbor: Society for College and University Planning, 1995.

Hawkins, Brian L. "Technology, Higher Education, and a Very Foggy Crystal Ball," *Educause Review* 35, no. 6 (2000), 65–73.

Wulf, William A. "Warning: Information Technology Will Transform the University." *Issues in Science and Technology* 11, no. 4. Washington, DC: National Academy Press, 1995, 46–52.

ONLINE EDUCATION (DISTANCE LEARNING)

"Books, Bricks, and Bytes." *Daedelus* 125, no, 4 (1996).

Bourne, John, ed. *On-Line Education: Learning Effectiveness and Faculty Satisfaction*. Nashville: Center for Asynchronous Learning Networks, 2000.

Dillenbourg, P., ed. *Collaborative Learning: Cognitive and Computational Approaches*. Oxford: Pergamon, 1999.

Goodman, Paul, ed. *Technology Enhanced Learning: Opportunities for Change*. New York: Erlbaum, 2001.

Graves, William H. "Virtual Operations." *Educause Review* 36, no. 2, (March/April 2001), 46–56.

Massey, William F. Massey. "Life on the Wired Campus: How Information Technology Will Shape Institutional Futures." In *The Learning Revolution*, edited by Diana Oblinger and Sean C. Bolton. Boston: Anker Publishing Co., 1997, 46–56.

Oblinger, Diana G., Carole A. Barone, and Brian L. Hawkins. *Distributed Education and its Challenges: An Overview*. Washington, DC: American Council on Education-Educause, 2001.

Steinbach, Shelly. *Developing a Distance Education Policy for 21st Century Learning*. Washington, DC: American Council on Education, 2000.

Twigg, Carol A. *Who Owns Online Courses and Course Materials? Intellectual Property Policies for a New Learning Environment*. Pew Symposium on Learning and Technology, 2000.

IT STRATEGIES IN HIGHER EDUCATION

Devlin, Maureen, Richard Larson, and Joel Meyerson, eds. *The Internet and the University*. Forum for the Future of Higher Education 2000. Boulder: Educause, 2000.

Grossman, Lawrence K., and Newton N. Minnow. *A Digital Gift to the Nation: Fulfilling the Promise of the Digital and Internet Age*. New York: Carnegie Corporation, 2000.

McRobbie, Michael A., and Judith G. Palmer. "Strategic and Financial Planning for Information Technology in Higher Education." In *Forum Futures 2000*, edited by Maureen E. Devlin and Joel W. Meyerson. San Francisco: Jossey-Bass, 2001.

The Millennium Partnership Initiative. Washington, DC: National Association of State Universities and Land Grant Colleges, 2000.

Olsen, Florence. "How Big a 'Pipe'? Colleges Struggle to Provide Network Bandwidth," *The Chronicle of Higher Education* (November 2, 2001).

Roche, James. "Checking the Radar: Survey Identifies Key IT Issues," *Educause Quarterly*, no. 2 (2000), 4–16.

Vest, Charles M. *Disturbing the Educational University: Universities in the Digital Age: Dinosaurs or Prometheans?* Cambridge: MIT Press, 2001.

THE COMPETITIVE MARKETPLACE

Collis, David. "When Industries Change: Scenarios for Higher Education." In *Forum Futures* (2001), 11–14.

———. "New Business Models for Higher Education." In *The Internet and the University*, edited by Maureen Devlin, Richard Larson, and Joel Meyerson. Cambridge: Educause, 2000.

Davis, Stan, and Jim Botkin. *The Monster under the Bed*. New York: Touchstone, 1994.

Downs, Larry, and Chunka Mui. *Killer App*. Cambridge: Harvard Business School Press, 1998.

Katz, Richard N., ed. *Dancing with the Devil: Information Technology and the New Competition in Higher Education*. San Francisco: Jossey-Bass Publishers, 1999.

Katz, Richard N., and Diana G. Oblinger, eds. *The "E" Is for Everything*. Vol. 2. Educause Leadership Strategies. San Francisco: Jossey-Bass, 2000.

Moe, Michael. *The Knowledge Web: People Power—Fuel for the New Economy*. New York: Merrill-Lynch, 2000.

Newman, Frank, and Lara K. Couturier. "The New Competitive Arena: Market Forces Invade the Academy." *Change* 33, no. 5 (September 2001), 11–17. [For an excellent example of such virtual universities, see the Web site for the Michigan Virtual Automotive College at <http://www.mvac.org> and the article by Scott Bernato, "Big 3 U," *University Business* (September–October 1998), 20–27.]

Peterson, Marvin W., and David Dill. "Understanding the Competitive Environment of the Postsecondary Knowledge Industry." In *Planning and Management for a Changing Environment: A Handbook on Redesigning Post-secondary Institutions*, edited by M. Peterson, D. Dill, and L. Mets. San Francisco: Jossey-Bass, 1997.

Swahney, Mohan, and Jeff Zahn. *The Seven Steps to Nirvana: Strategic Insights into Business Transformation*. New York: McGraw-Hill, 2001.

Zemsky, Robert. "Rumbling." *Policy Perspectives*. The Pew Higher Education Roundtable, sponsored by the Pew Charitable Trusts. April 1997.

Zemsky, Robert, and Gregory Wegner. "A Very Public Agenda." *Policy Perspectives* 8, no. 2. Knight Higher Education Collaborative, Philadelphia, 1998.

SCIENCE FICTION VISIONS OF LEARNING IN THE DIGITAL AGE

Gibson, William. *Neuromancer*. New York: Ace, 1984.

Stephenson, Neal. *Snow Crash*. New York: Bantam Books, 1992.

———. *The Diamond Age*. New York: Bantam Spectrum Books, 2000.

OTHER GENERAL SOURCES
Periodicals

Change, The Magazine of Higher Education, American Council on Education
Monthly and Quarterly Publications of EDUCAUSE

EDUCAUSE Review

EDUCAUSE Quarterly

Weekly section in Information Technology in *The Chronicle of Higher Education*

Useful Websites

Asynchronous Learning Networks: http://www.aln.org/
Cardean University: http://www.cardean.edu
Distance Learning Resource Network: http://www.dlrn.org
Duke University's Fuqua School of Business: http://www.fuqua.duke.edu
eARMYu (U.S. Army's Virtual University): http:www.eArmyu.com
EDUCAUSE: http://www.educause.edu/
Fathom: http://www.fathom.com
Forum for the Future of Higher Education
The Futures Project: Policy for Higher Education in a Changing World: http://www.futuresproject.org/
Internet2: http://www.internet2.org/
Jones International University: http://www.jonesinternational.edu/
The Michigan Virtual University: http://www.mivu.org/
The Millennium Project at the University of Michigan: http://milproj.ummu.umich.edu/
MIT Center for Advanced Educational Services: http://www-caes.mit.edu/
National Technological University: http://www.ntu.edu
Sylvan Learning Systems: http://educate.com
Universitas 21: http://www.universitas.edu.au

University of Maryland University College: http://www.umuc.edu
University of Phoenix: http://www.uophx.edu/online/
Vision 2010: Scenario Planning for Higher Education: http://www.si.umich.edu/
    V2010/
Western Governors University: http://www.wgu.edu

About the Authors

JAMES J. DUDERSTADT is Professor at the University of Michigan.

DANIEL E. ATKINS is Professor at the University of Michigan.

DOUGLAS VAN HOUWELING is Professor at the University of Michigan.